Cromwell Hath the Honour, but . . .

Significant places in the second Civil War

Cromwell Hath
the Honour, but . . .

Major-General Lambert's Campaigns
in the North, 1648

P. R. Hill and J. M. Watkinson

Foreword by
David J. Breeze

Frontline Books, London

Cromwell Hath the Honour, but . . .
Major–General Lambert's Campaigns in the North, 1648

This edition published in 2012 by Frontline Books,
an imprint of Pen & Sword Books Ltd,
47 Church Street, Barnsley, S. Yorkshire, S70 2AS
www.frontline-books.com

ISBN: 978-1-84832-654-5

CIP data records for this title are available from the British Library

For more information on our books, please visit
www.frontline-books.com, email info@frontline-books.com
or write to us at the above address.

Printed in the UK by MPG Books Group

Designed and typeset by Wordsense Ltd, Edinburgh in Bembo 10/13

CONTENTS

ILLUSTRATIONS

MAPS, FIGURES AND TABLES

Maps

Figures

Frontispiece: Significant Places in the second Civil War

Tables

Maps, Figures and Tables

TIMELINE

Date	Action or event
Note: The dates given are sometimes those when the actions were reported rather than when they took place. Some dates are approximate, using one of the alternatives given in the text	
1642	Civil War begins
Jan 1645	Lambert appointed Commissary-General of the Northern Army under Lord Fairfax
14 June 1645	Battle of Naseby
March 1646	King handed over to the English Parliament by the Scots
1647	
25 May	Commons vote to begin disbanding of the army on 1 June
2 June	Cornet Joyce removes the king from Holdenby and takes him to the Army HQ at Newmarket
5 June	The Scots Commissioners declare readiness to join the English Parliament to rescue the king
11 June	Parliament votes that forces be raised for defence against the army Fairfax announces that the Army will move towards London
17 July	The Northern Association Army to be brought into the New Model under Lambert
30 July	Following rioting, Independent MPs and both Speakers go to the army for safety.
6 August	Fairfax and the army lead the Speakers and Independent Members back to Westminster
end December	King signs an Engagement with the Scots in return for their military support
1648	
January	The Committee of Both Kingdoms replaced by the Committee of Both Houses (Derby House)
3 January	Vote of No Addresses

Timeline

April	Riots at Easter in London and southeast against high taxes and for the freedom of the king Colonel Fleming killed in south Wales, replaced by Colonel Horton
28 April	Sir Marmaduke Langdale takes Berwick for the king
29 April	Sir Philip Musgrave takes Carlisle for the king
May	Demonstrations in Kent grow into armed revolt, troops are sent into Kent, Suffolk, and Essex
1 May	Cromwell ordered to south Wales with 2 regiments of horse and 3 of foot
3 May	Scots Parliament votes to raise 30,000 foot and 6,000 horse under the Duke of Hamilton
8 May	Colonel Horton defeats rebels in south Wales at St. Fagans
9 May	Fairfax, with three regiments of horse and some foot, ordered to march north
16 May	Ireton recommends that Hesilrige abandon Northumberland
19 May	Fairfax sends Harrison's horse and others to Cheshire and then Lancashire Cromwell sends five troops of horse and some dragoons to the north
28 May	Fairfax ordered to return south to deal with troubles in Kent Seven ships of the navy go over to the Royalists
3 June	Pontefract Castle taken by Royalists
8 June	Langdale skirmishes with Lambert's advance guard at Greta Bridge, retreats to Brough
9 June	Lambert advances to Brough, Langdale retreats to Kirkby Thore
10 June	Lambert advances, besieges Appleby, and drives Langdale's army north of Penrith
11 June	Langdale retreats to Carlisle
14 June	Lambert advances to Carlisle
16 June	Lambert retires towards Penrith
17 June	Appleby Castle surrenders to Harrison
19 June	Skirmish at Ferrybridge
24 June	Pontefract garrison plunders Isle of Axholme, then marches to Lincoln
25 June	Lancashire reinforcements join Lambert, who advances and takes Warwick Bridge
26 June	Lambert takes Stanwix
last week June	Cromwell sends four troops of horse and two of dragoons to the north
1 July	Colonel Robert Lilburne successfully attacks Royalist forces in Northumberland

4 July	Lambert begins withdrawal to Penrith
5 July	Battle of Willoughby Field
8 July	The Scots army crosses the border.
11 July	Pembroke Castle falls to Cromwell
c.14 July	Cromwell begins his march north from Pembroke
15 July	Lambert withdraws to Appleby
17 July	Hamilton advances to Appleby, driven off after heavy skirmishing
18 July	Lambert retreats to Bowes, Hamilton besieges Appleby
last week July	Governor of Scarborough defects to the Royalists
29 July	Appleby Castle surrenders to Hamilton
1 August	Hamilton begins his march south
2 August	Lambert marches south from Barnard Castle to parallel Hamilton's march
9 August	Colonel Henry Lilburne seizes Tynemouth Castle for the king
10 August	Cromwell takes Pontefract town
11 August	Tynemouth Castle recaptured by Hesilrige
12 August	Lambert's and Cromwell's armies meet
13 August	Langdale reaches Settle with 3,000 foot and 600 horse
14 August	Langdale clashes with Cromwell's outposts near Skipton
17 August	Opening day of the battle of Preston The Commons repeals the Vote of No Addresses
19 August	Scots foot surrenders at Warrington
c.23 August	Cromwell turns north to follow Monro
24 August	Hamilton surrenders to Lambert at Uttoxeter
c.26 August	Lambert follows Cromwell north
28 August	Colchester surrenders to Fairfax
end August	Cockermouth Castle besieged by Royalists
15 September	Scarborough town taken from Royalists
28 September	Lambert approaches Edinburgh with 6 regiments of horse and 1 of dragoons
29 September	Siege of Cockermouth Castle relieved, Royalists flee to Appleby New Scottish government orders surrender of Berwick and Carlisle

Timeline

4 October	Cromwell and Lambert enter Edinburgh
9 October	Cromwell leaves Scotland for Carlisle, Lambert stays to assist the new government Appleby Castle surrenders to Ashton
13 October	Pontefract town taken by besiegers
20 October	Fairfax sends the Remonstrance of the Army to the Commons
29 October	Death of Colonel Rainsborough
30 October	Cromwell arrives at Pontefract Commons rejects the Remonstrance of the Army
8 November	Lambert begins withdrawal from Scotland
20 November	Lambert reaches Pontefract ahead of his regiments
28 November	Lambert's 3 horse regiments reach Pontefract area
29 November	Cromwell leaves Pontefract, Lambert takes over the siege
30 November	Army removes the king from Carisbrooke to Hurst Castle
1 December	Army begins to occupy London
5 December	Commons vote to accept the king's concessions as a basis for agreement
6 December	Commons purged by Colonels Pride and Rich, Cromwell arrives there in the evening
12 December	The army before Pontefract supports the Remonstrance of the Army
16 December	The king is brought to Windsor and all ceremonial towards him is stopped
19 December	Scarborough Castle surrenders
1649	
6 January	Commons orders a new Great Seal celebrating Freedom
8 January	Commons acting alone passes an Act to try the king
20 January	The king's trial begins
30 January	The king is executed
early February	Some of the heavy siege guns at Pontefract come into action Fever breaks out in the garrison during February
19 February	Lambert sets out conditions for his Commissioners to discuss surrender of Pontefract Castle
16 March	Surrender of Pontefract agreed
25 March	Pontefract garrison leaves the castle
9 April	Demolition of Pontefract Castle begins

GLOSSARY

Brigade	Two or three regiments acting under one command.
Commanded party	A group of men selected from different troops, companies, or regiments for a particular purpose.
Company (Coy)	Basic division of a foot regiment, nominally around a hundred men, with ten to a New Model regiment.
Compounding	Charge levied on Royalist supporters by which they were allowed to keep all or part of their property.
Council of War	A body of officers which gave advice to the general on further action, and as needed would form a court-martial.
Covenant	Also known as the National Covenant, and based on an oath taken by Scots in 1581 to defend their established church against its enemies, this document was drawn up after Charles I tried to impose the Prayer Book on the Scottish church. From February 1638 members of all social classes across Scotland put their signatures on it, to show their opposition to the king's religious and political control of the country. *See also* Solemn League and Covenant.
Dragoons	Soldiers who rode to battle (on inferior horses) but normally fought on foot. They formed a single regiment, 1,000 strong divided into ten companies (often called troops).
Drake	An artillery piece, with bores ranging from 3½ to 6½ inches.
Drum	A common term for the drummer in an infantry regiment, especially when carrying messages, a duty on which they were often employed.
Excepted	A person surrendering at *mercy* as opposed to the generality surrendering on *quarter*.

Glossary

Foot	Infantry soldiers, organised in regiments of around 1,000.
Forlorn hope	A party of men sent ahead of the main body to initiate an attack, or to break up attacks by the enemy.
Horse	Mounted soldiers, in regiments of 500–600, who fought from horseback, technically not including dragoons.
Indemnity, Act of	An act to protect soldiers from being charged with offences committed during the war.
Independents	In contrast to the *Presbyterians*, Independents were against any form of national religion in England, and in favour of a church system based on local groupings of congregations. Support came from the army and the more radical MPs.
Key shot	A bunch of small pieces of metal, strung together to make one load, fired at close range with the effect of a large shotgun.
Mercy, to yield on mercy	'By rendring to Mercy we understand; That they be rendred, or render themselves to the Lord General, or whom he shall appoint, without certain Assurance of Quarter; so as the Lord General may be free to put some immediately to the Sword, if he see Cause. . . (Rushworth, 1248, 31st August 1648). This usually affected only the more senior officers – see also *Quarter*.
Militia	Locally raised and trained troops, paid by the county organisation rather than by Parliament. Regiments were usually much smaller than those of the New Model.
New Model	The reorganised army raised in 1644-5 from existing armies, but with better training and discipline.
Pass	An obstruction to the line of march, whether a bridge, narrow road, or other defended point.
Presbyterian	An adherent of Presbyterianism, the Scottish national religion which is not controlled by the monarch, bishops or the state.
Post, Riding Post	The 'Post' was a series of stations where horses could be changed at short intervals, in order to sustain a high speed.
Quarter, to yield on quarter	'By fair Quarter we understand, That with Quarter for their Lives they shall be free from wounding or beating, shall enjoy warm Cloaths to cover them and keep them warm; shall be main tained with Victuals fit for Prisoners' (Rushworth, 1248, 31st August 1648). By the rules then in use giving quarter was optional.

Quarters	Lodgings which might be paid for at the time or taken on Free Quarter, paid by means of a draft on the government which might take years to be paid.
Reformado	A previously discharged or surplus officer, often used for one who had re-enlisted or otherwise served in a lower rank.
Saps and Parallels	Trenches which zig-zagged towards a fortified site, allowing besiegers to close in with reduced risk of injury.
Self-denying Ordinance	A resolution of Parliament that Members could not serve in the army; it was not universally applied.
Slighting	Destroying sufficient of a castle or fortified house to make it indefensible in the future.
Solemn League and Covenant	An agreement made in 1643 by which the Scots sent an army to fight for the English Parliament, in return for the latter imposing Presbyterianism on England and Ireland.
Summons	A call for a besieged force to surrender. By the informal Rules of War then in use, lives need not be spared if a reasonable summons was refused.
Trained Band	The predecessors to the *militia*, usually less well-trained except for those raised in London.
Troop	The basic division of a cavalry regiment, nominally 80–100 strong in the second Civil War, with six to a New Model regiment.
Troops	A generic term covering a group of any type of fighting men, not defined by quantity.

ACKNOWLEDGEMENTS

THANKS ARE DUE TO Dr C. D. Watkinson who, while consistently claiming that the seventeenth century was 'not his period', frequently pointed the authors in the direction of useful material. We would also like to thank Mr Martin Sowerby of Cumbria Archaeology, Long Marton, Appleby, who provided information on the river Eden at Appleby, and Mr Neill Croll who advised on the elucidation of some place names. Particular thanks are due to Mr Rollo Bruce who read the text in draft and made a number of very useful suggestions, leaving any errors, repetitions and infelicities the responsibility of the authors.

Material has been consulted in several institutions including the British Library, the National Library of Scotland, the Library of the Literary and Philosophical Society of Newcastle upon Tyne, and the Special Collections Departments of Durham University Library and of the Library of the University of St Andrews. Thanks are extended to staff in all these libraries but particularly to those in the last named for their forbearance. The staff of Leicester Archives were very helpful in giving access to the Hesilrige Letters, and the authors are grateful to His Grace the Duke of Northumberland for permission to consult the Archives in Alnwick Castle, and to the Archivist, Mr Christopher Hunwick, for his assistance.

The cover drawing is from the title page of *Bloody Nevves rom* [sic] *the Scottish Army* . . . (RB m. 307(19)) by permission of the Trustees of the National Library of Scotland.

FOREWORD

W̲A̲R̲ ̲I̲S̲ ̲A̲ ̲G̲R̲E̲A̲T̲ catalyst for change. It speeds social and economic evolution and encourages new inventions. It can lead to the creation of new military tactics and new weapons. It also throws up new generals. This occurs even in military societies such as the Roman Republic. A Scipio Africanus was needed to defeat Hannibal, a Pompey to deal with Mithridates while the empire was effectively founded by the most famous general (and politician) of the Republic, Julius Caesar.

Britain in the seventeenth century, however, was not a military society. It had no standing army, only a king's bodyguard. James VI and I and his son Charles I had been careful to avoid war. England had lost Calais, her last toehold in France, in 1558 and had avoided continental adventures since, apart from supporting the Dutch in their struggle for independence, while the Union of the Crowns in 1603 had removed the necessity for military engagement on her northern frontier. Scotland's militarily minded sons had gone abroad to fight. The eruption of the Civil War in 1642 brought several of them home, perhaps most notably David Leslie. Others came too, including the king's nephew, Rupert of the Palatinate.

But war has its own dynamics and creates its own generals. Oliver Cromwell would have remained an obscure MP but for Charles I's obduracy and lack of political nous. In Cromwell, however, England, indeed Britain, produced a general who was also a politician. Having defeated his Parliament's enemies, he abolished the monarchy and executed the king. Having executed the king, he abolished the Parliament, or rather Parliaments, for those in Scotland and Ireland went too. And he ruled virtually as dictator, as had Caesar. However, Cromwell sought legitimacy. So he had himself declared as Lord Protector sitting on the Coronation Chair, which contained the Stone of Scone, in Westminster Hall.

Cromwell created the first united kingdom. From London he ruled all three kingdoms. He backed his rule by the construction of forts all of which embodied new military features and all carefully placed to control Scotland, as had the Romans over a thousand years before. Parts of some survive to this day, most notably Ayr Citadel, but also a gate at Leith. And he ruthlessly dealt with all opposition.

Cromwell did not achieve all this by himself. He was an astute politician certainly, a better politician than a general, but he also was supported by many good generals. One of these was John Lambert. A northerner, from Yorkshire, Lambert was successful in the first Civil War and started the second Civil War in 1648 commanding the forces in northern England. Here he faced the Scottish army and, if he had failed in his duty, the history of Britain would have been rather different. As it was, Cromwell was in the better position to take the glory of victory and even Lambert's presence at the battle of Preston failed to receive mention in Cromwell's dispatch.

In writing history, the greater men tend to receive the greater attention. Furthermore, the more political the general, the easier he can manipulate the reporting to his advantage. Blucher's actions in 1815 were essential to the victory at Waterloo, but how much do we remember that in relation to Wellington's glory? Worse, the activities of the 'lesser' men are seldom revisited by historians who – not least because time is short – so often repeat the judgements of their predecessors. Yet it is always worth the effort to revisit the original sources as the authors have done here, reconsider the evidence and offer a balanced view unclouded by the mask of time.

The story of the 'lesser' men can be as much if not more interesting as those of the great, and this is certainly true in the case of Lambert. His story is made even more attractive because he was his own man, refusing to bend the knee to Cromwell when the Lord Protector required total obedience and suffering for his conscience. He was also humane, refusing to undertake the harsh actions indulged in by Cromwell, which even today cast a long shadow. He is a man well worth studying and this twelve-month episode in his military life is well told by Peter Hill and Jane Watkinson. John Lambert could well earn the sobriquet of being a 'man for all seasons'.

David J. Breeze, 2012
Honorary Professor of Archaeology, Durham, Edinburgh and Newcastle

INTRODUCTION

'Cromwell hath the honor, but Lambert's discreet, humble, ingenious, sweet and civil
deportment gains him more hugs and ingenious respect . . . I could give you a large
character of that man's great wisdom and valour . . .'[1]
This quotation refers specifically to the reception of Oliver Cromwell and John
Lambert in Edinburgh in October 1648, but it seems to sum up very well the
perceived relative importance of the two men in the second Civil War.

THE FIRST CIVIL WAR and its battles and skirmishes between 1642 and 1646 have received
much detailed attention in print, but the second war tends to be treated in more cursory
fashion. Those works that do consider the second Civil War (1648–1649) in detail have an
emphasis on events in the south, and especially those close to London. The war in the north
comes a poor second, to the point where the first full-length treatment of the Parliamentary
victory at the battle of Preston was not published until 1998.[2]

This book sets out to give a detailed, factual explanation of the day-to-day military
actions in the north of England conducted by Major-General John Lambert in 1648–1649.
Military events in the south, and various political moves in both England and Scotland, are
referred to in order to sketch in a background but no more. In general, speculation as to the
political intentions of the participants has been avoided in favour of factual analysis of what
was actually happening. It relies almost entirely on the examination of original sources
rather than using more modern commentaries, except for the political and military events
in the south.

The second Civil War was by no means merely a tidying-up of left-over business, but
rather a serious and at times desperate series of campaigns: '. . . victory at Preston was
neither guaranteed nor unnecessary. The future of the three kingdoms hung more in the
balance than at any time since Marston Moor and perhaps since the 1st battle of Newbury.'[3]

Before the spring of 1648 there was always the possibility of some compromise and
reconciliation, but what was seen at the time by many as the unnecessary bloodshed of the
second Civil War led almost inevitably to the king's execution in January 1649.

Binns points out that many historians 'have followed Clarendon's habit of confusing geographical remoteness with military and political significance. The further away from London and Oxford the less it matters.'[4] One writer even refers to Sir Arthur Hesilrige's service as governor of Newcastle upon Tyne, only 280 miles from London, as 'in the far north'. Other writers seem to have a tenuous grasp of the geography: for example, it is not clear how troops sent to Coventry in May 1648 were of assistance in actions 200 miles to the north.[5] They are not alone, as will be seen: some contemporary news reports also show unfamiliarity with the north of England.

For several months in 1648, the commander of Parliament's army, General Sir Thomas Fairfax (Lord Fairfax from March 1648), was putting down revolts in Essex; Lieutenant-General Oliver Cromwell was fighting in south Wales, principally at the siege of Pembroke, and not until that was over was he ordered to the north. The contemporary campaign of Major-General John Lambert, who was holding off first Sir Marmaduke Langdale and then the Duke of Hamilton, has to some extent been glossed over, albeit with some words of praise for his tactics. Lambert was also responsible for the conduct of the sieges of Pontefract and Scarborough, events which are sometimes ignored altogether.

Cromwell's defeat of the Royalists at Preston could not have happened if Lambert had allowed his army to be destroyed by Langdale, or by Hamilton who greatly outnumbered him. Cromwell brought with him no more than half of the numbers Lambert had already under his immediate command, or one-third of the whole (see Chapter 1). Cromwell's political achievements have given him a reputation in the historical record which has perhaps magnified his military accomplishments, and overshadowed Lambert's very considerable successes in the field.

Then, as now, the population at large in London was not greatly concerned about the north, but in this case with good reason. As will be shown in Chapter 2, in the middle of 1647 they had been threatened by their own mutinous soldiers seeking redress for injustices, which led to the army taking control of the capital for a short time. In 1648 the newsbooks were aware of the possibility of counter-revolutionary soldiers coming into the city, which must have focused minds on local events rather than on those 300 miles away. However, those responsible for the conduct of the war, the Committee of Both Houses (usually referred to simply as Derby House, from their meeting place), were very much alive to the danger from the north. During the fighting in Wales and southeast England, frequent requests were made to the armies in the south, and to a number of County Committees, to release troops for service in the north.

Many of the actions that will be described were no more than small skirmishes, but to those taking part they were no less important than battles, especially for the dead and wounded. The final stages of a campaign may be dismissed as 'mopping-up' but can be at least as dangerous for those taking part. Although none of Ashton's regiment was killed when they were sent to relieve Cockermouth at the end of September 1648, they had to march 120 miles with poor quarters and worse rations just to get to the scene of action. In the event they were not needed there, but instead had to march another forty miles to Appleby.

This book is intended for the general reader as well as the serious student, and can be read without recourse to the notes, which are largely devoted to sources of information and quoted material. References are not usually given for Captain Samuel Birch's 'diary' (reproduced in part in Appendix 4), nor for Captain John Hodgson's *Memoirs*, nor for Major John Sanderson's diary where there is no discussion of the entry, as the dates of the quotations provide easy reference.

At a number of places in the text there is detailed discussion of times, distances and alternative interpretations of the evidence. In one or two peripheral instances these points have been relegated to endnotes, but the authors believe that in most cases these details form an essential part of the examination of the campaign and are best left in the narrative.

Ranks and regiments

The rank, and where possible Christian name, of individuals are given at the first mention, but thereafter are usually dropped except where differentiation might be difficult. Thus Major-General John Lambert generally reverts to his surname only, but Colonel Robert Lilburne and his cousin Captain Thomas Lilburne (both in Lilburne's regiment of horse) retain their rank unless the identification is clear. Lord Fairfax's regiment of foot is referred to (as then) as the Lord General's to avoid confusion with his uncle Colonel Charles Fairfax's regiment of foot. Lord Fairfax himself is referred to as General Fairfax, and Colonel Fairfax also retains his rank unless the distinction is obvious.

Ranks were not always consistent even in official documents: Lambert is sometimes referred to as Major-General and sometimes as Colonel. Most ranks in the seventeenth century were roughly equivalent to those in use today, although there are some differences. 'Serjeant-Major', a commissioned rather than non-commissioned officer, is now simply Major (as was already common at the time); Ensign (Foot regiments) and Cornet (Horse regiments) are now Lieutenant; a Corporal of Horse was equivalent to Sergeant (as it still is in the Household Cavalry); Field-Marshall was then a senior officer who disposed troops on the battlefield, not the commander of armies. There was also an occasional rank, not in modern use, of Colonel-General, approximately equivalent to Brigadier.

Regiments are referred to by the surname in the possessive case of their current commander, as there was no other identification at the time.

Maps

Compared to modern maps those of the mid-seventeenth century tend to be sketches, not to say sketchy. A map that proved so useful that it became known as the Quartermasters'

Map (plate 25) has very few roads, shows hills pictorially and rarely indicates bridges. An eighteenth-century traveller in Scotland made this comment on it: 'Newtown-Stewart is a neat little town . . . On the 3rd I went two miles to Garlais Castle in the middle of a wood . . . What is called Cromwell's map, or the Quartermasters', is so imperfect in these parts that I shall not attempt to correct it . . .'[6] There was nothing to compare with Ogilby's post-war route maps, which were a great advance, showing for the first time the location of bridges and whether they were of wood or stone, as well as side roads and their destination; they were also drawn to a consistent scale of 1 inch to 1 mile, but showed routes as strip maps of roads, rather than whole areas, and were in any case not published until twenty-five years after the second Civil War.

The sketch maps in this book show the principal places mentioned in the text with some modern roads on routes that probably existed in the seventeenth century. Ministry of Transport road numbers are occasionally given as an aid to location. The old county boundaries are shown where they are relevant to the narrative. The single symbol for a city, town or village makes no attempt to discriminate between places of different size. Castles that played some part in the events are marked as such; others, whether in active commission or not, are marked simply as places. The maps are grouped together in geographical sequence and keyed to a map of northern Britain, apart from a few very specific maps and plans which are inserted in the appropriate place in the text. The frontispiece map provides a quick reference to the more important places.

Dates

At this time England was officially still using the Julian calendar, with the new year beginning on 25 March. Scotland and continental countries had already changed to the new Gregorian calendar in which the year began on 1 January. Many people in England, although not all, chose to use the Gregorian style year and therefore dates given in letters and newsbooks can vary. Thus, *The Moderate Intelligencer Numb. 207 From Thursday March 1 to Thursday March 8, 1649* (*TT* E546/13) refers to the same month and year as *The Kingdomes Weekly Intelligencer Numb. 302 From Tuesday March 6 to Tuesday March the 13 1648* (*TT* E546/18). Dates given in direct quotations are given in their original style, and where there is room for doubt the modern year is given in brackets thus: 1648[9].

It was common, but by no means universal, in the seventeenth century for dates to be given in the form August 14. 1648. Except in direct quotations this has been modernised to current standard English usage of day followed by month, as 14 August 1648.

Intelligence

Apart from the details of his own army, the most important matter to a general on campaign has always been to discover the whereabouts, strength and intentions of his enemy. Over the last few decades, satellite and aerial reconnaissance, wireless intercepts and telephone tapping have provided perhaps the bulk of the raw data of intelligence. Instant dissemination of the information by telephone and wireless is second nature and the latest troop movements can be flashed halfway around the world in seconds.

Until the end of the nineteenth century the situation was quite different. The only way to see what was over the next hill was to ride or walk to the top, and then to return in the same manner. Cromwell's initial account of the opening of the battle of Preston was obliged to say: 'We *understand* Colonel-General Ashton's are at Whalley; we have seven troops of horse and dragoons that we *believe* lie at or near Clitheroe' (emphasis added).[7] Any enquiry as to their actual whereabouts would take time – Whalley and Clitheroe are four miles apart and thirteen and seventeen miles respectively from Preston, where the battle started – and answers might be several hours old when they reached the questioner.

It was not necessarily just a matter of sending the nearest two or three men forward in the hope that they would report accurately on what they saw. The Parliamentary army saw scouting as a sufficiently important and specialist function to have a Scoutmaster-General, paid at £4 per day for himself, his servants and assistants.[8] Parliamentary forces are generally reckoned to have had much better intelligence than the Royalists. When at Penrith, Lambert was receiving intelligence from spies in Hamilton's army, but whether these were men sent for the purpose or more haphazardly reporting on what was happening is not clear.[9]

However, Lambert and his secretary Thomas Margetts mentioned the lack of scouts with the Parliamentary forces in the north from April 1648 onwards.[10] Amazingly, it was not until late July that Derby House began to take any steps to remedy the situation, by reporting: 'Also that money is wanted for intelligence and other incident charges. That general officers are wanted . . . as a Scoutmaster-General and a Quartermaster-General.'[11] There is no indication that the posts were ever established.

Seventeenth-century warfare

At the time of the Civil War the 'Rules of War', which were in any case informal rather than a codified Convention, were very different from those of today. Principally, it was not then seen as essential to take prisoners: quarter (mercy) could be given or not during a battle according to how the superior force saw the situation. For example, at Preston the Parliamentary army gave no quarter for the first hour or so of fighting.[12] In a siege, a garrison that failed to yield when summoned could all be put to death when the place was finally taken, although this did not by any means always happen. It was not uncommon for the senior officers to be forced to surrender 'at mercy', meaning that their lives might or might not be spared.

The first Civil War had many instances of consideration given, but in the second war the army, which had endured several years of fighting only to have it start all over again, was much less forgiving. Prisoners were not always well treated. In July 1648 Captain Henry Ogle, a Parliamentary officer prisoner, was 'used so coarsly' that Sir Arthur Hesilrige had the prisoners in Tynemouth moved to Duns Lodge and sent word 'that as they meated, they must expect'.[13]

After the battle of Preston, Cromwell ordered that the prisoners in the town were to be killed if the town were attacked by the Scots, and had no need to explain the reasoning in his despatch to the Speaker.[14] The killing of around sixty men found hiding in a barn near Appleby in July (see Chapter 6) was a brutal act, but should not be viewed from a modern perspective as a war crime. Wanklyn points out that warfare in Europe and even Scotland at this time was far more costly in lives than the more gentlemanly manner of fighting in England.[15] Participants knew what to expect, as they knew what they could mete out without attracting obloquy.

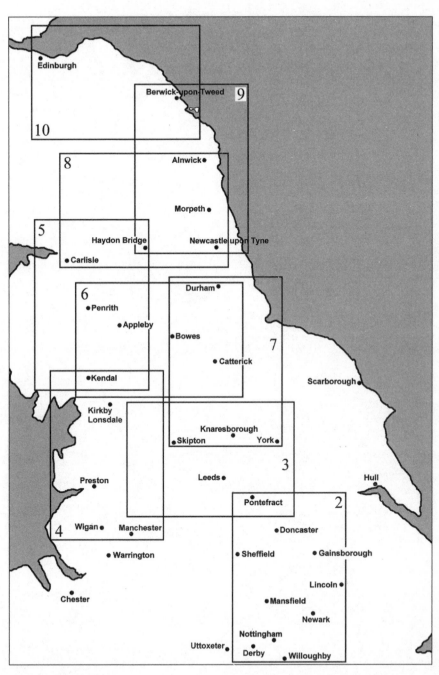

MAP I: *Key to map sections*

Maps

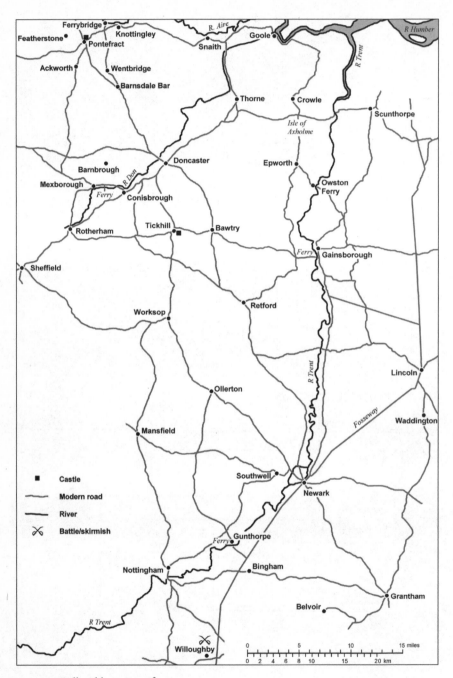

MAP 2: *Willoughby to Pontefract*

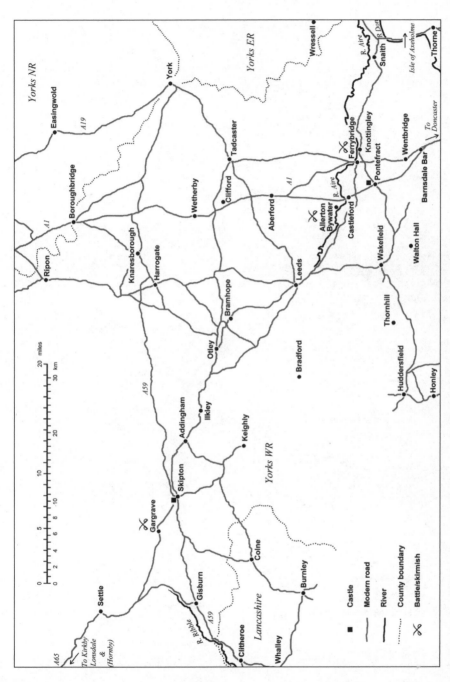

MAP 3: *York to Clitheroe*

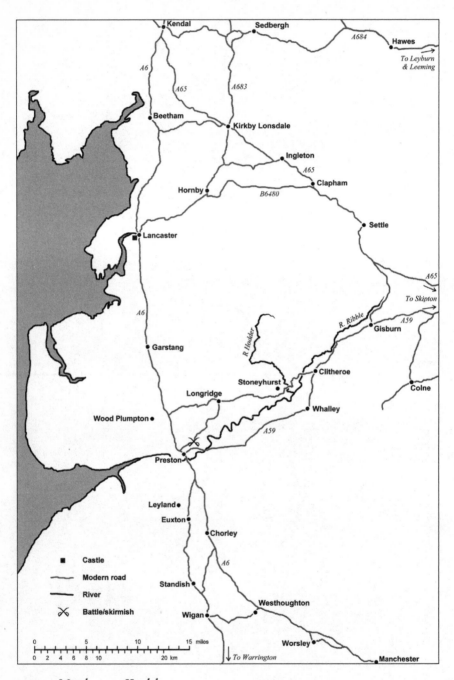

MAP 4: *Manchester to Kendal*

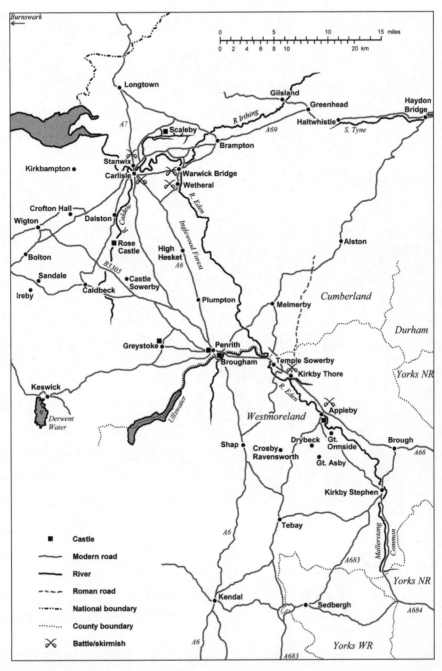

Burnswark

0   5   10   15 miles
0 2 4 6 8 10   20 km

Longtown

Gilsland

Greenhead

Haydon Bridge

R. Irthing

A69

Haltwhistle

S. Tyne

Scaleby

A7

Brampton

Stanwix

Carlisle

Warwick Bridge

Wetheral

Kirkbampton

R. Eden

Crofton Hall

Dalston

Wigton

R. Caldew

Inglewood Forest

Alston

Rose Castle

High Hesket

A6

Bolton

B5305

Sandale

Castle Sowerby

Caldbeck

Ireby

Plumpton

Melmerby

Cumberland

Durham

Greystoke

Penrith

Brougham

Temple Sowerby

Kirkby Thore

Yorks NR

Keswick

Derwent Water

Ullswater

R. Eden

Appleby

Westmoreland

Shap

Crosby Ravensworth

Drybeck

Gt. Ormside

Gt. Asby

Brough

A66

Kirkby Stephen

Mallerstang

Common

Tebay

A6

Castle

Modern road

River

Roman road

National boundary

County boundary

Battle/skirmish

A683

Yorks NR

Kendal

Sedbergh

A684

A6

Yorks WR

A683

MAP 5: *Kendal to Carlisle*

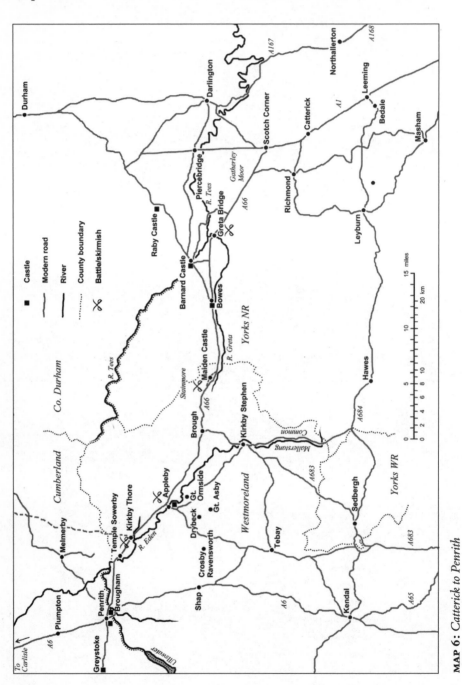

MAP 6: *Catterick to Penrith*

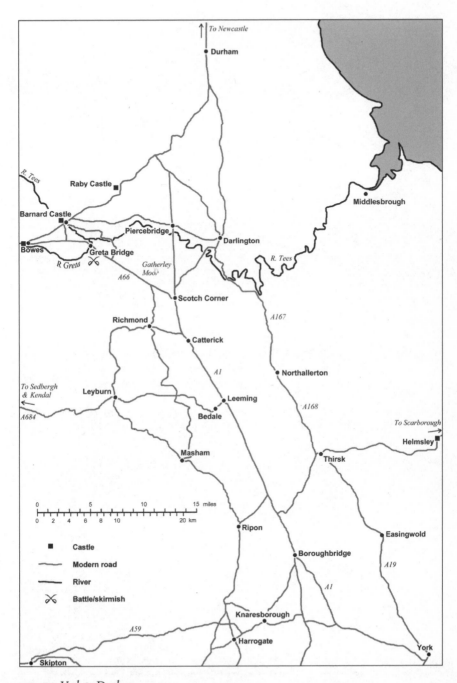

MAP 7: *York to Durham*

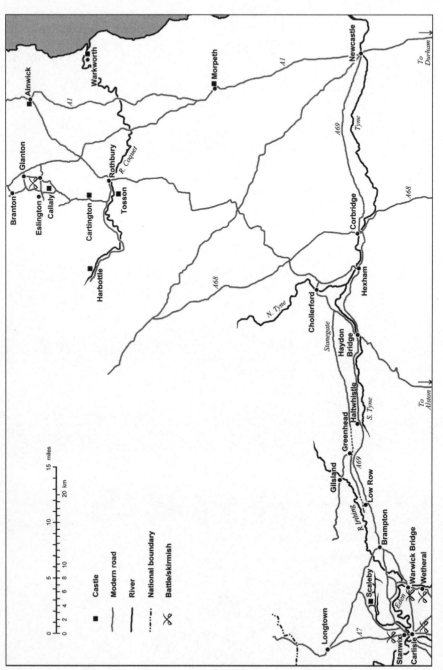

MAP 8: *Newcastle to Carlisle*

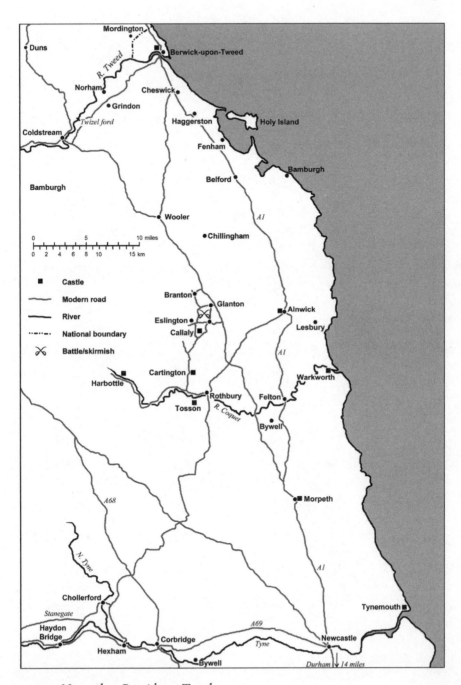

MAP 9: *Newcastle to Berwick-on-Tweed*

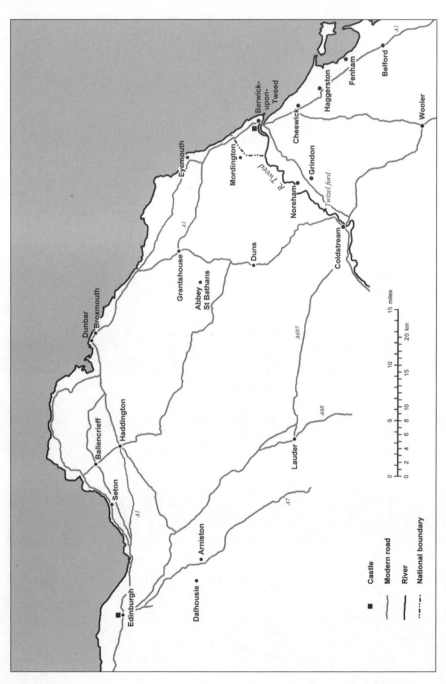

MAP 10: *Berwick-on-Tweed to Edinburgh*

Chapter 1

LAMBERT AND HIS ARMY

John Lambert

THIS CHAPTER INTRODUCES MAJOR-GENERAL Lambert, the task he faced in the north of England in 1648, and the forces available to him to meet the various threats. It also looks briefly at his later life, and his reputation.

The Lambert family was provincial gentry which had risen in the sixteenth century and declined somewhat in the seventeenth. John Lambert was born in 1619 at Calton in the West Riding of Yorkshire, some seven miles northwest of Skipton. He was probably educated at Cambridge, and then in one of the Inns of Court, perhaps Grays.

In 1638 he married Frances, daughter of Sir William Lister, giving him a connection to one of the more powerful Yorkshire families, who in their turn were linked to the Fairfaxes. Lambert's father was already acquainted with Sir Thomas Fairfax's father, Ferdinando, Lord Fairfax, as they both served as JPs in Skipton in the early years of the century.

Lambert, in company with Sir Thomas Fairfax and many other northern gentry, was involved in various petitions and approaches to the king at York in 1642. After negotiations failed he began his military career when he entered Sir Thomas's regiment as a cornet. Lord Fairfax commanded the Northern Army (later the Northern Association Army) and under the two Fairfaxes Lambert was involved in fighting almost from the beginning of the war.

By the end of 1642 he was a captain, and a colonel by March 1643 when he began to make a name for himself. He was very active in a number of skirmishes in the north, from Hull to Nantwich; in February 1644 he retook Bradford from the Royalists, and under the command of the Fairfaxes took part in the battle of Selby. He fought at Marston Moor, and was one of the two officers sent into York to begin arrangements for the surrender of the city. In October 1644 he and Colonel Sandys attacked the enemy quarters in Plumpton and took 120 horses and some prisoners.[1] The following month he went to London to recuperate from an illness, discussed below.

In January 1645 Lambert was posted to the Northern Association Army as Commissary-General, a signal promotion at the age of twenty-six. This was a Command rather than a Supply appointment, as the Commons order makes clear: 'to Colonell Lambert now in Towne, to speed down into the North, to the end that Sir Thomas Fairefax comming up, he may take care to command the forces there, being Commissary Generall of the Lord Fairefax army'.[2] He thus replaced Sir Thomas as deputy to Lord Fairfax, who continued to command the Northern Army until replaced in June of the same year by Sydenham Poyntz.

In February raiders from the garrison of Skipton went to Keighley (map 3). Lambert caught them, recovered a hundred prisoners and sixty horses, took a captain and killed his lieutenant and fifteen men, for the loss of a captain and eight men. He was then defeated at Wentbridge in March by Sir Marmaduke Langdale, who came to relieve the siege of Pontefract, and he was wounded by a shot in the thigh.

All reports suggest, rightly or wrongly, that the defeat was in part due to the actions of an untrustworthy man, Siddell/Syddall/Siddall, who gave misleading information as to the whereabouts of the enemy: 'Yet the vigilant Col. Lambert, mistrusting both the man [Siddall] and his intelligence, went with a forlorne hope to discover the certainty.' The injury does not seem to have been serious, for Lambert remained in the vicinity of Pontefract.[3]

Later he was moved south and reached Naseby on 15 June 1645, the day after the battle. He was sent with Sir Thomas Fairfax to the southwest, where he took part in the sieges and surrenders of Dartmouth, Truro and Exeter. He then conducted the siege of Oxford where he negotiated its surrender and was made governor. The terms were said to be generous and included safeguards for the buildings and artistic treasures of the city. Bulstrode Whitelocke MP, who had hoped to be made governor himself, observed that the terms were most carefully observed. During the troubles between Parliament and the army in 1647 Lambert played a very prominent part on the side of the army, and in July of that year he was appointed to the command of the Northern Army. This army, however, was to be taken into the New Model, now coming directly under Fairfax rather than Parliament. His military career from then to March 1649 is dealt with in the main body of the book.

★ ★ ★

After the capture of Pontefract in March 1649, Lambert was busy on both personal and military matters, including the settling of discontents in Oxford, and further disbanding of surplus forces. During the year he had some potential political problems. His friends believed that Hesilrige, either on his own or prompted by Cromwell, was trying to undermine Lambert's position in the north, although it is not possible to determine the truth behind the rumours.[4]

In 1650 he took part in the invasion of Scotland as Cromwell's second in command, and suffered lance wounds in his thigh and shoulder in an engagement at Musselburgh. At Dunbar he was responsible, perhaps with Cromwell, for the plan to attack the Scots army (Farr, p. 79 and *ODNB*, probably rightly, give all the credit to Lambert). By popular demand he took command of the Parliamentary army for the battle, on 3 September. His victories at Hamilton, southeast of Glasgow in December 1650, and at Inverkeithing in July 1651, whither he had ferried his army over the Forth to take Fife, showed his abilities to the full. Inverkeithing, after which he found two bullets between his breastplate and his coat, was a most significant victory which destroyed the hopes of the Scots and resulted in their army taking what seemed to be their only course, to march into England with Charles II. They used the same western route as in 1648 under the command of William, 2nd Duke of Hamilton whose brother had led them to disaster at Preston. Farr, in *ODNB*, quotes Ludlow's claim that at the subsequent battle of Worcester Lambert was prominent in the tactical decisions for the attack on the city, which battle finally ended the Civil Wars.

In April 1653 Cromwell used a file of musketeers to close the Rump Parliament, and in December Lambert disposed of its successor, the Barebones Parliament, in similar fashion. At the same time he presented a new Instrument of Government which put Cromwell in place as the Lord Protector, completing the military coup. He had great influence in the evolving systems of government, including the rule of the Major-Generals, and he was seen as a likely successor to Cromwell as Lord Protector. However, his opposition to Cromwell in 1657 (Farr believes that he stopped Cromwell taking the title of king) caused a rift between the two men, and his refusal to take the oath of loyalty to the new constitution led Cromwell to require Lambert to resign his offices and commands.

He retired to his house in Wimbledon, formerly owned by Queen Henrietta, where he cultivated his splendid gardens and pursued his many artistic and aesthetic interests. He had acquired a number of paintings from the royal collection, and was said to be a good painter himself. Lucy Hutchinson, who did not care for him, described him as working 'at the needle with his wife and maids'.[5]

He recovered some of his influence after Cromwell's death in 1658, and in 1659 was sent by Parliament to put down the rising of Sir George Booth in Cheshire. However, when he was involved in a petition calling for reforms in the army and government he was dismissed by Parliament. In response he sent troops to Westminster, and persuaded the forces protecting Parliament to join him. This restored his power and as a member of the Committee of Safety he was sent to resist the march from Scotland of Monk who had declared for Parliament. These efforts failed when Fairfax took the side of Parliament, and in March 1660 Lambert was sent to the Tower. He escaped in April, but was recaptured within a fortnight when a plan to raise forces failed.

At the restoration of Charles II, Lambert was tried for High Treason and sentenced to death, although the king remitted the sentence in favour of life imprisonment.

His military prowess is best summed up in the words of Farr, *ODNB*: 'Militarily he ranks with any of his contemporaries and during the Scottish campaign he arguably surpassed his older commander Cromwell as the leading general of the English forces. His evident military genius and care for his troops saw him worshipped by them and described by one contemporary as the "Armyes Darling" ' (Bodl. Oxf., MS Carte 131, fol. 189).

He was not only an excellent general but was also personally brave, his several wounds showing that he was not content to lead from the rear. He was also a good leader (not at

3

all the same thing as a good general), as evidenced by his ability to keep his army together and in good heart during the to-and-fro action between Barnard Castle and Carlisle in the dismal weather of 1648.

Lambert's campaigns and achievements in 1648 were not inconsiderable. If he had failed to hold Langdale and Hamilton there would have been no worthwhile force left to stop a successful invasion by the Scots. And once the Scots looked like being successful, Royalists among the northern gentry would have had the encouragement to rise up in support of the king. Lambert used his forces, tiny at first, with great skill, pushing forward when appropriate but knowing when to fall back quickly. Indeed his retreats from Penrith and from Appleby both left Hamilton wrong-footed and looking in vain for an enemy to fight.

Lambert's success seems to have been somewhat unsung even at the time, perhaps owing to the apparently lukewarm esteem in which he was held by the grandees of Derby House, and by Parliament of which he was not a member. He was also much overshadowed by Cromwell, whose vastly greater achievements in the political sphere have led to perhaps excessive regard for the latter's military successes owing to 'the natural tendency there always is to ante-date the greatness of a genius such as Cromwell'.[6] This is perhaps partly due to Cromwell's own reports which are selective in their praise for others. His deliberate omission of the names of Lambert and Lilburne from his Preston despatch is discussed in Chapter 7: 'more [of the battle of Preston] is attributed to some and less to others than they deserved'.[7]

Markham's statement that 'Cromwell was [Fairfax's] very efficient general of horse, but nothing more'[8] may be overstating the case, but it is true that during the first Civil War Cromwell had not had sole charge of a major campaign. It was the siege of Pembroke and particularly the battle of Preston which made his name as a general to add to his well-deserved reputation as a leader of men.

The first Civil War had given Cromwell wide military experience of skirmishes, sieges and of major battles at Marston Moor and Naseby where he made significant contributions, but it was not until the second Civil War that he was able to exercise command in his own right. His reputation deservedly stood high as a cavalry commander by the end of the first Civil War, and he was undoubtedly an extremely able trainer of cavalry, and introduced a greater discipline into the horse than had been seen in England before, or perhaps since. It was in this area, rather than his generalship or even his undoubted leadership, that Cromwell's greatest contribution was made to the success of the Parliamentary army. But it was between the wars and particularly after the second, when his actions were more political than military, that he really began to make his name. His real genius lay in his political acumen, albeit supported by his very great influence with the army, and this is what led him to greatness in the 1650s as a very public man. But, as Reece warns, 'it is essential . . . to avoid pre-dating Cromwell's pre-eminence'.[9]

Lambert undoubtedly made errors of judgement which have not come down in the written record, but if so he overcame them and kept his army whole and unharmed. More importantly he must have kept up their morale in what must have been an exhausting campaign in foul weather. As will be described in Chapter 6, the retreat from Penrith in very wet weather, the march south from Appleby of most of his men to find supplies, and their hurried return when Hamilton advanced, to spend what was left of the day in fighting, would have wearied any army. But in the early hours of the next day they began a march of twenty-eight miles over the bleak and windswept Stainmore road to Bowes. The fact that the army did not disintegrate, despite having their pay in arrears and little opportunity for loot, must be a reflection of Lambert's leadership as well as his generalship.

Lambert had something of a reputation as a humane commander, and he was certainly much liked by his men. The terms he gave to beaten enemies were generally very mild: those taken when Appleby Castle was captured in June were allowed to go to their homes, as were most of those captured at Scarborough. He was quite prepared to give Morris and the other five excepted men at Pontefract time to escape before the castle was surrendered, and had to be reminded several times to collect Morris and Blackburne from Lancaster, where they had been caught, and carry them to York for trial. As the army commander he must have played at least some part in sparing the lives of the deserters captured at Carlisle in June 1648. All these actions are described in their chronological order below.

He was also careful of the rights of civilians when his soldiers stepped over the line. In September and October 1647 he settled differences about quartering and insisted on an equal distribution of quartering of his soldiers, and gave orders for punishment by the gantelope (gauntlet) of those guilty of plundering.[10] Thomas Margetts was undoubtedly biased in Lambert's favour, but there seems to be justification of his summary of Lambert's character after a reception in Edinburgh in 1648.[11]

There are hints that he did not enjoy the best of health. He spent three months in London, November 1644 to January 1645, recovering from an unspecified illness. Dawson says he was in poor health, while Farr believes that he was wounded at Plumpton but evidence either way is lacking. The only record comes in a letter from Lambert to Sir Thomas Fairfax: 'I have hitherto been kept from waiting upon you by reason of my indisposition, but now, though not altogether so healthful as formerly, I shall be upon my journey this next week,' which perhaps sounds more like illness than wounds. In the middle of June 1648 it was reported that: 'Major-Generall Lambert is not very well, but you know he hath been long sickly, but is in the field, and victorious . . .'[12]

His portraits show him as a somewhat slender man with delicate features. While this is not serious evidence one way or the other, they do not show him as a large, robust individual living a hearty, outdoor life. On the contrary, without the armour he could very easily be taken for a scholar or a divine rather than a successful soldier. In 1647, Whitelocke described him as 'of a subtle and working Brain'.[13]

Despite his various high-profile positions Lambert seems at times a man not quite in the limelight, whether or not he would have preferred the latter. He had the administrative ability to organise a coup in favour of Cromwell as Lord Protector, but not the political power base to organise a successful one for himself. He was certainly something of an enigma to his contemporaries, and it is by no means clear how eager he was for personal power. His limited popularity among his seniors may in part have been due to his lukewarm approach to religion, and he certainly gave support to Quakers in the later 1650s. He was one of the great generals, a man of ability in many fields, whose life flowered very early. It was also in some ways a tragic life, which ended after twenty-four years of imprisonment at the age of sixty-five.

This very brief summary of Lambert's life owes very much, although not exclusively, to the work of Dawson and of Farr. Neither is wholly satisfactory, in that Dawson's is something of a now outdated hagiography, with few sources given for his material, and Farr (who says himself that his is not a definitive biography) concentrates very much on Lambert's links of family, kinship and political events. There is room for a new, fully-rounded portrait of the man.

Lambert's strength

As the commander of the Northern Army of Parliament it was Lambert's task to maintain the peace in the north, covering approximately the counties of Yorkshire, Lancashire, Cumberland and Westmoreland (now Cumbria), Northumberland and the Bishopric of Durham. In particular, he had to resist any invasion from Scotland, discourage the northern gentry from rising in support of the king, and to suppress the long-running activities of the so-called moss troopers along the Border. He did have some support from the governor of Newcastle, Sir Arthur Hesilrige, who had garrison troops under his command, and to a limited extent both men sent forces to support the other on specific occasions. Lambert, however, was the only general in the field.

The question of what forces were available to Lambert at various stages of his campaign is a vexed one. It is often unsafe to rely on contemporary figures in newsbooks which may range from intelligent estimates at best, through guesswork, to wishful thinking or propaganda, and errors. At times, the present authors' calculations of strength seem to match one or other contemporary figures, but whether this should bring a feeling of satisfaction or the realisation that the calculations must therefore be wrong is a matter for debate.

Modern commentaries have suggested various totals and some seventeenth-century errors have over the years inevitably become accepted as received wisdom. It is hoped that this attempt to cut through what is at times almost a mythology, by extrapolating from the incomplete and sometimes contradictory records, has resulted in a reasonable assessment. In addition to the text, the figures are summarised as a list in table 1 and shown graphically in two bar charts, tables 2 and 3.

Lambert's military strength is a somewhat complex discussion, and has therefore been separated from the chronological text, although troop movements are mentioned there as they occurred. Similarly, this section perforce mentions various stages in the campaign in outline, but the details are brought out in the proper place. The figures given include only those immediately available to Lambert to oppose first Langdale and then Hamilton's Scots, and they ignore the several hundred he had under his command besieging Pontefract and Scarborough, or based elsewhere. The focus is on the defence of the road from Carlisle to Yorkshire across Stainmore, which is where the main threat developed. The five dates chosen for calculating the increase in his army are based on the dates of known additions, but at times it is impossible to be certain that all the troops listed had yet reached him, rather that on the balance of probabilities they ought to have been there within a day or so. At the end is an estimate of the combined army after Lambert and Cromwell joined forces.

With the reduction in the size of horse and foot regiments in February 1648, they can all be assumed to be at full strength in March, that is 480 for horse regiments in six troops and 800 for foot regiments in ten companies.[14] However, it is known that in the middle of March Major John Sanderson, of Colonel Robert Lilburne's regiment of horse, was allocated an extra twenty troopers to bring his troop up to its war strength of a hundred.[15] It is most unlikely only one troop was so treated, and as the progress towards war intensified it is probable that all commanding officers were recruiting above their establishment. In the following discussion the horse is assumed to have an effective strength of eighty-five per troop or 510 in a regiment. There may well have been many more in some regiments but the figure allows for a few more men than the nominal establishment while keeping the estimates to a minimum. However, as Sanderson's troop is certainly known to be a hundred strong, Lilburne's total is given as 525 when Sanderson rejoined.

It was always harder to recruit and retain the foot, and it is assumed that they are all at their nominal establishment of 800 men, allowing for both a small increase and some desertion. It may be noted, however, that Bright's foot regiment was described as being 800–900 in May 1648, and Captain Samuel Birch of Colonel Ralph Ashton's militia foot had 135 soldiers rather than eighty in his company on 16 June 1648. Overton's, see below, were reported to be 1,200 strong before Tenby and this figure is used for them. The establishment for dragoons, and the figure used here, remained at a hundred in a company or troop – the former term is technically correct, but 'troop' was more often used in contemporary letters.

There are some indications that many if not all regiments had been brought up to their war strength, as in this comment from October 1648: 'there be also two Regiments of Horse consisting of 600 in a Regiment, to be ready upon all occasions to resist and oppose any Invasion.'[16] As the extent of the increase is not confirmed the lower figure suggested above has been used.

TABLE I **Calculated strength of forces under the command of Major General Lambert**

Horse and Dragoons		Foot		Total
March 1648, Northern Army regiments at the start of the second Civil War				
Lambert's (6 troops)	510	Bright's (10 coys)	800	
Lilburne's (6 troops)	525			
Total	**1,035**		**800**	**1,835**
Troops immediately available to Lambert to oppose Langdale and Hamilton				
11 May 1648				
Lambert's (4 troops)	340	Bright's (2 Coys)	160	
Lilburne's (1 troop)	85			
Total	**425**		**160**	**585**
Joined 24 May 1648				
Lambert's (1 troop)		Bright's (6 Coys)		
Lilburne's (3 troops)				
To give:				
Lambert's (5 troops)	425	Bright's (6 Coys)	480	
Lilburne's (4 troops)	340			
Total	**765**		**480**	**1,245**
Joined 6 June 1648				
Cromwell's (4 troops)		Lord General's foot (8 Coys)		
Harrison's		Bright's (2 Coys)		
Thornhaugh's (1 troop)				
Twistleton's (5 troops)				
Dragoons (1 troop)				

Horse and Dragoons		Foot		Total
To give:				
Cromwell's (4 troops)	340	Bright's	800	
Harrison's	510	Lord General's (8 Coys)	640	
Lambert's (5 troops)	425			
Lilburne's (4 troops)	340			
Thornhaugh's (1 troop)	85			
Twistleton's (5 troops)	425			
Dragoons (1 troop)	100			
Total	**2,225**		**1,440**	**3,665**
Joined 25 June 1648				
Lancashire horse		*Lancashire foot*		
Rigby's horse		Ashton's		
Shuttleworth's horse		Dodding's		
		Rigby's foot		
		Shuttleworth's foot		
		Standish's		
To give:				
Cromwell's (4 troops)	340	Bright's	800	
Harrison's	510	Lord General's (8 Coys)	640	
Lambert's (5 troops)	425	Ashton's *c*.300		
Lilburne's (4 troops)	340	Dodding's *c*.300		
Rigby's horse c.250		Rigby's foot *c*.300		
Shuttleworth's horse c. 250		Shuttleworth's foot *c*.300		
Lancashire horse total	500	Standish's *c*.300		
Thornhaugh's (1 troop)	85	Lancashire foot total	1,500	
Twistleton's (5 troops)	425			
Dragoons (1 troop)	100			
Total	**2,725**		**2,940**	**5,665**

Horse and Dragoons		Foot		Total
Detached at the end of June for service in Northumberland, for about one week				
Cromwell's (four troops)	-340			
Harrison's (six troops)	-510			
Lilburne's (four troops)	-340			
Total remaining	**1,535**		**2,940**	**4,475**
These were restored to Lambert by about 6 July				
Joined on, or in the week before, 27 July 1648				
Bethell's militia horse		Lascelles' foot		
Cromwell's horse (2 troops)		Lord General's foot (2 Coys)		
Harley's troop of horse		"Old foot" (3 or 4 Coys), say		
Lambert's horse (1 troop)		Person ("thin" Coy)		
Lilburne's (Sanderson's 2 troops)		Wastell's foot		
Pennyfeather's troop of Horton's (not left in Chester)				
Scroop's (3 troops)				
Twistleton's (1 troop)				
Dragoons (2 troops)				
Wren's Durham militia (5 troops)				
To give:				
Cromwell's	510	Bright's	800	
Harrison's	510	Lord General's	800	
Horton's (Pennyfeather's troop)	85	Lancashire	1,500	
Lambert's	510	Lascelles'	500	
Lilburne's	525	"Old foot", say	250	
Scroop's (3 troops)	255	Pearson's Coy, say	50	
Thornhaugh's (1 troop)	85	Wastell's	500	
Twistleton's	510			
Bethell's militia horse, say	300			
Harley's troop, say	50			
Lancashire horse	500			
Wren's Durham horse (5 troops)	250			
Dragoons (3 troops)	300			
Total	**4,390**		**4,400**	**8,790**

Horse and Dragoons		Foot		Total
Troops available for Preston				
1. Accompanying Lambert south, 2 August 1648				
Cromwell's	510	Bright's	800	
Harrison's	510	Lancashire	1,500	
Lambert's	510	Lascelles'	500	
Lancashire horse	500	Lord General's	800	
Lilburne's	530	"Old foot", say	250	
Pennyfeather's troop	85	Wastell's	500	
Scroop's (3 troops)	255			
Thornhaugh's (1 troop)	85			
Twistleton's	510			
Dragoons (3 troops)	300		3,795	
Total Lambert	**3,795**		**4,350**	**8,145**
2. Marching from Wales with, or collected by, Cromwell				
Thornhaugh's (5 troops)	425	Overton's	1,200	
Scroope's (3 troops)	255	Pride's	800	
Lord General's horse (1 troop)	85	Dean's	800	
Dolphin (1 troop)	85			
Dragoons (2 troops)	200			
Total Cromwell	**1,050**		**2,800**	**3,850**
3. 12 August 1648, under Cromwell to Preston	**4,845**		**7,150**	**11,995**

TABLE 2 Regiments of Horse available to Lambert, from May to August, and the joint Cromwell/Lambert army

Bars below the name of the regiment each represent the approximate equivalent of one New Model troop of 85 men

| Regiments | with Lambert | | | | | | | | | | | | | | Lambert and Cromwell | | |
| | May | | | | June | | | | July | | | | August | | |
	Wk 1	Wk 2	Wk 3	Wk 4	Wk 1	Wk 2	Wk 3	Wk 4	Wk 1	Wk 2	Wk 3	Wk 4	Wk 1 towards	Wk 2 Preston	Wk 3 Preston
Bethell's															
Cromwell's															
Dolphin's troop															
Harley's troop															
Harrison's															
Horton's (Pennyfeather)															
Lambert's															
Lancashire horse															

12

Regiments	May				June				July				August		
	Wk 1	Wk 2	Wk 3	Wk 4	Wk 1	Wk 2	Wk 3	Wk 4	Wk 1	Wk 2	Wk 3	Wk 4	Wk 1 towards	Wk 2 Preston	Wk 3 Preston
						with Lambert									Lambert and Cromwell
Lilburne's															
Lord General's															
Scroope's															
Thornhaugh's															
Twistleton's															
Wren's															
Dragoons															

Dark shading shows the presence of troops, lighter shading indicates some uncertainty

TABLE 3 Regiments of Foot available to Lambert, from May to August, and the joint Cromwell/Lambert army

Bars below the name of the regiment each represent the approximate equivalent of one New Model company of 80 men

Regiments	with Lambert												Lambert and Cromwell		
	May				June				July				August		
	Wk 1	Wk 2	Wk 3	Wk 4	Wk 1	Wk 2	Wk 3	Wk 4	Wk 1	Wk 2	Wk 3	Wk 4	Wk 1 towards	Wk 2 Preston	Wk 3 Preston
Bright's															
Dean's															
Lancashire															
Lascelles'															

Regiments	with Lambert												Lambert and Cromwell		
	May				June				July				August		
	Wk 1	Wk 2	Wk 3	Wk 4	Wk 1	Wk 2	Wk 3	Wk 4	Wk 1	Wk 2	Wk 3	Wk 4	Wk 1 towards	Wk 2 Preston	Wk 3 Preston
Lord General's															
"Old foot", say															
Overton's (Reade's)															
Person's Coy, say															
Pride's															
Wastell's															

Dark shading shows the presence of troops

15

The former Northern Association regiments of Lambert's and Lilburne's horse and Colonel John Bright's foot were formally put on the strength of the New Model when the revised establishment was accepted by Parliament in February 1648.[17] This gave him a nominal force of 1,835 horse and foot with which to oppose any moves southward from Berwick or Carlisle. There was also available to him the militia of Yorkshire, Durham and Northumberland, which played some part in his dispositions later in the campaign. The numbers in table 1 include the militia when this is recorded and of significance. There are some known (and probably many unknown) temporary absences elsewhere, but unless the numbers were large this is not shown in the table. For example, Sanderson patrolled Northumberland with his own troop and either Bradford's or Captain Lilburne's until the end of July, leaving Colonel Lilburne with only four troops as given in table 1. At times more troops were in Northumberland, but brief episodes are not recorded in the tables.

It is now necessary to look further afield to establish where various bodies of troops who were later on with Lambert, or with Cromwell, were stationed. On 19 May General Fairfax reported to the Lords on the disposition of the horse. He had sent Twistleton's horse to the north as part of his own intended move, and five troops of the regiment were now in Otley near Leeds; it is not known where the other troop was stationed, but it joined the rest towards the end of July. He also sent Harrison's horse to Cheshire and then Lancashire to oppose any move south by Langdale.[18]

There was also some movement of Thornhaugh's horse. According to Fairfax's report, in mid-May Thornhaugh's 'was appointed to have an Eye to *North Wales*, save one troop thereof which is assigned to *Coventry*'. There may be an error here, or perhaps a revision of orders, as in the event two troops of Thornhaugh's were ordered to Coventry, along with Colonel Isaac Ewer's regiment of foot, according to a letter from Cromwell dated 30 May.[19] This move was in response to a request from the town at the beginning of May for 'Capt Creed's [of Thornhaugh's] or some other troop and a regiment of foot'.[20] Within a few days of their arrival in Coventry, Ewer, 'with your regiment and the two troops of horse with you', was ordered to join Colonel Whalley in Waltham, Essex.[21] Both Whalley and Ewer were with General Fairfax at the siege of Colchester, and the two troops of Thornhaugh's may have been there also but such evidence as there is suggests that they were not.[22]

Fairfax also reported that one troop of Thornhaugh's had already been ordered by Cromwell to go into north Wales, together with four troops of Cromwell's horse and 'some dragoons'.[23] The dragoons are assumed here to amount to a full troop. Fairfax says that he was about to order this force to join Harrison. There is no indication that Harrison's horse was other than complete, giving him a brigade of twelve troops including the dragoons.[24]

These moves left three troops of Thornhaugh's in Wales, under the command of Major Saunders to whom Cromwell wrote on 17 June at Brecon ordering him to move south and east to arrest two Royalist plotters.[25] Thornhaugh himself was not with his regiment, but joined Cromwell on his march north in July. Presumably Cromwell brought with him the three troops from south Wales as he is said to have marched with Thornhaugh's.[26] The two troops last certainly heard of at Waltham may well have joined them, as discussed below.

11 MAY 1648

The start of serious campaigning may be said to be the beginning of May, following the seizure by Royalists of Berwick and Carlisle at the end of April. By 11 May Bright's foot had been moved up from York to Northumberland;[27] eight companies are known from Sanderson's diary to have been at Alnwick, with the other two perhaps in York or left at Barnard Castle. Some of Lambert's horse went north with Bright's; Sanderson mentions them only as 'Captaine Goodrick . . . marched from us' on 16 May, so presumably just one troop was sent. Two troops of Lilburne's were left permanently in Northumberland under Major Sanderson during May, June and July. Three more troops of Lilburne's were briefly in Northumberland in mid-May, arriving there on the 11th: Major Smithson with his own, Colonel Lilburne's and Captain Bradford's. This left Lambert with only one troop of Lilburne's, Major Cholmley's. One troop of Lambert's was based elsewhere until July, probably in Yorkshire, leaving him with four.[28] Lambert, at Barnard Castle, thus had fewer than 600 horse and foot to control the road over Stainmore, the likeliest route for an invader from Carlisle.

Barnard Castle, incidentally, was ideally placed as a base from which to prevent movement over Stainmore or to block an invasion down the east side of the country through Newcastle and Durham (see plate 3 and map 6). Although the castle was no longer fully functional (see appendix 2) it probably still had a defensive capability if needed, and could provide at least some accommodation.

24 MAY

A letter from Newcastle dated 25 May says that Hesilrige had the day before received news that 800–900 Yorkshire horse had come down from Northumberland to Barnard Castle, at the same time as Lambert arrived there probably from Newcastle where he was on the 12th. The reason for the move south was said to be 'upon the disturbance to the Parliament', probably referring to the threat to the Parliamentary army from Langdale who was now in Carlisle.[29] Whether Lambert had accompanied these troops or had come from elsewhere is not clear. At about the same time, three of Lilburne's and two of Lambert's also came south, and Sanderson's two troops had been on their way south to Newcastle when they had to turn back to resist a minor incursion from Berwick.[30] Lambert was drawing his forces together to deal with what appeared to be the main threat.

However, there is no other record of so many Yorkshire horse being in Northumberland, or indeed anywhere else, and while Yorkshire was making arrangements to raise forces at this time they would not yet have been available to go on patrol in Northumberland. On the other hand, Bright's foot, which had been based in York at the beginning of the campaign, moved into Northumberland on 11 May as noted above and, according to Sanderson, six companies of the regiment left Alnwick on the 18th to join Lambert. It would have taken about six days, allowing for rest, to cover the seventy-five miles, which is just about when the horse was supposed to have arrived. The strong likelihood is that 'horse' was written in error for 'foot', and that it was Bright's foot which came to Lambert. Sanderson's diary makes no mention of Yorkshire horse at all, but does mention Bright's foot at precisely this time along with the return to Lambert of Smithson's, Colonel Lilburne's and Captain Lilburne's troops. The 'Yorkshire Horse' has therefore not been included in the table or charts. Two companies of Bright's were left at Alnwick and marched from there for Newcastle on 3 June, probably to join the rest of the regiment with Lambert at Barnard Castle.[31]

6 JUNE 1648

At the end of May Langdale began to move eastwards across the Pennines. Lambert withdrew from Barnard Castle to Catterick and brought up Harrison's brigade, consisting of his own regiment, four troops of Cromwell's, one of Thornhaugh's and one of dragoons, from Lancashire together with the five troops of Twistleton's from Otley, and concentrated his army at Catterick.[32] He was joined there by eight companies of the Lord-General's regiment of foot and two of Bright's.[33] This gave him almost 1,400 extra horse and 800 extra foot to make a respectable force of about 3,700 men. On 1 June he was reported to have 'about 4,000 horse and foot', which is reasonably close to the calculated figure. However, on 12 June the figures are given as 1,500 horse and 1,200 foot, a deficit of 1,000, which sounds like an intermediate and somewhat outdated estimate.[34] Lambert had had to leave troops under Harrison to mask Appleby Castle from 11 June until the 17th, but as the numbers are not known this brief detachment has been disregarded. It is possible that they account for the missing 1,000 men.

In the face of Lambert's increased numbers and obvious determination Langdale retreated, and over the next week was driven back into Carlisle. On 15 June he was said to have at least 6,000 armed men, and as many more unarmed, against 6,000 of Lambert's, but both these figures were probably very rough estimates at best.[35]

25 JUNE

On 25 June Lambert, now at Hesket Moor, south of Carlisle, was further reinforced by seven Lancashire regiments, two of horse and five of foot. However, these were militia units and their total strength is given as 500 horse and 1,500 foot, or 'one Regiment of good

Horse, and two Regiments of Foot'.[36] Dividing the numbers equally gives 250 each for the horse and 300 each for the foot; they are so shown in tables 1 and 2.

These additions were said to bring Lambert's total strength up to 8,000 men.[37] This is 2,500 more than shown in table 1 and it is difficult to ascribe the difference to anything but ignorance, optimism or propaganda to deter the enemy. A month later, Lambert was said to be 'not yet 5,000' against at least 12,000 Scots and Royalist English.[38] The letter was written from York to Members of the Commons and could reflect either losses through sickness, or a different kind of propaganda in order to encourage the Commons to provide more men. In fact he seems to have had a nominal total of about 5,700 so perhaps the estimate was not so very pessimistic.

More men were certainly needed as Lambert's small army had to be spread very thinly over the north of England. At the end of June Colonel Lilburne and his four troops were sent to Northumberland to deal with a Royalist pincer movement from Berwick and Carlisle, arriving at Haydon Bridge by 29th. On 1 July all of Harrison's and the four troops of Cromwell's were sent to reinforce Lilburne, arriving at Meldon on 3 July.[39] This temporary detachment of 1,200 horse was part of the balancing act that Lambert had to perform throughout May, June and July. This large depletion, which reduced him to about 4,500 men, is significant enough to merit its own entry in the tables.

Lambert was certainly not happy with the number of men he had. In a letter to his father-in-law of 4 July he says he has only twenty-three troops of horse immediately to hand, with two more in Northumberland and four in Yorkshire.[40] Furthermore, some were very small due to parties being elsewhere, there were many sick, many horses were unfit, and some men had run away. He ought to have had thirty-two troops in total, including one of dragoons, less the fourteen temporarily moved to Northumberland, leaving a balance of eighteen with him. Although the two Lancashire horse regiments amounted in total to only one New Model regiment, they could have been divided into up to ten or twelve troops of forty to fifty, which would make up the numbers of troops and explain in part why Lambert said that some troops were very small.

The total figures Lambert gives for his army are 2,600 horse and 2,200 foot. This may be compared with the figures calculated in table 1: 2,725 horse and 2,940 foot. The horse compares well enough, despite 'the abundance of horses sick and lame', although for some reason he has reduced the Lancashire horse from 500 to 300. The discrepancy of 700 in the foot remains to be explained; perhaps some of the former besieging force at Appleby were still stationed there and not immediately available. It is as certain as can be that he had Bright's, eight companies of the Lord General's and 1,500 Lancashire foot. Possibly the major desertions were in the foot, as was not uncommon, and perhaps some sickness as well, but it does still seem a wide discrepancy.

WEEK ENDING 27 JULY 1648

Cromwell, in a letter dated 28 June, said that 'some few days since' he had sent two troops of dragoons and four troops of horse to the north via West Chester (i.e. Chester), the horse specified as Captain Pennyfeather's troop and three of Scroope's.[41] Pennyfeather's was to stay at Chester and the rest to go to Leeds and thence to take orders from the Committee in York (not, rather oddly, from Lambert). It seems that Pennyfeather was not needed in Chester for it was reported from York on the 20th, following the taking of Thornhill Hall on the 18th, that 'Col. Wastell and Col. Losseth, their Regiments go not now to Pomfract, but to M. G. Lambert they will make about 1,000. Also the 6. Troopes from Wales, one of Col. Twistletons, and 2 of the Lieutenant-Generals, and one of M.G. Lamberts, these will be ready to joyn. And Col. Bethels new Regiment are ordered to march also, with 3. or 4. Companies of the old foote.'[42]

All of the six troops sent by Cromwell were certainly expected in the north, as a slightly earlier report says: 'The 600 horse and dragoons sent by Chester not yet come to him.'[43] The date of despatch of the final two troops of Cromwell's own horse regiment from Pembroke is not recorded, but it seems to have been at about the same time as the other six troops as they were all together in the Thornhill or York area.[44]

The distance from Pembroke to Thornhill via Chester is 240 miles. Marching from Scotland to Pontefract in November, Sanderson took twenty-one days to cover about the same distance, including four days of rest. If Cromwell's detachment of horse were despatched on 26 June and marched at the same rate, an average of about eleven miles a day including rest days, they would have reached Thornhill around 16 July, in time to assist in the attack (the surrender was on 18 July) and to be reported from York on the 20th.

If the horse and foot then marched north together from Thornhill they could have covered the eighty-odd miles to Bowes via Pontefract in five or six days. They seem to have reached Lambert over a period, from perhaps 23 to 27 July.[45] On 15 July two companies of the Lord General's foot marched north from York.[46]

Lambert was clearly expecting each of the six troops sent by Cromwell to be a hundred strong, which may not have been the case, and taking the most conservative estimate the additions – two troops of dragoons, one of Twistleton's, one of Lambert's, two of Cromwell's, three of Scroope's and Pennyfeather's troop – come to 880, and by analogy with the Lancashire horse, Colonel Hugh Bethell's Yorkshire militia horse may have added 300, or the equivalent of almost four New Model troops. Also, Sanderson's two troops of Lilburne's, at least 185 strong, had been called down from Northumberland, and five troops of Wren's Durham horse, perhaps 250 strong, were at Bowes when Lambert reached there on 18 July, along with Captain Harley's troop and Captain Pearson's 'thin' company from York.[47] The additional horse come to around 1,700 and the foot to nearly 1,500. The total of 8,790 horse and foot with Lambert agrees well enough with the contemporary total of 9,000.[48] Fenwick's Northumberland horse appear to have remained in that county, as the only troops not part of the Newcastle garrison, and were not immediately available to Lambert.

Two sources, though both clearly from the same original, record that 1,000 foot came to Lambert from Cromwell.[49] The date of reporting suggests that this happened on 22 July at the latest. From Pembroke to Barnard Castle through Chester is 320 miles which, at an average of ten miles a day including rest days, slightly slower than the horse, means that they would have had to leave Pembroke around 20 June.[50] This was when Cromwell was in the middle of trying to take Pembroke, an operation that needed infantry. He had set out for Wales with his own regiment of horse and three regiments of foot – Pride's, Ewer's and Dean's. Ewer's was posted to Coventry and Cromwell came north with Pride's, Dean's and Overton's. Before Pembroke he had, by his own reckoning, no more than 2,400 foot, and while he records sending the six troops of horse he does not mention sending any foot, which would have had to leave well before the horse.[51] He did not have the equivalent of a foot regiment to send to Lambert, and no record can be found of any orders issued to whatever regiments might have provided the 1,000 men.

Another source presents a different and perhaps more accurate picture: 'There are 2,000 horse and foot from Yorkshire joyned with us, which makes us 8,000.'[52] The horse from Yorkshire and from Cromwell, listed above, amounted to 1,100, and Lascelles' and Wastell's Yorkshire militia regiments of foot with a contemporary combined strength of 1,000 (note 42) fit very well for the additional foot, and 'foot from Cromwell' can be discounted.

There is another anomaly in the accepted figures. A letter from Lambert's quarters announced that 'Lieutenant-General Cromwell's Horse (consisting of thirty odd Troops) joined with Major-General Lambert [on] the 27th'.[53] Whatever their numerical strength, thirty troops make up five regiments of horse, which were simply not available to be sent anywhere. There were only fourteen regiments (eighty-four troops) of regular horse. Eight regiments of horse fought at Preston: Cromwell's, Harrison's, Lambert's, Lilburne's, Twistleton's, the Lancashire horse and at least parts of Scroope's and Thornhaugh's. The first six of these were already with Lambert, apart from one or two odd troops, at the end of June. Also, adding together all the regiments and odd troops known to have joined Lambert at the end of July, the total is only twenty-four including five troops of Wren's Durham militia, which had nothing at all to do with Cromwell. There must have been a misreading of the original letter. An alternative of 'thirty troop*ers*' would be hardly worth reporting; perhaps the original read 'three troops' although they cannot be identified unless it was a reference to the three from Scrope's who joined about this time with the Yorkshire troops. The total number of troops joining Lambert at around this time, including the equivalent from the Yorkshire and Durham militia, was around twenty. Only eight of these came from Cromwell.

**TABLE 4 Disposition of New Model Horse, July 1648
by numbers of troops**

Regiment	Southern England	Under Cromwell	Under Lambert
Cromwell		2	4
Fleetwood	6		
Gen. Fairfax	4	1	
Harrison			6
Horton		5	1
Ireton	6		
Lambert			6
Lilburne			6
Rich	6		
Scroope	3		3
Thornhaugh	2	3	1
Tomlinson*	6		
Twistleton			6
Whalley	6		
Totals	**39**	**11**	**33**

*in Devon and Cornwall

For clarity, the fourteen New Model horse regiments in being at the start of the second Civil War are listed in table 4, with their areas of activity in early July 1648. Some were already on their way to the north from their indicated locations. One troop of Fairfax's horse has been allocated to Cromwell on the basis of probabilities, and one cannot be accounted for, giving a total of eighty-three troops.

Lambert's and Cromwell's army

When Lambert marched south on 2 August to meet Cromwell he took with him most of his army, but there is no record of Fenwick's Northumberland horse, Wren's Durham horse, Pearson's company or Harley's troop accompanying him. Pennyfeather's troop is not mentioned either, but as part of the regular army it has been assumed that they went to Preston. Bethell's Yorkshire horse went at some unknown date to take charge of the siege of Scarborough rather than going with Lambert and was not at Preston. Cromwell mentions Wastell's and Lascelles' foot there, showing that they marched south with the rest. Lambert's numbers were thus 8,145 horse and foot.

It is not clear what happened to the 120 troopers from General Fairfax's horse, who were at Allerton Boat during the second week in July (see Chapter 5) and who might have been expected to join Lambert, or Cromwell on his way north. Lyndon (p. 145) says that there were only four troops of the regiment at Colchester, but there is no record of where the other two troops were stationed. One troop is included here in Cromwell's figures on the assumption that he collected them on the way north.

It was reported that Cromwell came north with 'his owne three Regiments of Foot, colonell Thornhaghs Regiment of Horse, and some Dragoons'.[54] Pride's, Dean's and Overton's foot had been with Cromwell in Wales and were all at Preston, so these must be the foot he brought north. His total strength was reported as 1,200 horse and 3,000 foot. [55]

Overton's, incidentally, was reported to have 1,200 men in it when attacking Tenby, an indication that this regiment at least had been recruiting up to war strength.[56] Eight companies of the regiment had been sent to reinforce Horton in the initial campaign.[57] Rushworth reported that: 'His Excellency hath also written to Lieut-Col. Rede at Bristol, to hasten the March of the Two Companies of Col. Overton's Regiment, designed for the Reducing of Pembroke-Castle, if they be not already there.'[58] The regiment was being commanded by Lieutenant-Colonel Reade, in the absence of Overton who was serving as governor of Hull, and Cromwell referred to it as Reade's in his despatches.

This gives at least 2,800 foot marching with Cromwell, close enough to the reported 3,000. However, of the 3,000 pairs of shoes ordered for him by Derby House, only 2,500 were supplied, and this may indicate that his actual number of foot was lower, or it may simply be that no more were available by the time he arrived.[59]

The reference to Cromwell bringing Thornhaugh's with him indicates that he brought the three troops of the regiment serving in Wales. Derby House had also offered Captain Richard Dolphin's troop from Herefordshire, and Cromwell presumably took up the offer.[60] This would give him 340 horse, to which he added others on the way.

Three troops of Colonel Adrian Scroope's regiment had been with Cromwell in Wales but were sent north by him at the end of June. The other three were in the east in early June, and in the second week in July had captured the Earl of Holland after the failed revolt of the Duke of Buckingham.[61] In his despatch to the Speaker after the battle of Preston Cromwell specifically refers to 'Colonel Scroope' in relation to orders given.[62] Scroope would hardly have marched alone from East Anglia to join the northern force without bringing reinforcements. On 21 July Derby House had asked General Fairfax to send a regiment of horse, or more, to Lambert.[63] Scroope is very likely to have taken his own three troops north with him as well as, probably, the two troops of Thornhaugh's which were last heard of at Waltham with Colonel Ewer.[64] Five troops would have gone a long way towards satisfying the request of Derby House, but as there is some doubt about their presence they are shown in lighter shading on the bar chart in table 2. The number of dragoons is also problematic. As already shown, Lambert was sent 'some dragoons' in June, taken here as one troop, and two troops towards the end of July. Cromwell came north with 'some dragoons', numbers unspecified but probably at least one troop.

In the initial stages of the battle of Preston, Major Smithson commanded the forlorn of 400 foot, 200 horse and two troops of dragoons.[65] On the same day, Cromwell noted that there were seven troops of horse and dragoons near Clitheroe, and on the following day Sanderson refers to three troops of dragoons being near him in the fight from Preston to Wigan.[66] These three may include the two who were in the forlorn, but those at Clitheroe must represent at least one other troop. So, there were at the minimum four troops of dragoons in Cromwell's army at Preston, including at least one coming up with Cromwell from Wales.

There could well have been more, as Cromwell's letter to Lord Fairfax towards the end of November refers to Okey's regiment in relation to his departure from Pontefract. Colonel Okey himself was certainly at Pontefract in November, perhaps with all or most of the regiment, but it is not known whether he came north only after Preston, nor what numbers came with him.[67] If Cromwell brought two troops with him the total of his mounted troops would be just over 1,000, still some way short of 'about 1,200' understood by Derby House.[68] To reach their figure, which is no doubt an estimate, all the troops of horse believed to have been brought with him would have to be at full war strength of a hundred, with three troops of dragoons. Two troops of dragoons is at least very likely and they are shown thus in table 1. The figures do argue very strongly that Cromwell was joined by the two troops of Thornhaugh's and three of Scroope's from the southeast, as well as Dolphin's troop, as otherwise his horse would be only 340 plus one or two hundred dragoons.

It has been said that Cromwell also brought with him troops from Pontefract, but there does not seem to be evidence for this. His careful mention of all regiments at Preston (Lambert's and Lilburne's apart) includes none from Yorkshire other than Wastell's and Lascelles' foot, both of which had already been ordered north to join Lambert before Cromwell arrived (see above 'Week ending 27 July'). It is sometimes said that he exchanged some raw recruits for more experienced men,[69] but all the troops with him had had considerable experience in south Wales and were surely rather more useful than the militia besiegers. He may have recruited the strength of his foot regiments from those besieging the castle, but that seems to be all. Certainly there is no indication that he took any complete regiments from the siege to accompany him.

On the contrary, the Account[70] of Capt Thomas Paulden gives the regiments left at Pontefract and their locations: White's and Hacker's were at Ackworth, Colonels Fairfax's and Rhodes' at Featherstone, and Sir Henry Cholmley's at Ferrybridge. Paulden does say that some of these marched for one day with Cromwell and then returned which, however unlikely a scenario, may have given rise to the belief that they went with him to Preston.

Cromwell did leave eleven troops of horse at Pontefract after taking the town, but these will have been from the militia forces of Nottinghamshire, Leicestershire, Lincolnshire, Northamptonshire, Derbyshire and some from Belvoir, a total of 660 ordered there by Derby House in mid-July.[71] This point is specifically made in a letter: 'The Forces of Nottingham and Derbyshire were conjoined, and marched up to Pontefract to release the forces that had surrounded that place, which by order were to advance to Maj. Gen. Lambert: there marches with the Lieutenant-Generall none but his own three Regiments of Foot, Colonell Thornhaughs Regiment of Horse, and some Dragoons.'[72] Colonel John Mauleverer's foot was on the way to join the siege before 15 July; under the same orders went Lascelles' and Wastell's foot, and Col. Bethell's horse, but the latter three were ordered north to join Lambert by 20 July,[73] and it seems to have been these regiments which were replaced by the militia ordered to Pontefract by Cromwell.[74] The regiments from and around Pontefract had been ordered north by Lambert twenty days before Cromwell arrived in the town on 10 August. At some point Bethell's was diverted to Scarborough.

There had been a proposal that Colonel Sir William Constable's regiment of foot might be sent from Gloucester to the north, but trouble in Gloucestershire and Herefordshire meant that this did not happen.[75]

In summary, Cromwell seems to have brought with him from Wales about 2,800 foot and probably 200 dragoons, with 340 horse made up of three troops of Thornhaugh's and Dolphin's troop. At some point on his march he was joined by Colonel Scroope with three of his own troops and two more of Thornhaugh's, and he is here assumed to have picked up one troop of the Lord General's horse from the Pontefract area, making a total of 1,050 horse, or 150 fewer than estimates.[76]

When joined with Lambert, the combined army will have consisted of almost 5,000 mounted men and over 7,000 foot, or a total of almost exactly 12,000. The calculation, it must be remembered, has been made using minimum unit strengths and the total may well have been somewhat higher. These figures cannot be said to be either final or accurate beyond dispute, but they do present, based squarely on available evidence, a realistic view of the numbers Cromwell led to Preston.

Cromwell himself said in his despatch to the Speaker that he had a total of 8,600 horse and foot made up of 2,500 horse and dragoons and 4,000 foot, all from 'your old army' plus 500 Lancashire horse and 1,600 Lancashire foot.[77] He was perhaps following a successful general's usual routine of giving an exaggerated view of a hard-earned success against vastly superior numbers. Certainly he seems to have ignored Wastell's and Lascelles' militia foot, but subtracting all the militia forces from the calculated totals still leaves 4,345 New Model horse and 4,400 New Model foot. The discrepancy of almost 2,000 horse cannot be explained. Gentles suggests that the total was in the order of 14,000, perhaps a little too great but more realistic than Cromwell's own figures.[78] Lucy Hutchinson gave a figure of about 10,000, and Ashley has estimated 9,000.[79] The truth may lie in the region of 12,000–13,000.

Hamilton's forces at Preston are even more difficult to ascertain. Cromwell says that Langdale had 4,000 and Hamilton 17,000, a total of 21,000 horse and foot. Turner says the Scots never amounted to more than 14,000 horse and foot, which, with the 3,600 that Langdale says he had, comes to 17,600.[80] The best estimate, and that may be putting it too generously, is something over 12,000 Scots horse and foot, with a further 3,600 or so under Langdale, to give a total of somewhere between 15,000 and 18,000.[81]

Chapter 2

THE CONDITION OF ENGLAND BEFORE
THE SECOND CIVIL WAR

THE RESOUNDING DEFEAT OF the Royalists at Naseby in June 1645 led, after more fighting in the west country, to their final collapse. On 5 May 1646 the king left his headquarters in Oxford and made his way to Southwell where he surrendered to the Scottish army which was besieging Newark (map 2), and ordered the surrender of his forces. The Scots handed him over to the English Parliament at the beginning of 1647, in return for a subsidy of £400,000, and went back to Scotland.

The Scots, who had been fighting on the side of the English Parliament, were still active in the affairs of England. They had had Commissioners, principally the earls of Loudon, Lauderdale and Lanark, in London since 1644 and they continued to negotiate for a settlement with the king based on the so-called Newcastle Propositions. In broad terms these demanded the king's signature on the Solemn League and Covenant, the removal of armed forces from his control, abolition of Catholicism, and the continuation of the war in Ireland but without the Scots. Parliament had agreed to the Covenant in 1643, in return for 20,000 Scottish troops who were to be paid for by England, but the king was now doing his best to avoid a measure that imposed Presbyterianism on the Church of England.

For their part, the Scots were not united in their desire for the Covenant. The Duke of Hamilton was prepared to accept compromise, the Marquis of Argyll in particular saw the king's adherence to the Covenant as an absolute necessity, while others including the Marquis of Montrose and the Highland clansmen rebelled against it militarily. This caused eight regiments of horse, one of dragoons and 500 musketeers to be withdrawn from the Scottish army in England late in 1645.[1]

By 1647 the Presbyterian majority in the English Parliament were becoming mistrustful of the victorious New Model, the Scots were mistrustful of both the army and the Independents in Parliament, and the king was attempting to play off all sides against the others.

When the Scots handed over the king in January 1647 the fighting in England had been over for eight months, but this was a truce rather than a formal treaty between the king and Parliament, and until the king agreed to a settlement there could be no permanent peace. The king, however, prevaricated and made half-promises to all sides in an effort to delay agreement, hoping to recover his original autocratic status. In these conditions, peace became more and more precarious, especially with the Scots being determined to retain the king in power, albeit with some limitations, as a symbol and figurehead of the unity between the two countries. It must not be forgotten than the union of the crowns had taken place less than fifty years earlier, when Charles I's father James VI of Scotland became also James I of England., and the Scots did not want to see their king deposed. The events of 1647 were to inflame the Scots' suspicions of the English army's intentions, and vice versa, as well as leading indirectly to the victory over the Scots at Preston and the execution of the king.

England in 1647

Although there was still fighting in Ireland in 1647, there was no clear enemy left in England. The Presbyterian majority in Parliament, led by Denzil Holles, were determined to disband most of Parliament's New Model army to which the people were becoming increasingly hostile. Free quarter and high taxes were significant factors in their dissatisfaction, as were the encroachments into civilian affairs of the County Committees, originally formed to raise troops and to levy taxes for their support. However, little or no thought was given to dealing properly with the army's sometimes substantial arrears of pay. It was now calculated that from the time of the New Modelling in early 1645 to 1 February 1647 the army was in arrears to the tune of forty-three weeks for horse and dragoons, and eighteen weeks for the foot, a total of £331,000, and this does not include the separate Northern Association army. The latter had been formed by the northern counties of England in support of Parliament, and was paid by locally raised taxes known as assessments or 'sesses'. Sanderson mentions applying to the local sessions for these in his entry for 12 January 1648.

On 5 March 1647 a move by the Presbyterians to replace Sir Thomas Fairfax, who had commanded the New Model since its foundation, was only narrowly lost. Three days later, in a repeat of the Self Denying Ordinance, the Commons resolved that no member of the House might hold a commission in the army. Parliament was clearly apprehensive about the army's intentions, for on 17 March it pointed out to General Fairfax that some of the army had quarters much nearer to London than the agreed twenty-five-mile limit and asked him to remedy this. A week later a conference between Lords and Commons led to the recommendation that the forces under Fairfax should be disbanded.[2]

The increasingly radical soldiers began to agitate, refusing to accept disbanding before they were paid in full, demanding legal indemnity for acts committed during their military service, and insisting on no conscription for service overseas. There were petitions and demonstrations on the part of the soldiers, who had the more or less discreet support of many senior officers. The Commons responded first by asking General Fairfax to stop the raising of petitions, and then on 29 March 1647 resolved to disband all the foot, save garrison troops, in the New Model and the Northern Association.[3] The following day both Houses issued a declaration that soldiers who in future caused any disruption would be declared 'Enemies to the State, and Disturbers of the Public Peace'.[4]

This could only inflame the situation, and it was soon clear that the army was no longer fully under the control of Parliament. Throughout April and May messengers went to and from Parliament to the army at Saffron Walden in an attempt to resolve the impasse. It took until the end of April for Parliament to appreciate the temper of the army, and on the 30th Lieutenant-General Cromwell, Field-Marshall Skippon, Commissary Henry Ireton and Colonel Charles Fleetwood were asked to do their best to quiet the army, to tell them that an Act of Indemnity was quickly to be brought in, and that a considerable portion of their arrears was to be paid upon disbanding.[5]

Parliament now seems to have been doing its best to placate the army. During May the Ordinance for Indemnity was passed and an extra two weeks' pay on disbanding was added to the six weeks previously agreed.[6] Cromwell had secured all of his own arrears, amounting to almost £2,000, by warrant signed on 27 May 1647.[7] On 25 May the Commons formally voted to begin disbanding the foot.[8] The first to go, on 1 June, was to be the Lord General's own regiment which has the ring of a deliberate insult to the general. Whether this was so or not the army was still not happy, and on 1 June the Lords received a letter from Fairfax expressing his officers' dissatisfaction and enclosing their Resolution which said that they were 'unsatisfied', 'amazed' and 'startled' at the votes passed by Parliament.[9]

On 2 June 1647 the army took the initiative and, acting at least in part on Cromwell's orders, Cornet Joyce with a commanded party of 500 men seized the king from Holdenby, Northamptonshire, where he was guarded by Major-General Brown, a Parliamentary Commissioner.* The king was taken to Newmarket (frontispiece map) where the army had rendezvoused in a spirit of enthusiastic unity between senior officers and men.

On 3 June the Commissioners for Disbanding reported that they had been unable to proceed as the army was 'in a Distemper'. On the same day Parliament attempted to appease the army by expunging from the record their declaration that anyone causing disruption was an enemy of the state.[10] But the Presbyterians were still determined to have their way and there were moves to oppose the army by raising forces, based on the Trained Bands and on the large numbers of former officers and soldiers in the capital awaiting payment.[11]

In this atmosphere of impending rift between the army and the Parliament, on 5 June the Scottish Commissioners made it plain that they were prepared to join the English Parliament 'for rescuing and defending his Majesty's Person . . . and for maintaining the

---

* Holdenby Palace (as it then was) was the largest private house in England, built by Sir Christopher Hatton, Queen Elizabeth's favourite.

Privileges of Parliament'.[12] This will have bolstered the confidence of the large Presbyterian faction in the Commons, but will not have reassured the army as to their intentions.

Friday 11 June was a day of great activity and significance. First, it was resolved by Parliament that men should be encouraged to desert from the army, and that those who did desert should be paid some of their arrears in the same manner as those still with the army, and have indemnity from courts martial. Parliament's not wholly unreasonable view was that the deserters were being obedient to the Parliament rather than to a rebellious army. Secondly, a formal Ordinance was passed that forces should be organised and raised for the defence of Parliament and the City. A letter from the Lords ordered that no part of the army under Fairfax should come nearer to London than forty miles.

But also on 11th a letter to the Lord Mayor of London, signed by General Fairfax, Cromwell, Lambert, Colonel Thomas Rainsborough and others, announced that the army was to move closer to London to obtain their desires. If the City did not resist, no harm would come to anyone, but if there were opposition 'we have freed ourselves from all the Ruin which may befal that great and populous City, having hereby washed our Hands thereof'. This was a stark warning that the army was determined to have its way against what it saw as counter-revolutionaries, and effectively threatened the start of another Civil War. The next day the headquarters of the army moved to St Albans, twenty miles from London.[13] 'Within the space of three months the army had moved from being an organisation on strike for pay and privileges to being a revolutionary movement more representative of the people than Parliament.'[14] The senior officers of the army were negotiating with the king for a peaceful solution, and indeed offered him better terms than were available from Parliament, while the king was looking for support anywhere it might be found, including Scotland, Ireland and France.[15]

Throughout June there were demands from Fairfax that Parliament should stop both encouraging deserters and raising forces to oppose the army, pleas which always met with the response that Parliament had no knowledge of any such actions. For its part, Parliament gave frequent orders that the army move away from London, which Fairfax said they would do when they were satisfied. In the middle of June Parliament ordered Fairfax to move the king to Richmond, an order that he ignored, and it was believed in some quarters that the Northern Association army had orders to move against the New Model if he did not obey.[16] On 16 June the army demanded the impeachment of eleven Presbyterian Members, headed by Holles, who were seen as their principal enemies.[17]

At the end of June the army moved to Uxbridge, only fifteen miles from Westminster, and the Commons gave leave for the eleven Members to be absent, at which they appear to have gone into hiding. Fairfax demanded that Parliament recall the declaration encouraging desertion, and pay the army what had been paid to deserters; that the many reformadoes (discharged officers) gathered in London be sent away; that Parliament should not suggest that the king be moved any closer to London than they allowed the army to be; and that the impeached Members be suspended from sitting until full charges could be laid. Among precedents he cited for impeachment, presumably as an implied threat, was that of the Earl of Strafford who was executed in May 1641.[18]

On the same day, 28 June, the Commons gave in and voted to pay the army as requested and declared that no officer or soldier should leave the army without permission of the general. In response, on the 30th Fairfax announced that his headquarters would move to Wickham, sixty miles west of London.[19] They later moved to Reading, about forty miles from London.

The commander of the Northern Association army, Colonel-General Sydenham Poyntz, had been much troubled by agitators from the New Model, and his more radical soldiers were petitioning General Fairfax with their grievances even though they came under the direct command of Parliament rather than the New Model. One of their requests was that they should be associated with the New Model rather than remaining independent, a view which Fairfax also recommended to Parliament. Indeed Fairfax seems to have been rather enthusiastically supporting the agitators, despite his own later denials and claims that he had acted under the duress of his own army.[20] On 8 July Poyntz was seized by his own men and taken first to Pontefract and then to Fairfax at Reading. He was immediately released, but Parliament ordered that he be discharged from his command. On 17 July 1647, Fairfax was appointed commander of all land forces rather than just the New Model, and at about this time Colonel John Lambert was given command of what was now the Northern Army of Parliament under him. Lambert met his new command on 4 August, and after being at first received in silence was later given a loud acclamation.[21]

On 2 July the Lords and Commons followed the army's request and voted not to ask that the king be brought nearer to London than they would allow the army to be. The army clearly had the upper hand at this point, and Commissioners were appointed from both sides to negotiate what, significantly, was described as a Treaty between army and Parliament. Throughout July the army kept up pressure for a settlement of all their demands.

On 6 July the formal charges of impeachment were laid against the eleven Presbyterian Members, and on the 20th the Speaker was empowered to give them passes to go abroad.[22] One of the demands of the army was for the release of those wrongly held in prison. More significantly they demanded that the London Militia be put back into the hands of those who had controlled it until May, that is to say, the Independents rather than the Presbyterians. Parliament gave in to this on 22 July, which led to riots on the 26th when a mob of 'Apprentices and many other rude Boys and mean Fellows' forced both Houses to repeal the new Militia order.[23]

Independent Members and the Speakers of both Lords and Commons thereupon left London for the protection of the army, leaving the Presbyterians in control. They elected a new Speaker for the Commons and lost little time in making their position clear: the Militia was given greater powers and ordered to protect Parliament and the city; Fairfax was told to give 'exact obedience' to an order not to come within thirty miles of London as this was likely to lead to fighting; it was to be broadcast with trumpets that Fairfax's command did not extend to the Trained Bands and garrisons; the king was invited to come away from the army and Parliament would make peace with him.[24] They also made clear what would today be called the Rules of Engagement: the Militia, and forces raised from mariners by Trinity House, were authorised to 'Kill and Slay all such as are or shall be in Arms against the King, the Kingdom, Parliament and City'. The reformadoes and others were to be put into regiments with Major-General Edward Massey as commander-in-chief. Another Civil War was feared.[25]

General Fairfax for his part announced that he intended to enter the city in order to protect Parliament, and put the blame for the riots firmly on the Lord Mayor of London's dereliction of duty. He also called up the Hertfordshire forces and ordered provisions from the Hundred of Cashor: 'Four Hundred Dozen of Bread, Four Hundred Pounds of Cheese, Four Hundred Pounds of Bacon and Ten Hogsheads of Beer' all to be delivered by eight o'clock the next morning.[26] This amounts to one and a third ounces each of cheese and bacon and seven-eighths of a pint of beer, to each loaf.

On 3 August Parliament sent another very strong letter to Fairfax, again ordering him to move the army at least thirty miles from London, to cease attacking forces in the city, capturing forts and raising money, all of which was 'tending to the Terror and Astonishment of the City'.[27]

This had no effect at all, as on the same day the army drew up on Hounslow Heath with 20,000 horse and foot complete with the artillery train. The City, as opposed to Parliament, ordered all the gates to be opened to the army, and on 4 August Colonels Rainsborough, Pride, Hewson and Twistleton marched unopposed into Southwark and pointed two pieces of ordnance at the raised drawbridge of London Bridge; it was promptly lowered. On Friday 6 August 1647 Lord Fairfax led the Speakers and dispossessed Members back to Westminster in a procession of four regiments, all with laurel branches in their hats, to the salute of the Common Council.[28] Fairfax received a vote of thanks from both Houses, and was made Constable of the Tower. The actions of the army were vindicated in a declaration of Parliament, and all reformadoes were ordered to leave the city.[29] The political situation had totally changed, following the submission of Parliament to *force majeure*.

In fact, it took a fortnight before the Commons agreed to repeal the votes taken between 26 July and 6 August and to restore the Militia to Independent control.[30] The fortifications around London, built during the first Civil War, were demolished, and the only outstanding question was the arrears of money for the army. It may be noted that the City had long been the greatest defaulter in the assessments for support of the army. Satisfied with progress, the army moved out of London to Putney, south of the river and five miles from Westminster, where they were joined by Fairfax who moved closer in from his headquarters at Kingston.[31]

Parliament agreed on 18 September 1647 to disband militia forces, but to maintain a standing army of 7,200 horse, 1,000 dragoons and 18,000 foot in England and Wales, plus the forces in Ireland.[32]

Many ordinary soldiers were still not convinced of the correctness of the path the army was following. The more radical agitators in the army forced a series of discussions (the Putney Debates) with senior officers, and there was danger of splits in the ranks of the army. The issues were settled, despite a mutiny in November which led to one soldier being executed by way of example, and many radicals were excluded from the army which returned to duty. An agreement was reached to have no further negotiations with the king, and that something approaching half the army would be disbanded, chiefly provincial – non-New Model – regiments and garrison troops.

At this point the king escaped from his new quarters at Hampton Court to the Isle of Wight, where he was recaptured and kept in custody in Carisbrooke Castle while fruitless efforts were made to negotiate with him. At the end of 1647 he signed an Engagement with the Scots, agreeing to bring in Presbyterianism for three years, although there was to be no compulsion for anyone to accept the Covenant. The Scots were to be allowed to occupy Berwick, Carlisle, Newcastle and Hartlepool until the king had been restored and peace achieved. The king was to resume control of the militia and his power to veto bills, and should Parliament not agree to the Engagement the Scots would bring in an army to compel it to do so.[33] The Engagement was subject to approval by the Committee of Estates and the Kirk in Scotland, which in the end was not readily forthcoming. In response to the Engagement, Parliament forbade further discussions (the Vote of No Addresses).[34] The Commons were to make no further approaches to the king, and anyone who did would be guilty of High Treason.

These events of 1647 are important for an understanding of what was to happen during 1648. The army having flexed its muscles with considerable success, and given many senior officers some share in government, Members of Parliament were no longer entirely free agents. The rebellion of the New Model army meant that it survived the attempted disbanding, and was available to defeat the Royalist risings and invasions in 1648. Knowing its power, it was able to control Parliament with impunity whenever it felt the need; without this, there may not have been the confidence to carry out the purge of its Members in December 1648 under Colonel Pride, and thus to execute the king. From now until the Restoration of the monarchy in 1660 Parliament was ultimately subject to the will of the army, which sometimes used the disguise of a velvet glove but at other times simply produced the iron fist.

Chapter 3

ESCALATION TO WAR

JANUARY AND FEBRUARY 1648

FROM ITS BEGINNING, 1648 was a difficult year for those now ruling in London, with the threat of invasion, risings, disturbances and plots, real and actual, proliferating throughout the country.

The Scots Commissioners had been secretly negotiating with Royalists and Presbyterians and encouraging risings to coincide with a future Scottish invasion. When they left London for home in January 1648, they confided in certain of the gentry along the way that they intended to raise an army to invade England to restore the king. The Commissioners were followed to Edinburgh by Sir Marmaduke Langdale and Sir Philip Musgrave, who held secret meetings with the erstwhile Commissioners. It was agreed that the Royalists should take Carlisle and Berwick and hand them over to the Scots on demand.[1]

In 1644 when Scotland was allied with Parliament, a Committee of Both Kingdoms had been set up to direct the strategy of the war. Subsequent distrust of the Scots led to the abolition of the Committee in January 1648, and its replacement by the Committee of Both Houses, which began work on 20 January. It met in Derby House, by which name it was generally known.[2]

During the first two months of 1648 Parliament carried out the agreed reduction in the size of the army in an attempt to reduce the tax burden, and the opportunity was taken to remove some of the more radical agitators from its ranks. Something like 20,000 men, or about half the total army, were disbanded, chiefly from the militia and garrisons. At the same time the army was reorganised 'so as to have more Officers at less Pay than now, and fewer Soldiers, which may be suddenly filled up as there shall be occasion'.[3] The treatment of the Horse exemplifies this: the twelve regiments with six troops of a hundred were changed to fourteen regiments with six troops of eighty.[4] The saving in troopers' pay was not great – a reduction in numbers from 7,200 to 6,720 – and the number of officers in a regiment remained the same. But this gave a wider base on which an increase in manpower could quickly be achieved if needed. The restoration of troop numbers to a hundred would increase the total by 1,680, a militarily much more efficient way than creating three new regiments in an emergency. It also ensured that officers of proven loyalty and efficiency could be kept in pay.[5]

There were numbers of independent troops and companies, so-called as they were not attached to a regiment. Some were disbanded and others were taken into existing, presumably under-strength, Northern Association regiments as they were reorganised on New Model lines. For example, the independent troops of Major John Sanderson, Major Cholmley, Captain Thomas Lilburne and Captain Francis Wilkinson were drawn into a depleted regiment of horse to be commanded by Colonel Robert Lilburne. Colonel Lilburne, formerly governor of Newcastle, went from there to York to take command of his new regiment towards the end of March.[6] Lambert appears to have been given a regiment of horse at around this time, probably the one formerly commanded by General Poyntz.

The reduction in the army did not produce any reward for Parliament by way of increased popularity. At the end of 1647 there had been riots or disturbances in Canterbury, Ipswich, London and elsewhere against the abolition of Christmas. Later there were several deaths when Easter riots in London against high taxes had to be put down by armed horsemen, and there were demands for the king's freedom as a move to restore lost liberties and forbidden customs. Essex, Suffolk and Norwich had riots and petitions, the West Country was in something of a ferment, and there was a need to guard against trouble from across the Scottish border, all of which put considerable pressure on the smaller army.

Almost from the beginning of 1648 the *Calendar of State Papers Domestic* has many references to anticipated inconveniences, mischiefs, tumults and insurrections, by those opposed to the new government. From May onwards these are mostly referred to as 'designs' and occur all over the country.[7] Derby House showed much concern for the reduction of castles and fortified houses which might be occupied by 'many malignants . . . secretly lurking'. Between January and the end of May designs were anticipated or discovered at: Aldeburgh, Ashby-de-la-Zouch, Belvoir Castle, Bristol, Carnarvon, Conway, Coventry, Croyland, Gloucester, Hereford, Holy Island, Kent, Leicester, Netley Abbey, Newark, Newport Pagnell, Parliament, Scarborough, Tilbury, the Tower and Winchester. There is an air of tension in the record, and an awareness of how tenuous the Parliament's hold might be in the face of uprisings. The revolutionary government was clearly not feeling secure and depended very much on the support of the reduced army. Gentles well describes the Derby House minutes in May as showing 'barely controlled consternation'.[8]

On 24 January Derby House was given authority: 'to prevent and suppress all Insurrections and Tumults within the Kingdom of England, Dominion of Wales and Town of Berwicke: And, to that Purpose, have Power to give Order and Direction to all the Militias and Forces of the Kingdom . . .'[9]

The north of England was relatively quiet, although it was not free of rumours about the intentions of the Scots. The Scottish Commissioners, who had negotiated the Engagement with the king at the turn of the year, returned to Scotland to argue for its approval while the English Parliament sent a Commission to Edinburgh to argue against it. The Duke of Hamilton, who led support for the Engagement, had a substantial majority over the Marquis of Argyll and the Covenanters who led the opposition to it; only the Kirk wholeheartedly sided with Argyll.

It was in these uncertain times that more serious trouble broke out when Colonel John Poyer, commanding the Parliamentary garrison of Pembroke, refused an order to disband on the grounds that their pay was in arrears. Later he disobeyed orders to hand over the castle to Colonel Fleming. Similar complaints struck the spark of opposition among several local regiments which soon flared up into support for the Royalist cause.

As early as the end of January there were reports from Berwick that the Scots soldiers were cheerfully anticipating another invasion, and a little later letters from Scotland announced that many Englishmen who were disaffected to the Parliament were flocking to Edinburgh.[10]

MARCH 1648

In the middle of March there was concern over English soldiers marching north to join the Scots. These were Captain Edward Wogan, of Okey's regiment of dragoons, and his troop which had been ordered to disband. They were travelling under orders forged in General Fairfax's name, and Lambert was ordered to stop them but was unsuccessful. Initially they were not received on their entry to Scotland, although by 14 March Wogan was in Edinburgh beginning to raise a regiment.[11]

Conditions in Northumberland were deteriorating with horses being stolen by the Scots on some scale: 'and for Horses, we in Northumberland can hardly keep any; the High-Sheriff and Two Justices of the Peace, having had stolen, or taken and carried into Scotland, above Twenty'.[12] Also at this time a plot was uncovered to seize Berwick-upon-Tweed by those gathering under the pretence of attending a race meeting, which was promptly cancelled.[13]

Late in March there was news that 'the Army is to march into the North but false'.[14] At the same time, the Scots were discussing the raising of 40,000 troops to go into England, while a letter from York was confident that the Parliamentary forces there were ready to oppose invaders.[15]

APRIL 1648

On 7 April Colonel Thomas Horton, who had been assisting with disbanding in South Wales, was given orders to suppress the revolt there and promised reinforcements.[16] There was initially a lack of success, and the Parliamentary adjutant-general, Colonel Fleming, was killed at Llandeilo at the end of April.

Early in the month apprehension was growing in the north, for it was reported that in Northumberland Major Sanderson was keeping a watch on Royalists, who were fearful of being questioned again.[17] One of the problems for Lambert, as commander in the north, was that information was difficult to come by: 'Our intelligence from there is meere accidental, not certaine; having no scoutmaster or other intelligences.'[18] This complaint was repeated by Margetts in May and in a report from Appleby in July.[19]

On 12 April the English Commissioners in Scotland finally received a refusal to answer long-standing questions about the return of Sir Philip Musgrave, Sir Thomas Glemham and Captain Wogan. All three were in Scotland where the number of English troops was said to be 2,000. Irish forces under Sir George Monro were ready to support the Scots, and were sent a fortnight's pay in response to their offer.[20]

A letter of 25 April invited Parliamentary supporters to meet for discussions on matters of mutual safety.[21] By the end of the month the new governor of Newcastle, Sir Arthur Hesilrige, was taking steps to ensure the safety of the town and region; he also arranged a meeting in Richmond to discuss putting the north in a state of defence. The cavaliers were said to have high expectations of the Scots and English sympathisers coming into England.[22]

The situation then began to deteriorate rapidly. On 28 April Sir Marmaduke Langdale seized Berwick, and on the following day Sir Thomas Glemham and Sir Philip Musgrave took Carlisle.[23]

MAY 1648

Owing to Horton's initial lack of success in South Wales, on 1 May General Fairfax, as commander of all land forces, ordered Cromwell, Lieutenant-General of the New Model, to take command there with an additional two regiments of horse and three of foot.[24] However, Horton had in the meantime defeated the rebels in the field at St Fagans on 8 May, and thereafter operations were largely limited to besieging castles. Cromwell's troops took Carmarthen Castle on the 20th. Colonel Isaac Ewer took Chepstow on the 25th and Tenby fell to Colonel Robert Overton on the 31st.[25] Now only Pembroke held out, enabling Cromwell to release some of his cavalry for service in the north, as described in Chapter 1.[26]

Early in May Hesilrige also sent supplies to Holy Island, apparently just in time to encourage the governor, Captain Robert Batten, not to respond to approaches from Langdale and the Prince of Wales. Although Batten's loyalty was later seen as having been in some doubt, Langdale was unsuccessful. The Commons, on 9 May, went to some trouble to keep Batten on side, asking Hesilrige to reimburse him for money he had spent out of his own purse, and to give other assistance. A week earlier Derby House had asked General Fairfax to send more troops to the island in view of its importance. It was perhaps in response to this that it was reported on the 18th that Royalists from Berwick had garrisoned Haggerston tower, which guarded the approach to the island (map 9).[27]

On 2 May it was made known that Fairfax was to go north with an army, an indication that Parliament took the potential troubles there very seriously, although they did not actually give the instruction until the 9th.[28] In the first few days of the month Langdale was alarming the neighbourhood of Morpeth (map 9), although he said that he would not join with the Scots but act only on a commission from the Prince of Wales.[29] On 5 May Sanderson had news that Major Sir Gilbert Errington, who was later described as 'late Capt of the Mosse Troopers',[30] was putting a garrison into Cartington Castle, and Sanderson attempted unsuccessfully to eject him. Errington left on the 7th, but the following day there was a report that he had occupied Harbottle Castle less than seven miles to the west; Sanderson at once occupied the vacant Cartington. The report added that Sir Philip Musgrave was marching towards Penrith with 500 horse, intending to take Appleby. Meanwhile, Lambert had fortified Appleby and Raby castles (map 6), and Walton Hall in Yorkshire, seven miles southwest of Pontefract (map 3), and Hesilrige put horse and foot into Warkworth under Captain Pie (map 9).[31] Later in May Lambert gave orders for a garrison of sixty men to be put into Wressell Castle, eighteen miles north east of Pontefract (map 3), to the dismay of the Earl of Northumberland's tenants.[32]

At the beginning of May Lambert was at Somerset House, the London quarters of General Fairfax, from where he wrote to Colonel Charles Fairfax at York in reply to a letter about the recruitment of the latter's new regiment, and promising arms and men.[33] By 12 May Lambert was in Newcastle.[34]

The 'Popish and Malignant Party' from Northumberland and Berwick were concentrating in Berwick, and a rendezvous for sympathisers was arranged at Hedgely Moor near Alnwick.[35] At about this time came a report that Morpeth and Alnwick (map 9) had been taken by 'Malignant gentry' who were chased off by horse and foot sent by Hesilrige, taking six prisoners in the pursuit. It is not clear whether these Royalists were from Westmoreland under Sir Robert Strickland, from Berwick under Langdale, or local men. Sanderson, who was in the immediate area at the time, makes no mention of this and it may have been no more than a rumour, or at most a very brief occupation.[36] There was an almost identical event on 1 and 2 June, see below.

Despite all these alarms, the Commons found time to instruct their Commissioners in Scotland to make a complaint to the Scottish Parliament about the form of address used by them: 'The said letter being addressed thus: "To the Right Honble the Speaker of the House of Peers pro tempore, to be communicated to the Lords and Commons assembled in the Parliament of England at Westminster." That the Houses take notice of and very much resent this unusual address, it being not the style which hath been and is used to the Houses of this Parliament.'[37]

A letter from Newcastle of 11 May refers to part of Lambert's horse and Bright's foot passing through the town to join a troop already near the border.[38] The troop was Sanderson's which had marched from Whittingham on to Alnwick on the 13th, where Bright's had already arrived. The letter concludes with an expression of joy to hear that Fairfax was coming north. Meanwhile, another letter from the same place emphasised the dangers: 'The high Sheriffe of Northumberland, and many Justices of Peace, are inforced to flie to Newcastle for the safety of their persons, leaving their houses and goods exposed to the danger of the enemy.' The letter also incorrectly announced that about 1,000 of Lambert's horse were to go to Northumberland and Cumberland, while the remainder stayed in Yorkshire.[39] This number would have been the total of Lambert's horse. At about this time Cartington Castle was abandoned by Parliament as untenable, and its house (probably the hall and solar) dismantled.[40]

Things were little better elsewhere. A letter from Margetts in York mentions threats to the city[41] and speaks of the Cavaliers being full of pride and confidence as a result of the taking of Berwick and Carlisle. However, Major Cholmley and his troop dampened their enthusiasm by raiding their quarters, apparently in Westmoreland, and seizing some of the rebels.[42]

More fighting broke out in the second week of May in Cumberland when Musgrave marched as far as his house near Kirkby Stephen and forced Cholmley over Stainmore (map 6).[43] It is not known where Cholmley had been based (Appleby and Brough are likely candidates) but once pushed east of Brough he would have had to retreat to Bowes as there was nowhere between the two towns for quarter. The letter adds that Bright had gone to Raby Castle for safety. Bright, however, had been in Alnwick from 13 May, and on the 15th wrote a joint letter from there with Major George Smithson of Lilburne's.[44] Sanderson says that six companies of Bright's left on the 18th, something which cannot have been known in London before the 22nd. Bright's move to Raby was en route to join Lambert at Barnard Castle, rather than running for safety as the letter implies.

The reason for Bright and Smithson's letter was to report to Hesilrige on whether Chillingham and Bamburgh castles were suitable for garrisons (map 9). The result was decidedly negative: Chillingham was 'not fitt to place any men therein; for Bamburgh itt is altogether ruined; and decayed; the low roomes filld with sand; the gates burnt upp; and not one peice of timber in all the castle'.[45] Sanderson was one of those who inspected Chillingham, although he does not mention the reason himself, but it is not known who went to Bamburgh.

Lambert's base in Barnard Castle was ideally placed to block an invasion either from Berwick down the east coast or through Carlisle and across Stainmore. The castle had been partly dismantled, but was still usable. Lambert would probably also have had guards at Bowes, as he did at the end of July. The castle there, although no longer defensible, will have provided at least some shelter in the keep (plates 3 and 4, and appendix 2)

On 15 May General Fairfax's army set out for the north, with the general expected to follow shortly. Further detail comes in a letter of the 16th from Commissary-General Henry Ireton to Hesilrige, which explains that Fairfax would march with three regiments of horse and some foot after dealing with insurrections at Bury, Suffolk. One of the regiments of horse, Colonel Phillip Twistleton's which was based at Newark, had left three or four days earlier, but the other two, the Lord General's and Colonel Edward Whalley's, were later diverted south.[46]

The situation in the north was becoming so serious that in the same letter Ireton recommended Hesilrige to abandon Northumberland to the enemy and concentrate on preventing the Royalists moving south from Carlisle. His somewhat impassionate, almost frenetic, view is worth quoting at some length:

> ... the enemye by the waye of Carlisle hath an open waye and free range,
> through Cumberland, Westmerlande and Lancashire into the very bowells
> of Englande or into Wales. Sir I beseach doe not weigh Northumberlande in
> ballance with the wholle kingdome; rather give the enemy for the present
> all that parte beyond Tyne and all the monyes and strength they can rayse
> in it, then leave them unstopt on Carlisle-side ... From Barwicke and
> Northumberlande Newcastle and the River Tyne is a barre to theyre further
> progresse, but on Carlisle-side, there is no stop to them but by a force in
> the feild.[47]

The west and northwest of the county may have been relatively sparsely populated, but to contemplate abandoning the whole 2,000 square miles, including Morpeth and Alnwick in the east, was an indication of the seriousness of the situation. Clearly Parliament saw the gravity of it, for with the lieutenant-general busy in south Wales it was deemed worthy of the attention of General Fairfax himself. Ireton understood that there was one regiment of horse and one of foot in Northumberland, which would be Bright's foot (probably eight companies), five troops of Lilburne's horse (Colonel and Captain Lilburne's, Smithson's, Sanderson's and Captain William Bradford's) and one of Lambert's horse under Captain Goodricke.

There was need for close attention, for on 3 May the Scottish Parliament finally voted for a levy of 30,000 foot and 6,000 horse to form an army to invade England. After some changes, the Duke of Hamilton was to be general, with Earl Callander as second in command, John Middleton as lieutenant-general of horse and William Baillie as lieutenant-general of foot.[48] The levy proved very difficult with the Kirk speaking out against it. Argyll and other Covenanters not only encouraged resistance to it, but also, according to Bishop Henry Guthry, are even said to have sent Major Strachan to Cromwell to encourage him to send troops to Scotland to support the anti-engagement party.[49] This seems an unlikely move, but the point is not refuted by Turner who otherwise called Guthry's account a 'most malicious and lying pamphlet'.[50] At Mauchline Muir outside Kilmarnock (twenty miles southwest of Glasgow), resistance flared into conflict in the second week in June, when 2,000 anti-

Engagement Covenanters faced ten troops of horse under Middleton. The Covenanters were driven off only when Callander came up with another 1,000 horse.

The withdrawal from Northumberland of most of Bright's left only Sanderson's two troops of horse (his own and Bradford's) and two companies of Bright's foot, identified by Sanderson as those of Major Legard and Captain Challenor.[51] The other three troops from Lilburne's, and the one from Lambert's, had been withdrawn at about the same time as most of Bright's foot.[52] North of the garrison town of Newcastle, Northumberland was defended by no more than 400 men of the regular army.[53]

In an account to the House of Lords, 19 May, of the disposition of horse and dragoons, General Fairfax reported intelligence that Langdale had taken Warrington (of which there is no other report), and that to resist any further advance he had sent Colonel Thomas Harrison's horse and some others to Cheshire;[54] Harrison later moved into Lancashire.

General Fairfax left Windsor for the north on 20 May, following that part of his army which had already departed. To add to Poyer's rebellion in south Wales and the growing problems in the southeast of England, there now was a failed attempt to take Pontefract Castle; details are given below at the beginning of June. On the other hand, Lancashire, Yorkshire and Cheshire were raising forces to support Parliament.[55]

On 25 May it was said that 800–900 Yorkshire horse had been drawn back to Barnard Castle, but the unit was in fact Bright's foot as discussed in Chapter 1. They were much needed, for Langdale moved from Berwick to Carlisle in the middle of May to combine with Sir Philip Musgrave. By the end of May their force, estimated at 7,000–8,000, was around Kendal and Appleby and was obviously raiding across Stainmore: 'On Saturday last [20th] a Gentleman was fetched away out of his bed by a party of them, within a Mile of Barnard Castle, and some Houses were also plundered there by them.'[56]

Thomas Margetts wrote a long and usefully detailed letter from York on 27 May summarising the current situation.[57] Langdale was still in Cumberland and Westmorland and understood to be doing no more than making occasional raids. His strength, whatever was being said in the press, was not known: 'and how strong they are our intelligence is so bad wee cannot certainly learne'.

Margetts explained that Lambert had moved one troop of horse well in advance of the rest, right on the enemy's borders, with nine troops in a body on the border of Westmoreland, but they were not attacked by Langdale. Indeed, they took five of Langdale's men with valuable horses and arms, which had been an encouragement to the soldiers. The opportunities for loot were an important factor in an army whose pay, according to Margetts, was in arrears by six weeks more that the rest of the army.

Margetts' description of Lambert's advanced position can perhaps be related to the local terrain. The summit of Stainmore, where the Roman fortlet of Maiden Castle has views towards Brough and Appleby, is a mile and a half west of the Durham–Westmorland border (map 6 and fig. 1). There is no room there to accommodate nine troops of horse, but just to the east of the border is the Roman marching camp of Rey Cross, in and around which is twenty or thirty acres of level ground. One troop on the summit and nine more just under two miles to the east would fit well enough with the description, and it is not easy to see where else they could have been stationed. However, the details given are so sketchy that this location can be no more than a suggestion.

Margetts also says that Lambert left Colonel Lilburne in command at Barnard Castle and went to York where he arrived on 25 May, and there met Colonel Twistleton whose regiment was quartered in Otley. Meanwhile, a commanded party of 140 under Major Cholmley was sent over Stainmore towards the enemy quarters at Kirkby Stephen with orders to engage if he judged it advantageous; Colonel Lilburne was to 'second or secure him as occasion shall arise'. This is a good example of the organisation of the New Model, with a strong skirmishing party sent out and a reserve ready to support them or cover their retreat. A letter from someone in Cholmley's troop confirms Margetts' report: 'Our Forces are so disposed that they cannot come into Yorkshire and Lancashire, which they so aim at. We have of late taken some prisoners, with Horse and Armes; yesterday morning our Troope were appointed to March into Westmerland, to fall upon their quarters; Col. *Lilburne* commands our Troops in absence of the general.'[58] This letter also adds that 'Capt *Iakson* is well and his castle safe'. Jackson could be Captain Robert Jackson,[59] in which case the unidentified castle was Appleby, which Lambert had fortified early in May. However, if this were so it must have been given up very soon thereafter as it had to be retaken for Parliament in mid-June.

Margetts goes on to say that Lancashire had reached a treaty with the Cavaliers and would not hurt one another, and thus it was expected that the Royalists would advance through Yorkshire with their flank secure. It was anticipated that Harrison and Twistleton would join with Lambert, and in addition three regiments of foot, under Colonel Legard, Colonel Charles Fairfax and another, and one of horse under Colonel Hugh Bethell, were to be raised in Yorkshire. Fairfax was already busy raising his regiment at the beginning of May.[60]

At sometime in May the castle at Skipton was surprised by Royalists. Dawson suggests that this was in the middle of May as the Parish Register records that on the 16th 'many were slayne at this time'.[61] There was a suspicion that Langdale might avoid Lambert by reaching Pontefract using a route other than that over Stainmore, in which case the road through Skipton would have been the most likely.[62] A letter from York dated 1 June says that: 'Major Gen. Lambert marched this day towards Skipton, and hath regained the castle.'[63] As noted above, Thomas Margetts says that Lambert arrived in York from Barnard Castle on 25 May. His movements over the next few days are not known, but he could easily have been in Skipton, just over forty miles away, in ample time to take and complete brisk action against the castle on 1 June.

On 30 May Derby House copied to Lambert a letter to the Deputy Lieutenants of Lancashire asking them to give assistance to Lambert by sending whatever forces they could spare, and on 6 June appointed Colonel Ashton to command those forces.[64] This gives a different picture of Lancashire from that outlined by Margetts.[65]

At the end of May a party of Royalists under a Colonel Carnaby achieved a minor coup when a party from Cumberland captured Major Shaftoe and sixteen of his men who were recruiting at 'Beywell' on 26 May.[66] The place is perhaps more likely to be the tiny settlement of Bywell, 2½ miles southwest of Felton and forty miles from Berwick (map 9), rather than the better-known Bywell on the Tyne only fourteen miles from Newcastle. Shaftoe was taken to Carlisle, a distance of some seventy miles largely on side roads and small tracks (there is no direct route), which gives some indication of the very tenuous hold the Parliamentary forces had over Northumberland. In fact, after the first ten miles or so his captors would have been to the west of the area patrolled by Sanderson's two troops, the only Parliamentary force in the area about which we have detailed information. Shaftoe's capture was said to have been a great discouragement to those who were arming themselves against the Royalists.

The same source refers to difficulties in Scotland but concludes that these will be no barrier to raising the army there. In Cumberland there was fear of Langdale and of the Scots who were now expected within eight or nine days. Country gentlemen and others were rising in Langdale's favour, and Presbyterians were fleeing from the county. At the same time came a report that Langdale had taken an unnamed house in Westmoreland said to be the 'chiefe Magazeen of that County'. A second report may relate to the same incident: 'In *Westmerland* they have taken in the Isle seven brasse canon, 4,000 Armes; and a great deal of Silver and Plate, they are 7,000 strong, many of them armed.'[67]

This place was almost certainly St Herbert's Isle in Derwent Water, to where ordnance from Carlisle was ordered to be sent at the beginning of May. The Sheriff of Cumberland had fled there in mid-May, and even though it was surrounded by water five or six fathoms deep it was expected to be taken.[68]

The situation was clearly looking serious even though morale in the army was said to be high. The Scots were raising forces as quickly as they were able, although the Kirk was still hindering this so far as it could.[69]

During May problems were growing in the southeast of England. Petitioners from Surrey rioted in London, and the city was held in control only by Major-General Skippon and the London Trained Bands. At this time demonstrations and petitions in Kent grew into an open, armed revolt, and from mid-May onwards there is an almost continuous record of more troops being sent into Kent, Suffolk and Essex, as well as to counties north of London. The troubles in Kent began on 11 May as a celebration of the discharge of men accused of playing football at Christmas. It became more serious with 20,000 signatures on a petition demanding that the army be disbanded, taxation reformed, and that government should be by means of established laws. Some local gentry supported the petition, but little of a practical nature was done until the Earl of Norwich returned from exile. On 21 May he raised 10,000 men who marched on London. They were joined by many former Royalist soldiers, and moved to Essex where Sir Charles Lucas, Sir George Lisle and Sir Bernard Gascoigne had begun their own rising at Chelmsford.

There was a further blow to Parliament when it was reported on 28 May that Vice-Admiral Rainsborough's squadron of seven ships in the Downs (an anchorage off Deal in Kent) had declared for the king and had taken three castles, Deal, Sandown and Weymouth. Two more ships from the North Sea squadron joined the mutineers, who eventually sailed for Holland and the king's cause. The Earl of Warwick was re-appointed Lord High Admiral and, followed by Sir William Batten who had previously commanded the fleet in succession to Warwick and prior to Rainsborough, went to Portsmouth to dissuade the ships there from joining the mutiny. However, in July Batten, who had been in correspondence with the king, took a privateer to join the Prince of Wales.[70]

The following day, the 29th, Derby House instructed General Fairfax to deal with the troubles in Kent rather than to continue his journey north. He had left on 20 May, and even if he were marching with some of the foot he should have been several miles north of Leicester by this time. The major part of his army, which left on the 13th, ought by then to have been in the neighbourhood of Doncaster, 160 miles from London. This assumes one rest day in four, and an overall marching rate of ten miles a day, but there is no indication of how far they had actually marched.

In Essex the rebels were growing in number, despite some desertions, and marched to Colchester to carry out more recruiting. Fairfax was now in pursuit, but on 11 June the Royalists got into the town after some very hard and vicious fighting, and Fairfax was forced to settle down to a siege.

It is not clear whether this armed rising was due, at least in part, to the encouragement of the Scots Commissioners (see beginning of this chapter), but the coincidence of trouble flaring up less than two weeks after the taking of Berwick and Carlisle seems too great to be ignored. It was certainly successful in keeping the Lord General and a significant part of the New Model in southeast England when the greatest threat to the government was in the north.

JUNE 1648

Early in the morning of 3 June, Pontefract Castle, one of the strongest in the north, was captured by Royalists.[71] An attempt in May had failed, as the corporal who promised to be on guard to give assistance was drunk and not on duty. A scaling ladder was discovered the next day and the governor decided to bring in those of his soldiers who had been lodging in the town, and sent out for beds to accommodate them.[72] A letter written fifty years later by

Captain Thomas Paulden, and his undated account (referred to as Letter and Account) give details of how the castle was taken.[73]

Lieutenant-Colonel Morris, a former Parliamentary officer, with ten men including Captain William Paulden, Thomas's brother, brought in beds and overcame the guards after sending some of them out to buy drink. The governor, Major John Cotterell, was seized in his bedroom after a fight in which he was wounded, and was locked up with the guards.[74]

The fact that eleven men could so easily take such a large and strong castle is on the face of it rather surprising. But only those on duty were sleeping in the castle, while the rest quartered in the town. Morris had been a close friend of the former governor, Colonel Robert Overton, and indeed Holmes suggests that Overton would have declared for the king if he had not been transferred to the governorship of Hull in November 1647. Although Morris is not known to have been friendly with Cotterell (Paulden says 'little or no acquaintance'), he would have been a familiar face to the garrison and appears to have caused no suspicion when he sent men out for drink. Morris had been behind the attempted scaling of the walls in May, and had been investigated for an attempt on the castle eighteen months earlier, but this does not seem to have had any effect on his access.[75]

It was said that, when the castle was taken, an alarm of the enemy approaching was given, and market traders were encouraged to bring their goods into the castle for security, and thus the rebels gained a good store of provisions.[76] Captain Thomas Paulden came in on 6 June with 300 horse and foot to make a total of 500 men.

Fox says that Sir John Digby was made the nominal governor while Morris commanded in practice.[77] Certainly some letters from the besiegers were addressed to Digby.

It was suggested that Langdale was behind the coup: 'Many of the North being ill affected, they did connive at a party of Langdales that march obscurely in the night, upon the Moore out of Cumberland into Yorkshire, having some private engagements from some perfidious men that were in trust in Pomfret Castle.' That many were ill-affected indicates the degree of support in the north for the king, but it is remarkable if men did indeed come from Cumberland, about a hundred miles as the crow flies, to assist the garrison.

Lambert was in Knaresborough on the morning of 3 June probably, as shown above, on his way back from Skipton to York. In a letter of that date, written at nine o'clock in the morning, Colonel Thomas Stockdale wrote: 'This morning early I understand Sir Marmaduke Langdale is coming down from Appleby and Kirkby Stephen towards Barna[rd] Castle and so to Yorkshire, and will fall upon our forces thereabout before our body get together so Colonel Lambert is gone this morning to Otley to meet Colonel Harrison, whose regiment is still in Lancashire.' A postscript adds that Langdale will bring 2,000 horse and 2,000 foot, if he were able.[78] The sense of the letter is that Lambert had been with Stockdale, perhaps staying overnight at the latter's family seat of Bilton Hall about a mile west of Knaresborough, and while there received news of Langdale's projected advance.

Paulden's Account says that three troops of Parliamentary horse were marching from Pontefract towards York when they met Lambert.[79] This can hardly have been other than between Tadcaster and York, as the roads to York from Pontefract and from Otley, whence Lambert must have been returning, do not meet until Tadcaster (map 3), only ten miles from York. When told of the taking of the castle Lambert must have wondered whether there would be any end to bad news. At least he had the advantage of familiarity with Pontefract following his part in the previous siege in 1645 (see Chapter 1).

It would seem, then, that on the day that Pontefract was taken Lambert rode thirteen miles from Bilton Hall to Otley, twenty miles from Otley to at least Tadcaster, and then seventeen miles from there to Pontefract, where he lay all night in the field directing operations after riding fifty miles. The following day he was at Ferrybridge, two miles to the east, from where he wrote to Colonel Charles Fairfax in Leeds with directions for prosecuting the siege of Pontefract. He had ordered three companies of foot from Skipton to Leeds, and asked Fairfax to send them on to Ferrybridge.[80] Little time was wasted in formalising the siege, for within a day or so sixty pickaxes were being sent to Colonel Fairfax, presumably for digging entrenchments.[81]

It was probably on 4 June that Lambert wrote from Ferrybridge to the Commons concerning the military situation, although the details have not survived.[82] By 9 June 800 horse and foot were tied up in the siege, against a garrison of 250 horse and 400 foot in a pro-Royalist area. Defeat would 'so highten the King's partee in theis parts (which I think are twenty for one) then wee shall be in danger of loosing . . .'[83] Clearly the Royalists were thought to be very strong in the north, and the *Calendar of State Papers, Domestic . . . (CSPD)* shows Derby House increasing their calls for arms, ammunition, and men to be sent from the south, especially Wales.

At about the time that Pontefract was taken, another group made an attempt on Helmsley Castle, by offering a soldier £100 down with £500 and a knighthood to follow, but he revealed the plan and the conspirators were captured and confined to the castle dungeon.[84] At the beginning of June Langdale was active in Westmorland, issuing orders for the conscription of 600 men aged between sixteen and sixty.[85] To add to the army's manpower problems, there were revolts in Cornwall which had to be put down by Colonel Sir Hardresse Waller.

Chapter 4

GATHERLEY MOOR TO CARLISLE
AND PENRITH

Gatherley Moor to Carlisle

A LETTER FROM NEWCASTLE dated 1 June 1648 reports that Colonel Lilburne went towards Langdale's quarters in Cumberland and faced a considerable party of his troops, but the latter refused action. This sounds like a report of the raid across Stainmore by Cholmley supported by Lilburne in the last week of May, as described above. The same report refers to Graydan and Errington bringing two troops of Scots horse across the Tweed, into Northumberland.[1]

Langdale was also continuing to raid over Stainmore. A Royalist letter, dated 7 June at Carlisle, says that: 'Our men were as farr as Barnie Castle . . . tooke one of their skouts . . . wee are now in Westmerland, neer Brugh.'[2]

This was probably the opening move in Langdale's march towards Barnard Castle of which, it will be recalled, Lambert had had news while staying with Colonel Stockdale in Knaresborough. A letter from Durham, dated 8 June, records that Lambert withdrew his army twelve miles from Barnard Castle to Catterick on the advance of Langdale, in order to 'draw the enemy from the mountains to the more Champion parts', i.e. regions of arable cultivation still largely given over to unenclosed common fields.[3] It is true that Catterick lies on a plain which is less broken by small valleys than the surroundings of Barnard Castle, but the real reason for the withdrawal was most likely to allow the conjunction with Harrison's brigade before the small force of around 1,200 at Barnard Castle came into contact with the 4,000 men Lambert believed that Langdale had with him. The fact that as soon as the conjunction had been made Lambert advanced to offer battle supports this view. The Royalist Sir Philip Musgrave, in his contemporary narrative on the Scots invasion of England, gives Langdale's total force as 3,000 armed foot, 700 ill-armed horse and 500 good horse, but that he brought only 1,500 horse and foot across Stainmore.[4]

If Lambert left Ferrybridge on the 4th, he could have been back in Barnard Castle (seventy miles away) on 5th to give the order for his forces there to withdraw on that day. Major Sanderson had no difficulty travelling just over sixty miles from Barnard Castle to York in two days on at least three occasions, and each time covered at least thirty-five miles on one of the days.[5]

Lambert's withdrawal to Catterick did probably take place on 5 June, as Captain John Hodgson implies that the army was already quartered at Catterick on the 6th. Harrison's and Twistleton's horse and the Lord General's foot joined them there on that day, after which they marched to Gatherley Moor, seven miles away, to meet Langdale.

Harrison's brigade had been quartered in Lancashire.[6] The nearest place in Lancashire to Otley, where Lambert met Harrison on the 3rd, is Colne, sixty miles from Catterick (maps 3, 7). If the brigade had been on short notice to march, which one would expect in view of the tense situation, they might have left during the 3rd and could have reached Catterick on the 6th at an average of around seventeen miles a day. This is quite brisk but sustainable for three or four days, and there was some urgency. Twistleton's had only forty miles to march from Otley and would have had no difficulty in reaching Catterick some time on the 6th.[7] It would have been as well to give time for the horses to rest, for shoeing and for general maintenance before continuing, and Lambert could have marched the seven miles from Catterick to Gatherley in a couple of hours late on the 7th, with his army now totalling around 2,200 horse and about 1,500 foot.

The letter from Durham of 8 June explains that Langdale came across Stainmore as far as Barnard Castle but advanced no further. When Lambert approached: 'Langdale retreated into Westmerland, where it is conceived they will halt unto such time as they see what they shall receive from Scotland.'[8] This sounds as though the events were still in progress, and thus Langdale's retreat began on the 8th. It is about twenty-six miles from Gatherley Moor to Durham, and there would have been time enough for news of the day's happenings to get there in the evening.

With Langdale still in or around Barnard Castle, Lambert's army stayed in the Gatherley area, eleven miles away; Lambert quartered at Ravensworth, about three miles west of Gatherley Moor,[9] and Hodgson quartered a mile to the south of him near Kirkby on the Hill.* The next day they 'marched towards Bowes, where the enemy was retreated'.

This non-event was reported by a Royalist newsbook as a total defeat of Lambert: 'Most of his Horse and Foot were killed, routed and dispersed to the number of 3,000 or thereabouts.' The same report says that Lambert was refused entry to York, which had declared for the king, and fled north to his defeat at the hands of Sir Thomas Glemham.[10] As an example of optimistic reporting, or plain propaganda, it is hardly to be bettered in terms of its distance from the facts. The report may have been built upon strong rumours of a Royalist rising in York in mid-May, which were stoked up when a troop of Parliamentary horse happened to come into town and were mistaken by Royalists, who cried out: 'Glenham was come'. The troop agreed to remain until local horse and foot were raised, and it was believed that had they not done so the Royalists might have risen and taken the city.[11]

---

* Kirkby Hill, National Grid map reference NZ 140066.

To return to reality, there is a second account of events on 8 June which can be dovetailed with Hodgson. A letter from 'T. S.', dated 17 June at Penrith, is very confused as to both dates and geography but some sense may be teased out of it.[12] He says that Langdale came six miles beyond Bowes on the 15th and Lambert chased him as far as Carlisle by the 13th. This is clearly wrong, and as he refers to 'last Saturday being 17 June' it seems that the writer was a week out in the date of the meeting of the two armies. A letter from Lambert confirms that Langdale came east of Bowes on the 8th.[13] In an otherwise very confused sentence, T. S. is very definite that Langdale stood to engage at 'a bridge between Catterick and Bowes'. There is only one candidate, the bridge over the eponymous river at Greta Bridge, six miles east of Bowes (plate 5, map 6). After a skirmish between his scouts and a body of horse commanded by Harrison, apparently with his own and Twistleton's regiments, Langdale 'fled back so fast he could', initially as far as Brough nineteen miles away.

To sum up the confusing evidence, Lambert withdrew to Catterick on 5 June, Harrison's brigade and the Lord General's foot joined him there on the 6th, and the whole army advanced on the 7th and quartered near Gatherley Moor overnight. On the 8th Langdale began to move towards Yorkshire while Lambert's scouts probed westwards, leading to minor skirmishing around Greta Bridge. Langdale then began a hasty retreat over Stainmore.

Lambert pursued Langdale to the summit of the Stainmore pass (map 6, fig. 1, plate 6). In a letter to Hesilrige, written at Brough on Saturday 10 June, he says that 'upon Thursday last [8 June] we lay neere the Spittle on Stainmore'.[14] This was the Spital,* a hospital built by Marrick Abbey, which became an inn after the Dissolution.[15] From their overnight quarters near Gatherley Moor to the Spital is about twenty-one miles, or about seven hours' marching plus rest stops. This is a long day's march, and suggests that the Spital was not reached until late afternoon. Langdale also had a long day, with a march eastwards from Barnard Castle to Greta Bridge and then all the way over Stainmore to Brough, where he stayed the night, a total of around twenty-three miles.

In the evening, Lambert sent a party of 300 foot and 200 horse from the Spital to capture a strong point at the summit of the pass, 2½ miles to the west: 'a passage of advantage upon Stainmore called maidene castle'. Lambert is remarkably detailed about what little fighting took place: 'done and kept without any great difficulty or blowes except in a skirmish betwixt eight of oures and fourteen of theirs which indeed was very handsomely performed and one of theirs slaine and another taken prisoner, being both Northumberland gentlemen and reformadoes, one was a De La Veile and the other a Blaxton this without the least hurt to us.'[16] Hodgson says: 'Our men fell upon their rear', and that Langdale himself was present. This suggests that Langdale had not actually left men behind to occupy the summit, but was in the course of his march when Lambert's vanguard caught up with

---

* NY 911122, now Old Spital, a farm.

his rear. However, Hodgson incorrectly describes the Royalist attack at Appleby in similar terms, and may just be using stock phrases.

Maiden Castle is a Roman fortlet, probably dating from the early to the mid-second century, and encloses an area of about 115 feet by 145 feet on a natural terrace on the shoulder of Beloo Hill, at the summit of the 1,400-foot pass.[17] The walls are now represented by a rubble mound up to five foot seven inches high externally and three foot seven inches high internally; at various uncertain times there has been disturbance and robbing of the fortlet, and in the seventeenth century the potential for defence may have been greater. An internal height of only five feet would have given a stable and protected firing position.

From its highest point about a mile short of Maiden Castle, the modern road diverges from the Roman route and drops down across the south side of the hill below the fortlet. The Roman road climbs a long, slow slope from the east, swings around the north side of the fortlet and drops much more steeply to the west (plates 6, 7, and fig. 1). The eighteenth-century turnpike road followed the Roman line, and it is probable that the seventeenth-century road took the same route. There are good views to the east and especially to the west from the fortlet, although these are of the countryside rather than the road.* As Lambert says in his letter, if the Royalists had held the fortlet: 'the enemy might probably have much troubled us if not stopt our passage'.

A good illustration of the timeless nature of military needs is provided by the concrete pill box built in 1940–1941 to control the Stainmore pass, only 1,100 yards southeast of this Roman and Civil War strongpoint (fig. 1 and plate 8).[18]

When Maiden Castle had been captured Lambert's forces stayed in the area overnight. It is hard to imagine a more desolate area in which to camp, with very few dwellings between Bowes and Maiden Castle. The Spital could have provided accommodation for the senior officers but apart from that there were probably no more than a few sheepfolds to break the wind for those troops quick enough to take possession of them.

The next day, 9 June, the army went on to Brough in weather that Lambert called 'very bad and rainy all day from mourning to night' and Hodgson 'tempestuous'. At Brough it was found that Langdale had already retreated to Kirby Thore and so Lambert's force was able to quarter in 'five townes'. By this was meant centres of population: in addition to Brough itself, Church Brough, Brough Sowerby, Great Musgrave, Rookby, Helgrave, Winton and Warcop are but seven of a number of possible candidates within three miles. The castle at Brough was in ruins, giving Langdale nowhere to leave a garrison to oppose Lambert (see plate 10 and appendix 2).

While these events were unfolding, there was much activity elsewhere. In Northumberland Parliamentary forces under Major Sanderson were ordered to abandon

---

* A Roman fortlet would normally include a tower around 30 feet high, which would have greatly improved the view of the road, but very limited excavations have found no sign of such a structure.

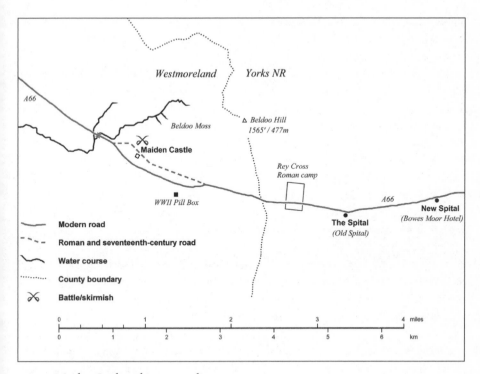

FIG. I *Maiden Castle and its surroundings.*

Alnwick on 1 June and march towards Newcastle. When 140 horse and 120 Royalist dragoons came down from Berwick Sanderson turned back with three troops of horse, one newly raised, and on the 3rd forced a fight in which two of the enemy were killed, some prisoners taken and the invaders chased back to Berwick.[19] On 9 June, a party consisting of some of Colonel George Fenwick's Northumberland horse, with the three troops under Sanderson, perhaps 400–500 men in total, rode south from Cartington to Chollerford on the North Tyne to intercept a force of Royalists. They chased them westwards to within fourteen miles of Carlisle, somewhere around Low Row (map 8), a day's ride of nearly sixty miles.[20]

Despite his pursuit of Langdale and the need to mask Pontefract, Lambert was still doing his best to hold Northumberland, rather than abandon it, now with a total of seven troops of horse and one of dragoons.[21] These seem to have been Sanderson's two troops from Lilburne's, the newly raised one and four of the Northumberland militia horse; the dragoons may have been supplied by Hesilrige mounting some of his infantry.

During the first two weeks of June the Committee at Derby House took notice of, and did their best to provide troops for, tumults or alarms in many places: Coventry,

Huntingdon, Isle of Ely, Isle of Wight, Leicester, Lincoln, Norfolk, North Wales, Rutland, Salisbury, Stamford and Waltham Cross.[22] Derby House must have felt as if they were trying to put out brush fires everywhere.

On 6 June Derby House authorised Lambert to announce that, if any of the enemy deserted and laid down their arms within ten days, the Committee would do their best to secure indemnity for them.[23] Such a conditional promise might not sound very appetising, but there were already reports of Langdale's men having deserted before they could have heard of the offer.[24]

On the same day, the Committee was confident that Pembroke would soon fall and that General Fairfax would speedily take care of the north. In the event, Pembroke did not fall for more than a month, and Fairfax was besieging Colchester until mid-August.

On 8 June the Committee of the County of Lancashire ordered two regiments of horse and five of foot to join Lambert under the command of Colonel Ashton.[25] The total number of men was around 500 horse and 1,500 foot, as described in Chapter 1.

On the 9th, Derby House wrote to Cromwell asking him to send what forces he could to the north, and that he should go with them himself 'or send such commander with them as he shall think fit'.[26] Although Cromwell was senior to Lambert, anyone he might send in his place would most likely be Lambert's junior. The Committee could just have been advising the appointment of a commander for the reinforcements while en route, but Cromwell hardly needed prompting to do that, and it perhaps implies suspicion of, or a lack of confidence in, Lambert on the part of Derby House. On the same day that they sent their instructions to Cromwell, they wrote to the Committee at York in the same terms and also informed them that Fairfax was unable to spare anyone from his own force.

To return to progress in the north, on 10 June Lambert advanced eight miles from Brough to Appleby, and then on to Penrith. Langdale had garrisoned Appleby Castle, and Lambert was obliged to leave a masking force under Harrison in order to prevent the road being blocked behind him. Lambert had garrisoned Appleby himself in mid-May and the castle must have been evacuated, or captured, on some unrecorded occasion. From Appleby, the rest of his army began the fourteen-mile march to Penrith, despite a shortage of ammunition. He asked Hesilrige to send twenty barrels of powder, with bullet and match, to Raby Castle by Tuesday next [13th], from where Lambert would arrange to collect it as convenient. He had already ordered the troop of Bishopric horse to Durham to convoy it to Raby.[27] Raby was perhaps chosen for the magazine as Barnard Castle was not in good repair (see appendix 2), and Raby was seven miles further from the Stainmore road should Langdale push Lambert back over Stainmore.

Near Kirkby Thore, about one-third of the way from Appleby to Penrith (map 6), Lambert found the road held by most of Langdale's horse, which were soon beaten off by the forlorn hope. Langdale's foot was quartered in Kirkby Thore but marched away along with the horse before Lambert could close on them. A rearguard of horse stood, but soon gave ground against 'a very smalle party of our forlorne'. Five of the latter, being well mounted, gave chase and killed two while the rest ran as far as the two bridges on the east side of Penrith.[28] Langdale was there in personal command of a reserve and tried to make a stand, but they gave way and were pursued for three miles beyond Penrith on the Carlisle road without any resistance. This took the Royalists twenty-five miles from their starting point at Brough, and they will have stayed where they were on the night of the 10th. They probably marched the fifteen miles to Carlisle, which had walls they could shelter behind, on the 11th. Hodgson's account of Langdale's retreat is brief, but adds the information that the enemy was caught at Whinfield Park,* about four miles beyond Kirkby Thore, 'where our horse fell upon their rear, and did execution'.

A Royalist garrison had been left in Brougham Castle (plate 11), which was then in poor condition (appendix 2), but yielded on quarter as soon as summoned, probably during the march to Penrith on 10 June. Lambert, who gave these details in his letter of the 11th,[29] had hopes that Appleby and Greystoke would fall as easily. He describes the day as one of 'sore marches and terrable weather' and for this reason was resting for a day in Penrith. A report from Penrith on 16 June announced that two castles had been seized.[30] The unnamed castles were probably Brougham, and perhaps Greystoke, which was taken in June; it lies less than six miles from Penrith and could have been captured from that base. A letter published on 26 June reports the taking of an unnamed castle and Greystoke (plate 12), the latter apparently unopposed.[31]

Another letter from Penrith says that Lambert's advance guard, at an unnamed place, 'fell into the Quarters of a Regiment newly levied, which we have totally dispersed and broken; the Officers fled after Langdale and the Soldiers threw down, most of them, their Arms, and ran home, seeming to be very glad of the opportunity'. The letter adds that inhabitants of Carlisle would rather die than receive Langdale's army, lest they be forced to eat horseflesh as in the siege during the first Civil War, but it seems they were given little choice. The letter also says that Lambert was 'not very well, but you know he hath beene long sickly'.[32]

A letter from Kendal betrays unfamiliarity with the local geography.[33] It describes Lambert as marching through Mallerstang Forest, which is an area some ten miles south of Kirkby Stephen:† a less likely route is difficult to imagine (maps 5, 6). It does say that he 'had some assistance from the Country who are as weary of the Cavaliers, as fearfull of the Scots' and describes Langdale (correctly) as marching through Inglewood Forest, which is between Penrith and Carlisle. The writer expected the Lancashire forces to join on Thursday, that is, 15 June. In fact, according to Birch, they arrived in Kendal on the 20th after diverting to capture Beetham House (map 4).

---

* Whinfell Forest, NY 580270.

† Around SD 770980.

Lambert's letter also said that Langdale endeavoured to keep his foot together by telling them that they retreated not out of fear but in order to join with 20,000 Scots, when 'they shall all receive full armes'.[34] Other reports also suggest that half of Langdale's men were unarmed, in which case it is hardly surprising that they were reluctant to stand and fight.[35] Lambert went on to say that he hoped that two companies of foot (unidentified), which Hesilrige had promised, would soon be at Appleby. He added that his messenger would bring the ammunition from Raby Castle on horseback for more speed and less trouble, an indication of the state of the roads. He also asked for four or five suits of armour as many officers were without. These were backs and breasts, rather than full armour such as a cuirassier would wear, as he made clear in his next letter to Hesilrige on the 17th.[36]

The army rested at Penrith. In the late sixteenth century the castle gatehouse was said to be in ruinous condition but two towers and the domestic quarters were in good repair, and Lambert probably used it as his headquarters at intervals until mid-July (plate 13). There is no suggestion that the Royalists put a garrison into it, which confirms that it was probably indefensible during the Civil War (appendix 2). The weather continued to be poor and provisions were scarce: 'Through the exceeding unseasonablenesse of the weather . . . we have done little but secured our own quarters at this Town which are now eaten up.'[37]

The whole of Lambert's army, horse and foot, marched out of Penrith at about one o'clock in the morning, on either 13 or 14 June (see below), and came to within a mile of Carlisle by about five o'clock (map 5).[38] The position would have been around the point where the main road, now A6, crosses the Petteril, a minor tributary of the river Eden. It was a moonless night and the sun did not rise until 3.45 a.m.[39] There would have been light enough to march by 2.45, and perhaps a little earlier if the night were very clear, but at one o'clock it would have been very dark. The distance is about seventeen miles, to cover which in four hours, that is 4¼ miles an hour, is a fast march for infantry, especially in a large body and at night, and there must be some doubt as to the accuracy of the times given by Lambert. If his 'about one o'clock' and 'about five o'clock' can be taken as 12.30 and 5.30 then the march, at just under 3½ miles an hour, is more believable. At Carlisle Langdale drew out 500 horse and as many foot below the walls, with some others from 'the farre side of the watter', perhaps the river Caldew to the west but more likely the Eden to the north.

Lambert says that the two forces faced one another for four hours, with Langdale's men keeping close under the walls and unwilling to engage. Eventually Lambert began to withdraw, and Langdale's horse attacked the rearguard: 'Beeinge very gallantly mounted would keepe very neare to our last partyes, and upon there wheeleing about would careare in upon them fire there pistols and soe backe againe.' The Royalists killed one and took one prisoner, while Lambert's men killed three that he knew of and took five. Musgrave wrote on the 14th that the enemy was in sight and the two armies were facing one another, which reads as though Lambert had just arrived.[40] The letter giving the date as the 13th is the same one that confused the dates of Langdale arriving at Bowes,[41] and perhaps Musgrave's date is to be preferred. It certainly agrees better with Hodgson, who said the army had rested in Penrith for three or four days.

It was also said that Lambert stayed at Carlisle 'one night but finding the Countrey so bare, and impoverished by Langdale and his Army, he could not have provision for his men, and so retreated to Perith'. Langdale was also short of food for 'a penny loafe is sold for three pence in Carlile'.[42] However, another letter reports that Lambert lay outside Carlisle on the 13th, 14th and 15th. Certainly it is most unlikely that Lambert took his men back to Penrith on the evening of the day on which he had made a quick march up to Carlisle, but it is not clear whether he remained outside the city for one, two or three days. The letter also says that seven or eight of the enemy were killed and twenty taken prisoner.[43] Although this disagrees with Lambert's figures, Hodgson says that among the prisoners: 'Several soldiers were taken that had run away from us.' 'Several' sits better within a total of twenty taken rather than within five. The deserters, incidentally, were judged to be hanged, but were spared.

A correspondent 'R.S.' writing from headquarters near Penrith announced that Langdale had been pursued initially to within twelve miles of Carlisle. He gives Lambert's force as 3,000 horse and foot, with the Lancashire men expected soon.[44] Table 1 shows his calculated strength as just under 3,700. Although he wrote on the 16th, R.S. does not mention the march right up to Carlisle.

Lambert was aware that with his present force he was helpless while Langdale had the walls of Carlisle to retreat to, although he was confident that he could beat him in the field.[45] He noted that he had received the ammunition he had requested and, in view of the success Hesilrige had had in raising the Northumberland and Durham horse, asked for the return of one or both of the troops he had loaned (their identity is unknown, but they may be Sanderson's two from Lilburne's), preferably bringing with them the backs, breasts and pots (helmets) he had ordered. He was also able to announce the surrender, to Colonel Harrison at midday on 17 June, of Appleby Castle,[46] the garrison of which had been released so long as they returned to their homes promising never to fight against Parliament. The reason for its fall was said to be mutiny, and the deputy governor was shot for not opposing the mutineers, two of whom were hanged.[47] If true, the executions were presumably carried out once the garrison reached other Royalist forces. The castle provided Lambert with '300 musquests six barrells of powder 1,000 weight of match and all kinde of provisions', which must have been welcome to him.[48] At this time Derby House was doing its best to send ammunition to the north, by ordering a convoy for two ship-loads to go to Hull.[49]

After remaining outside Carlisle for one, two or three days, Lambert retired to Penrith to await the arrival of reinforcements from Lancashire under Colonel Ashton. Not all of his army had pulled back as far as Penrith, as the Lancashire forces joined (see below) at Hesket Moor, about eight miles north of Penrith on the 25th.

Two newsbook reports of 20 June mention the fighting and pursuit to Carlisle, and falsely report Langdale wounded and captured, and Lambert killed.[50]

In his letter Musgrave was sure that Lambert could do them no great harm, always provided that the Royalist horse could cope with being confined within the walls.[51] Shut in a town, horses have no opportunity to graze and must be fed wholly on imported forage. The seventeenth-century diet for a cavalry horse was around 14 lb of hay, 7 lb of straw, one peck of oats and half a peck of peas each day.[52] Just as important, cavalry horses have to be exercised daily or they rapidly lose condition.[53] Turner makes the point that as soon as the Scots army began to assemble Lambert drew his troops closer together, which allowed Langdale to get provisions for the men and grass for the horses.[54]

Within two days of Lambert arriving under the walls of Carlisle, Langdale had sent off almost half his horse, to the number of 500, into Northumberland under Sir Richard Tempest. He kept 200 Yorkshire reformadoes and seven other troops with him, and on Friday 16th despatched the Bishopric reformadoes and seven troops to Hexham, where they joined with the two troops of 'Colonel Carre and Davy Driveal' on Sunday 18th.[55]

On Monday they moved northeast to come between Sanderson and Newcastle; the plan was for Colonel Grey to come down from Berwick to attack from the north at the same time. Such a move, if successful, would have effectively destroyed Parliamentary control over Northumberland, for the two troops with Sanderson, five other troops including the Northumberland horse under Colonel Fenwick, and one troop of dragoons, until now masking Berwick, were the only forces available to Parliament.[56]

However, the plan failed owing to good intelligence, and Sanderson pulled back to Newcastle, probably with Fenwick but Sanderson does not mention him. On Hesilrige's orders, Colonel Francis Wren's Bishopric horse joined Sanderson at Newburn on 25 June, to give a total of perhaps 500 horse, or something over 600 if Fenwick was with them. Tempest and Grey, with a total of 1,200 horse, met at Alnwick and from there intended a move towards Newcastle.[57]

In consequence of these movements Hesilrige had been asking for troops to be sent to Northumberland, which Lambert had been forced to delay in the absence of Ashton's men. On the 22nd Lambert wrote assuring him the men would be sent as soon as possible, and that his second advance towards Carlisle would secure the route through Hexham. He suggested that Hesilrige find horses to mount one or two hundred of his foot as dragoons as a necessary support for his horse when they should arrive to relieve Northumberland.[58] Hesilrige did in fact do this at the end of June, as will be seen later. Lambert, it may be noted, had at this point no more than one troop of dragoons to support over 2,000 horse (see Chapter 1 and table 1).

When Lambert's army returned to Penrith from Carlisle, Bright's regiment of foot, in which Hodgson was then a lieutenant, was ordered back to Yorkshire and had got as far as Appleby when they were called back. Hodgson says that this was because the Lancashire men had reached Kendal but were unwilling to march further. No one else comments on this, and it may be no more than inter-regimental snarling, but while at Kendal Colonel Ashton did write to the Speaker with a petition from officers and men under his command asking for pay.[59] Birch's account gives space for no more than one day at most for delay, but some reluctance to march may have been rumoured. Whatever the reason, Hodgson and his regiment had to return to Penrith 'with all expedition' and on towards Carlisle.

Captain Birch and the rest of the Lancashire men left Kendal on 23 June and after a night at Penrith met up with Lambert's army at Hesket Moor on Sunday 25th. This brought in Lieutenant-Colonel Alexander Rigby's and Colonel Nicholas Shuttleworth's horse, and Colonel Ashton's, Colonel Dodding's, Colonel Standish's, Colonel Rigby's (under Colonel Standish) and Colonel Oughtred Shuttleworth's foot, a total of 500 horse and 1,500 foot, just the numbers Lambert was expecting.[60] His total force was said to be 8,000 men, probably including those now come from the siege of Appleby.[61] Table 1 gives a calculated total of about 5,700, against which Langdale had 3,000 foot and 1,200 horse.

Langdale had also heard of the arrival of the 1,500 men from Lancashire. He begged for some relief from Scottish forces as he feared that if Lambert returned to the Carlisle area his horses would be deprived of forage, and if they had to be moved away it would discourage the foot.[62] As he had already sent away half his horse, his fears must have been very real. Whitelocke says that the enemy would not fight again until the Scots came in.[63]

From this point it is possible to refer to Birch's 'diary' in following Lambert's movements.

Warwick Bridge

Hodgson was part of a detachment that marched to Rose Castle, a residence of the bishop of Carlisle (map 5 and plate 14). According to a letter of 24 June from Langdale, Rose Castle was taken on 23rd. A letter from Lambert's quarters says that Rose Castle was stormed by a commanded party of 200 foot and taken within two hours. Despite the fact that the governor had refused two summonses, quarter was given, and only one of the garrison of twenty musketeers was killed and one wounded.[64] The taking of the castle was described as a very big prize, and was then garrisoned by Major Cholmley's troop of horse and Captain Challenor's company of foot.[65] Cholmley was probably the captain in Lilburne's horse, and Challenor was in Bright's regiment.[66] Hodgson relates that twenty-five prisoners were taken in the action and that horse were included in the garrison 'to hinder Carlisle garrison from provision', precisely the action that Langdale feared.

Meanwhile, Birch marched with the rest of the army from Hesket Moor to Warwick Bridge (map 5 and plate 15), just over four miles to the east of Carlisle. Its strategic importance lay in the bridge over the Eden which carried, or could block, the main east–west route between Carlisle and Newcastle. From Penrith to Newcastle the shortest route (now A686) is sixty-five miles, marching diagonally over the high Pennines through Melmerby, while the alternative over Stainmore is ninety miles (maps 6, 8). Newcastle is only fifty-two miles from Warwick Bridge on a very easy route, and from there it was relatively simple to reinforce Hesilrige against incursions into Northumberland. Lambert made the point to Hesilrige when apologising for being unable to send reinforcements to Northumberland until the Lancashire forces had joined him: 'Our advance to Carlyle will secure the way by Hexam.'[67]

The attack on Warwick Bridge was a carefully planned operation: 'Our men marching very silent, and the Foot keeping their matches undiscovered, we were upon them before they were aware . . . This action hapned in the night, which saved the enemy many hundreds [of casualties] . . .'[68] After beating the enemy off the bridge, and taking 'divers prisoners', Birch and his comrades quartered in a barn 'in extremity of wet and foul wether and want of provisions'. Hodgson says it took place on Sunday morning which was 25 June. Birch gives the date as the 26th, a Monday, although a letter[69] describing the action is quite definite that it was on Sunday 25th, at night, and this date is to be preferred.

The action was certainly successful. A party of Parliamentary horse fell on a strong guard at the bridge and 'gave them so hot an Alarm, being in the Night, that from all their Quarters they ran both Horse and Foot to Carlisle, in so great a Confusion, that if it had been day, we had taken at least 1,000 of them'. One hundred prisoners and forty horse were taken for the loss of six of Lambert's men.[70]

The weather continued wet and cold, as Birch observed: 'A miserable time for the souldiers as I have seene at any time.' The letter from Lambert's quarters supported this view: 'We have had miserable Marches, and most pitiful Quarters in the barren and undone Countrey.'[71] With first Langdale's and then Lambert's forces scouring the countryside for provisions, the inhabitants must have been reduced to near-starvation level in a very wet year following on from a poor harvest in 1647.

It was at this point that the Parliamentary forces suffered an embarrassing loss: 'After this happy successe of Lambert, our Souldiers being secure in their quarters, and fearing nothing, a party of Langdales horse came into our quarters, and drove about fifty of major Cholmleyes horse from grasse, without any let or opposition that I can heare of.'[72] Although this suggests that the raid was on the main body of the army, it must have been in the vicinity of Rose Castle where Cholmley was in garrison. The report is from Manchester, and the writer probably did not know enough to discriminate.

The next morning, the 26th, Lambert's men advanced on Carlisle by way of Stanwix (map 5) where there was another crossing of the river Eden. Birch says that first they rendezvoused at 'Guillsland'. This cannot be Gilsland, which is thirteen miles away in the opposite direction; he could conceivably mean Gill House,* just north of the Brampton–Stanwix road, which they would probably have used, but there may be better candidates.

---

* NY 472606.

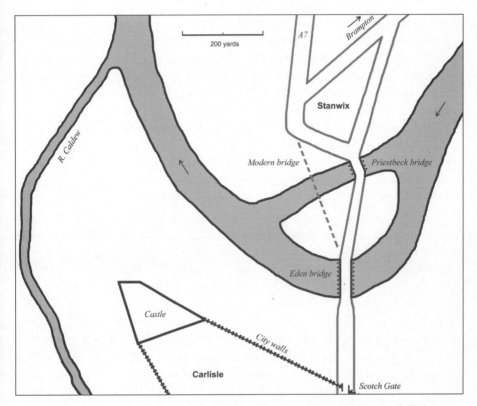

FIG. 2 *River Eden at Carlisle (after Hogg 1952). A causeway 200 yards long was built between the two bridges in 1733. The Priestbeck channel is the present course of the river Eden, the original course of which is now totally silted up.*

A forlorn hope of men from every company, with Birch's lieutenant, beat the enemy out of their entrenchments, the church and the town at Stanwix, and drove them into Carlisle. Sanderson, in a second-hand comment, says that this was on Sunday 26th; the day is obviously wrong, the date is probably correct.[73]

The suburb of Stanwix lies by the main road north into Scotland (now A7) and is separated from Carlisle by the river Eden. In the seventeenth century this was divided into two channels at that point, the northern known as the Priestbeck, which forms the modern channel, the southern as the Eden, now wholly silted up. The two streams had been formerly crossed on wooden bridges, which 'being in a state of decay were taken down in 1600, when two narrow stone bridges, were erected in their stead'.[74] The Eden bridge over the original, wider, channel had nine arches, while the Priestbeck had four arches on a different alignment (see fig. 2 and plate 16). They sprang from a substantial, though probably very low-lying island left between the two channels. In 1649 there is a reference to '400*l.* for building and repairs of Priestbeck bridge near Carlisle now destroyed, and 100*l*. for repair of the breach made by Gen. Lambert near the bridge'.[75] Birch says that he 'kept guard on the wooden bridge foote'. Birch has either misremembered the structure, or the stone bridge may indeed have been badly damaged and repaired with timber, although no other record of this is known. It is not clear what the breach made 'near the bridge' might mean, nor whether any destruction of Priestbeck bridge was also Lambert's work.

That night Birch quartered in Brunstock,* between Stanwix and Scaleby, with victuals in such short supply that officers and soldiers had nothing to drink but water. The following day, 27th, Birch returned to keep guard at Warwick Bridge.

Hodgson was also in the fighting at Stanwix, and remained there for five days keeping guard 'on Scotland-side' within musket shot of the town. The distance from the north end of the original Eden bridge to the town walls at Scotchgate is about 270 yards which was a long (and inaccurate) musket shot. A lesser road to the east leads from Stanwix to Brampton and so to Newcastle, and by holding both the former and Warwick Bridge Lambert put a stranglehold on movement to both north and east from Carlisle (map 5).

At about this time Scaleby Castle was captured; the date is uncertain, but was probably between 26 and 30 June:[76] 'Selby [Scaleby] Castle was taken by a Party of Horse only, they fired but one Piece, and one Trooper going up to the Walls and shewing his Pistol to them, and threatened what he would do if they fired any more, and that they should have no Quarter, they presently yealded.' The castle was probably not capable of serious defence (plate 17 and appendix 2). It was more likely to have been captured by a party from Stanwix rather than from Warwick Bridge, as there is no direct access from the latter owing to the marshy valley of the Brunstock Beck and its tributaries.

At this time matters were becoming serious in Northumberland. On the same day, 22 June, that Lambert wrote to Hesilrige assuring him that horse would be sent as soon as he was in a position to do so,[77] a letter from Northumberland to London announced that: 'Lambert was 3,000 Horse and 3,000 Foot, he hath sent Colonel Lilburn with 1,000 Horse towards us, they will be here on Saturday [24th] we hope'.[78] This was wishful thinking, for Lambert was then still in Penrith and in no position to do any such thing. Hodgson says that they were sent after Stanwix Bridge was taken, and while he is not always reliable or precise as to dates it was probably around the 26th or 27th that Lilburne left with three troops of his regiment. These must be his own, Smithson's and Captain Lilburne's, leaving Major Cholmley in Rose Castle. Bradford's was already in Northumberland with Sanderson. Sanderson in a letter of 3 July says that Colonel Lilburne was in Haydon Bridge on the 29th.

On the 26th Colonel Wren and the Durham militia horse with Sanderson and Bradford's troops manoeuvred to prevent the Royalists making a rendezvous at Chollerton, and three days later were at Hexham. On the 30th all the Parliamentary forces met at Chollerford.

---

* NY 418593.

The letter of the 22nd gives the total for Sanderson's troops and Fenwick's Northumberland militia horse as 500.[79] In addition, 300 horse were to be sent from Wren's Durham militia, but only 220 arrived[80] bringing the total to 720, with fifty dragoons. Lilburne was still expected with 1,000 more – the figure appears twice in the letter so the writer must have believed in it. However, the total for all Parliamentary forces at Chollerford was only 900.[81]

JULY 1648

The events of 1 July have been described in detail elsewhere,[82] but in brief Lilburne's force made an overnight march, surprised the Royalists at dawn and took Great Tosson Tower, Cartington and Callaly castles and Lurbottle Hall. Some 350 officers and men and 600 horses were captured and taken to Morpeth in the course of a march of between seventy-four and eighty miles in twenty-four hours. All this was achieved without loss. Parliament ordered: 'That a Letter of Thanks be written to Colonel Lilbourne, and Colonel Fenwicke, Major Sanderson and Colonel Wrenn, for their good Services, in the great Victory obtained in the North.' Public thanks to God were to be given in churches in the city of London on Sunday next, 9 July.[83] The Duke of Hamilton wrote to Langdale on 5 July expressing sorrow for the misfortune to his men in Northumberland.[84]

Hesilrige's letter to the Speaker[85] refers to the action as taking place along the river Coquet, which flows west to east, but while Lilburne's force did cross that river, from Great Tosson to Cartington, all the action was on a north–south alignment and not along the river (map 8). Other contemporary writers made the same error.[86] Northumberland was indeed an unknown area.

On 1 July Lambert also sent all six troops of Harrison's regiment of horse and four troops of Cromwell's horse to assist Lilburne, but by the time they arrived at Meldon on the 3rd the fighting was over.[87] It is uncertain whether they returned to Lambert quite soon thereafter (see below), or stayed with Lilburne who remained at Hexham for the time being.

During these troubles in Northumberland, Lambert remained at Warwick Bridge, but on news of Lilburne's success Hodgson and at least some of the army moved to Brampton in Gilsland, nine miles east of Carlisle. It was at Brampton that the two roads running east from Carlisle, through Stanwix and through Warwick Bridge, come together and thus the major route into Northumberland through Hexham was still tightly controlled (map 5).

Hodgson relates that the garrison of Carlisle took heart from this apparent retreat and followed with horse and foot. However, a Major Robinson from the Lancashire force hid behind a barn with a small party of horse and 'slashed them off the field . . . took eleven considerable men prisoner, one a captain of horse'.

Lambert's letter from Brampton gives a different account.[88] He withdrew from Stanwix on 30 June owing to the shortage of food, yet kept a strong guard at Warwick Bridge. In the retreat Robinson was shot in the face while commanding the rearguard against eighty horse who followed for two or three miles, and it was Major Haynes, with a commanded party of Twistleton's, who defended a 'second pass'. He drove them back and pursued them almost to Stanwix, dangerously wounding some, slaying two and taking twelve prisoners including Captain Sherburne. The remainder of the retreat was quiet. On 1 July Lambert wrote from Rickerby, a mile east of Stanwix, on the 2nd from Brampton, quoted above, and on the 4th from Wetheral, just over a mile south of Warwick Bridge. Clearly, the move to Brampton had not meant abandonment of the immediate environs of Carlisle, and was probably part of a search for quarters and provisions.[89]

From Carlisle to Penrith

On 4 July, Derby House wrote to Lambert asking why a house in Cleveland belonging to the Earl of Elgin had been garrisoned by Colonel Lascelles even though it was 'out of the way and very inconsiderable' and had not been garrisoned in the first war.[90] This was probably Whorlton Castle* eleven miles south of Middlesborough, thirty-five miles northwest of Scarborough, where Lascelles was involved in the siege (map 1). The castle was described as ruinous in 1343, but a two-storied house had been built against the northwest end of the gatehouse around 1600. It was doubtless proper of the Committee to ask the question of Lambert as Lascelles was in his command, but it must have been an irritation when he was busy opposing Langdale ninety-odd miles away.

He certainly had more serious matters to attend to. On 4 July he wrote to his father-in-law from Wetheral, giving his strength as about 2,600 horse and 2,200 foot, a total of 4,800 (see Chapter 1 for a discussion of these figures). Against him he reckoned the Scots could bring as many as 19,000 horse and foot, although this turned out to be an over-estimate.[91]

Late in June Cromwell had sent three troops of Colonel Scroope's, Captain Pennyfeather's troop and two troops of dragoons northwards through Chester where Pennyfeather's was to remain. The other five were to go on to Leeds, there 'to send to the Committee of York, or to him that commands the forces in chief there' for further orders.[92] It appears that in fact all six troops went on to join Lambert's army (see Chapter 1).

Lilburne's regiment was still in Northumberland, but Harrison's and the four troops of Cromwell's may have returned very promptly from there, for a letter to the Commons on 12 July, refers to the forces under Lilburne's command stationed at Hexham since 1 July, as 'being three Regiments, viz Northumberland's [Fenwick's], Bishoprick's [Wren's] and his own'.[93] The same letter reported that Lilburne was moving all three regiments to rejoin Lambert in view of a rumour that the Scots were within eight miles of Carlisle. There is a slight contradiction in another letter, which suggests that Harrison had remained with Lilburne as an invasion into Northumberland was anticipated. As this view had changed, Lilburne and Harrison with two more regiments of horse had been sent to join Lambert.[94]

---

* NZ 481024.

Which regiments these were is uncertain, as Wren's remained to guard the eastern end of Stainmore.[95] Major Fenwick was reporting to Parliament on the state of the north late in July, and Fenwick's was active in northern Northumberland at the beginning of September,[96] but they could have been temporarily withdrawn from there and returned only when Lambert took his army south early in August.

The Scots were indeed preparing to invade, on the west rather than through Northumberland. They were by no means ready to do so but were pressed to act in support of what they saw as the premature rising of Langdale and the other English Royalists. Early in July the Engager army mustered in Annandale, and it may have been at this time that a redoubt was constructed in the Iron Age fort on Burnswark.[97]

Hodgson moved to another Brampton, which he describes as being three miles from Carlisle and near the Eden (map 5). This place cannot be found, and the name may have been repeated in error. The nearest match is Kirkbampton* just over five miles due west of Carlisle and three miles from the Eden. On 6 July he quartered around Ireby,† and then moved on to Penrith.

On 4 July Birch was also on the move, to a place 'four miles on the other side Carlisle' perhaps somewhere on an arc between Dalston‡ and Kirkbampton. He still had little luck with supplies: 'Quartered in the field, noe provisions.' He then marched to Bolton§ (now Bolton Low Houses),[98] and quartered at Sandale near Boltongate, a mile from Hodgson's quarters at Ireby. By the 8th he was back in Penrith after an overnight stay between Caldbeck and Sowerby: 'Much rayne hath beene. Such wet time this time of year hath not been seen in the memory of man: the souldiers in great want of provisions.' The latter was despite having free quarter in Penrith and sending to the country for provisions, but the soldiers were short of pay. He had probably arrived at much the same time as Hodgson. It looks as though all Lambert's force moved in a body and spread out as little as possible for quarters. Their roundabout route may have been an attempt to get provisions and forage from parts not recently visited.

Most contemporary accounts of the events of the next few weeks are from the Parliamentary side, but a letter from a Royalist in Rotterdam dated 23 September gives perhaps the best overall view from the Royalist perspective. It will be referred to as *Letter from Holland*[99] to reduce the number of notes.

The Duke of Hamilton wrote to Lambert on 6 July, explaining that he wished only to free the king, and to disband the Parliamentary army in order to free Parliament from restraints and the people from the heavy taxation imposed upon them. He invited Lambert

---

* NY 566305.
† NY 390239.
‡ NY 370503.
§ NY 238444.

to join him in this undertaking. Lambert, quartered at Castle Sowerby (now Sowerby Row),* and probably on the point of leaving for Penrith, replied on 8 July. He made it clear that he would oppose to his utmost any forces other than those raised by command of the English Parliament, and hoped that Hamilton would assist him in this. On the day that Lambert replied, and before his letter can have been written let alone delivered, Hamilton crossed the border with an army of 2,500 horse and 2,000 foot at four o'clock in the morning, and quartered at Rockcliffe, four miles north of Carlisle. The figures and location are from *Letter from Holland*, but he may have been understating the numbers to explain the Royalists' poor success. Modern commentaries suggest figures more in the region of 3,000 horse and 6,000 foot, and the contemporary Thomas Reade[100] gives a total of 'about tenn thousand horse and foote' in his description of the events of 1648 found amongst Clarendon's papers. On the other hand, Reade also says that at Preston the Scots army was 25,000 strong, a distinct exaggeration, which along with other claims which he makes (such as having personally hindered the securing of Berwick and Carlisle by Parliament) cast doubt on the validity of the narrative.

Hamilton entered Carlisle on the evening of the 8th 'in the Van of the Scots Army, with his Trumpeters before him, all in scarlet cloaks full of silver lace, like a Prince in state. With the Duke did march a life-guard, of Scotch men, all very proper and well cloathed, with standards and Equipage like a Prince'.[101] But grand as the entrance was, the army was by no means complete, as Burnet explains: 'The Regiments were not full, many of the service exceeded half the number; and not the fifth man could handle Pike or Musket. The Horse were the best mounted that ever Scotland set out, yet most of the Troopers were raw and undisciplined.'[102] As an apologist for Hamilton, Burnet may be exaggerating but all sources agree that the Scots were under-strength.

The Scots army then took over Carlisle, while the greater part of it quartered around Wigton and Thursby, with the headquarters nearby at Crofton Hall (map 5 and plate 18), where they remained for several days in order to build up their numbers, as Lambert was seen as much the stronger.[103] Six days later they moved south to confront Lambert at Penrith. But before that, the Scots went down to Rose Castle, five or six miles away. It was not tenable and the Parliamentary garrison under Major Cholmley burnt it before they left. A Scottish newsbook says that this happened the day before the invasion, that is 7 July.[104] An express from Lambert received by the Commons on 18 July, the text of which is not fully recorded, says that Langdale and the Scots army joined at Rose Castle, making a total of about 12,000 horse and foot, while Lambert lay at Penrith 'from which place he intends not to budge'.[105]

It is now necessary to leave Lambert in the northwest to see what was happening elsewhere in his command during June and July.

* NY 392401.

Chapter 5

ACTIONS AROUND PONTEFRACT

IT WILL BE RECALLED that, in addition to keeping Langdale in check and holding down Northumberland, the siege of Pontefract was also in Lambert's purview, employing troops he could have better used further north. On 22 June a letter from Penrith mentioned 'the increase of the Enemy about Pontefret and their late indeavour to have surprized Notingham, Yorke, Helmslee and Bolton castles'.[1] This chapter discusses various actions near, or connected with, Pontefract.

On 10 June the Committee authorised Lambert to offer up to £2,000 to whoever commanded in Pontefract Castle, to be paid on surrender so long as this was within six days of the offer being made. This would have freed several hundred men from the besieging forces to join in opposing Langdale, that is the regiments of Sir Henry Cholmley's at Ferrybridge (in overall command of the siege); Colonel William White's and Colonel Francis Hacker's at Ackworth; and Colonel Charles Fairfax's and Colonel Sir Edward Rhodes's at Featherstone (map 2).[2] The offer was not accepted.

Axholme and Lincoln

About a week later a large part of the garrison broke out.[3] Paulden's Account[4] says that 400 horse and 200 foot, under the command of Sir Philip Monckton, marched to Doncaster. From there they moved into the Isle of Axholme, a recently drained area of nearly 200 square miles, twenty-odd miles east of Pontefract and immediately west of the river Trent at its junction with the Ouse (map 2). It is centred on Epworth and Crowle, the latter about thirty miles by road from Pontefract, so clearly the Royalists were acting with considerable freedom.

The date of the event is not certain. Rushworth reported the news of their arrival in the Isle of Axholme on 28 June, but as he was with General Fairfax around Colchester it is uncertain how long the letter might have taken to reach him, or whether it went through London on the way. A minimum of three and perhaps four days would have been needed. But the news had reached the garrison of Walton Hall by the 26th,[5] so Axholme must have been occupied by the 25th at the latest, and perhaps the 24th. It is twenty miles or a good day's march from Doncaster to a point midway between Crowle and Epworth, which means they left Doncaster on the 23rd or 24th. Although no other account mentions this point, Paulden says that they spent four or five days in Doncaster before being invited into Lincolnshire. If so, the breakout was probably on the 17th or 18th.

From Axholme, they were ferried over the Trent and marched to Lincoln on Friday 30 June; that date was probably when they reached Lincoln. The nearest crossing was from Owston Ferry, four miles from Epworth, to East Ferry, and using this route the distance from Epworth to Lincoln is about twenty-five miles, and from Crowle about thirty-five miles. Given that they had foot as well as horse it would have taken two days to reach Lincoln, indicating that they crossed the Trent on Thursday 29th.

In Lincoln they plundered the house of one Captain Pert who was with Lambert in Northumberland, released prisoners from the castle, broke open the Treasury and took £1,100 of public money, and attacked and partly burned the bishop's palace. The palace was defended for three hours by thirty men under Captain Bee (Whitelocke gives Bret), a woollen draper, who was captured along with Captain Fines (Fiennes) and others. An officer for Sequestrations, Mr Smith, was killed.[6]

A Royalist news sheet put this event in a manner designed to encourage and amuse its readers:

> The gallant Royalists in Pontefract Castle are now very numerous, they
> march up and down the Country at pleasure, and have so plagued the plaguy
> Roundheads of those parts, that the country is now cleare of them they have
> lately taken the City of Lincoln, and while Cap. Pet was busie in plundering
> the Royall party (whom he durst looke upon by stealth) in Northumberland,
> they cleansed his house of all those unnecessary bags of coins, as also of all the
> household stuffe, that the said Saint had gotten together (by sinister means)
> this seaven years.; they sent Mr Smith the Sequestrator, on a speedy message
> to Pluto, and drove Cap. Bee, who was so bold as to make head againe into his
> hive, and are at present in a very strong posture.[7]

The following day, Saturday 1 July, they marched to Gainsborough on their way back to Pontefract. Their progress from there will be examined shortly.

Ferrybridge

At about this time those left in the Pontefract garrison made an attack on Ferrybridge. A party under a Major Thimbleby came out from the castle to Ferrybridge, only two miles away, where there was a crossing of the river Aire (plate 19). Apart from Paulden's Account[8] there is one major contemporary printed source preserved by Thomason, as well as two or three less detailed ones, and a relatively modern copy of a letter from Colonel Fairfax to his wife.[9] According to the account in *TT* E452/31, when the approach of the Royalists was detected the sentries gave the alarm quietly and the guards opened fire. When this did not deter them, the Captain of the Guard (in the absence of the gunner) fired a drake loaded with key shot. This stopped the rebels who were chased back to Pontefract, their commander captured, and about twenty killed.

Paulden, in his Account, gives the same story from the Royalist viewpoint.[10] He describes how Major Thimbleby led a small party along back alleys to outflank the Parliamentary barricades but, failing to follow his orders, was confronted by a troop of horse and was captured, while his men were killed. The remainder of the party was then lured up to the barricade, and received several musket volleys and shots from two drakes.

Colonel Fairfax's letter relates that 'an attempt of desperat adventurers . . . was made upon us on Monday night . . . we amongst a people that made them passage thro' their crofts and houses'. The description of an advance through alleyways and the capture of Thimbleby are in both Paulden's and Colonel Fairfax's accounts, and the mention of the use of artillery in *TT* E452/31 and Paulden make it clear that all three accounts are describing the same incident. *TT* E449/21 adds the detail that after a hot encounter Colonel Fairfax led a party of horse over the bridge and charged the enemy in the streets, with over twenty of the garrison killed and six taken prisoner. *TT* E452/13, a letter from York, describes the attack being 'repulsed with great losse' and the capture of Thimbleby. *TT* E453/28, a Royalist account, makes the best of a bad job by saying only that they 'fell upon the guards at Ferry-Bridge, where there was a hot Conflict, and some killed and wounded on both sides'.

The event itself is reasonably clear, but the date is not immediately obvious. Paulden gives three conflicting dates: at the beginning of August, at the time of the battle of Willoughby Field (5 July), and at the time of the raid on Axholme. One might ignore this evidence altogether, except that he is very clear that the Ferrybridge action was made possible because most of the besieging force had marched into Lincolnshire. Although only Cholmley's move to Gainsborough is recorded, some other regiments may have followed him, and Paulden's evidence does have some logic to it.

An indication of the date comes in the undated report in *TT* E452/31 which gives the occasion as 'on Fryday night last' and the same report gives 'Fryday last' as the day of the capture of Warwick Bridge. Both events are said by others to have occurred on Sunday or Monday. Warwick Bridge, as described above, took place on Sunday 25 June 1648, which might indicate that the fight at Ferrybridge occurred around the same date.

The copy of Colonel Fairfax's letter is dated 5 June, which was the Monday two days after the capture of Pontefract Castle, so the raid cannot have been on the previous Monday; the date must be wrong through an error of Fairfax or the copyist. The error might have been in the month. If the letter were written by Fairfax on Wednesday 5 July referring to an event happening 'on Monday' it must be Monday 3 July. This seems to be supported by *TT* E452/13, a letter dated 8 July which says the action was 'on Monday night', apparently meaning 3 July. On the other hand, if the date should have been 25 June (Sunday), then Fairfax's 'Monday night' must be 19 June.

The letter in *TT* E449/21 is dated 19 June (a Monday) and says 'upon Sunday last, 3 in morning'. The reference to 'Sunday last' ought to mean the 11th, but it is quite possible that the editor of the pamphlet, which has a manuscript date 23 June [Friday] on the cover, added the word 'last' which would indicate Sunday 18th.

The date of the raid on Axholme may help to confirm the date. Paulden's recollection is that the raid on Ferrybridge took place when the besieging force had followed the Pontefract men towards Lincolnshire. As shown above, the garrison probably broke out on 17 or 18 June. A raid on Ferrybridge on the 18th/19th would then fit comfortably with some of the besieging force following the Royalists, leaving Ferrybridge less well protected than before. Colonel Fairfax's letter should almost certainly be dated 25 June.

This somewhat lengthy discussion is included to point up the problems of relying on one or even two or three contemporary sources. Without taking all the most relevant sources together and trying to account for the contradictions, there would be little hesitation in placing the action at the end of June. Some reports seem to have been conveying old news under the guise of recent events.

Willoughby Field

As shown, the raiders who had plundered Lincoln were on their way to Gainsborough, eighteen miles away, on Saturday 1 July, where they appear to have remained until ten o'clock on the night of Monday 3rd. The reason for this delay, and failure to cross the river Trent at Gainsborough, was that on the west bank Sir Henry Cholmley was waiting with 600 Yorkshire horse (*TT* E451/41). Neither side could cross as there was then no bridge and an opposed crossing by the ferry was not an option for either party. The Royalists then marched twenty-four miles south to Newark. Most crossings of the lower Trent in this period were by many small ferries, and the reason for the move to Newark may have been to make use of the bridge there.

On Friday 30 June news of the attack on Lincoln reached Colonel Rossiter at Belvoir Castle. He had been sent to the area on 5 June to deal with an enemy gathering at Stamford and, somewhat belatedly, on 4 July Derby House sent him orders to deal with the Pontefract raiders.[11] But Rossiter had already asked for assistance from the surrounding counties of Northampton, Leicester, Nottingham, Derby and Rutland, and on Monday 3rd marched towards Lincoln with 550 men, all newly raised.[12] They marched thirty miles and quartered at Waddington, five miles short of Lincoln, and at three o'clock on Tuesday morning marched through Lincoln towards Gainsborough. On the way, they were informed by an escaped prisoner that the enemy had gone to Newark, and they pursued for eighteen miles before stopping for the night in a field a mile from the town, where they received news that their quarry was six miles away at Bingham (map 2). On the morning of Wednesday 5 July, after resting for four or five hours, Rossiter sent 150 of his ablest men under a Captain Champion to ride ahead to engage the enemy and slow their retreat until the main body could come up. Meanwhile, the Royalists took food, drink and two horses from the home of the Parliamentary Colonel Hutchinson at Owthorpe.[13] It is sometimes said that the house was plundered, but Mrs Hutchinson is very clear that only a small party was sent to the house with clear instructions not to make any disturbance if Colonel Hutchinson were not there. The two horses were being exercised away from the house and taken more by chance than design. In any event, Champion made contact with the enemy rear after seven miles, and they were brought to bay on the north side of Willoughby-on-the-Wolds, Notts.* After a hard fight, with the outcome in doubt, Rossiter eventually 'routed their whole Party, consisting of about 1,000, took 600 Horse and their Riders, the Commander in chief, and all his Officers, all their Bag and baggage, the rest routed, but not many slain'.[14] Half the enemy were from the Pontefract garrison.

The Commons were sufficiently impressed by the action to order £2,000 to be sent to Rossiter, and for £100 to go to Captain Norwood who brought the news. Rossiter was wounded ('hurt in his thigh in the late fight, and the skin touched of one of his Codes, but is cheerful') and the Commons sent a physician, surgeon and apothecary to him.[15]

The distances given above from Lincoln onwards are taken from the contemporary account, and do not tally with actual distances, which are rather longer. Willoughby is about thirty-eight miles from Lincoln down the Fosse Way, a long way for a large body of men to march with no effective resistance.

Colonel Cholmley and the Yorkshire horse crossed the Trent by the bridge at Nottingham to join Rossiter after the battle. They had presumably been shadowing Monckton south on the west bank, discouraging him from crossing the Trent, at Newark or elsewhere, and making their way back to Pontefract.

In fact, it is not clear what destination the Pontefract men had in mind. Initially they were clearly intending to return to the castle, and when foiled at Gainsborough perhaps hoped to cross at Newark. Even if the Yorkshire Horse were at Newark before them, they ought to have been able to make an attempt to cross the bridge there. There was a ferry at Gunthorpe, but they seem to have ignored any possibility of crossing there as they marched south from Bingham. On their journey they appear to have changed their plans, as some of the prisoners taken said that the intention was to march south, encouraging others to rise, and ultimately to relieve the siege of Colchester. Although this sounds far-fetched, it was not impossible. Their numbers had apparently risen from 600 to 1,000 since leaving Pontefract,[16] and if they had picked up two or three thousand more they could have become a serious threat.

---

* SK 635265, ten miles southeast of Nottingham.

Allerton Boat

The Pontefract garrison was still determined to cause trouble, and early in July, perhaps in the second week, a convoy under a Captain Browne was attacked while crossing the river Aire by ferry at Allerton Boat, close to Allerton Bywater, five or six miles north of Pontefract (map 3). Paulden's Account[17] says that the escort was two troops of Lord Fairfax's lifeguard, but this unit had been disbanded in 1647 and Colonel Fairfax described them as 'some of the Lord General's troop . . . with lines being not above sixty in each'. It may be that 120 men formed the escort, half in front and half behind, but the meaning is unclear.[18]

They had unsaddled and swum the horses across (the saddles will have been taken by the ferry boat to keep them dry) when they were attacked by a force of Royalists under Sir William Byron and Captain William Paulden, while Browne and four men were still to cross. Those of Browne's men who could (i.e. had saddled their horses) mounted, retreated to reform, then charged the enemy and successfully drove them back. More Royalists appeared and, as Paulden said: 'In the third [charge] wee breake them, routed them, killed, tooke and drowned most of them, tooke both their colours, wounded Browne who com'anded them very desperately in the body.' Colonel Fairfax's account reports: 'Three of ours killed on the field, twenty horses, about six case of pistols, no backs or breasts [taken], two colours lost but not mounted, twenty wounded, six mortally inc Capt Brown.'[19]

Paulden believed that the numbers were about equal; Colonel Fairfax gave the enemy as about twelve score (240). Eleven Parliamentary troopers were taken prisoner and later exchanged after the siege of Thornhill House (see below). The loss of twenty horses against the death or mortal wounding of less than a dozen men shows up the greater target presented by horses. It is not clear what the description of the colours as 'not mounted' signifies, unless it simply means that they were being carried cased. The convoy appears to have been carrying military supplies and, although some items were taken, the back and breasts were saved, which indicates that the rout was not as complete as Paulden suggests. Carts or wagons are not mentioned, which might show that the goods were carried on pack horses. Perhaps the escort went over first to secure the opposite bank, and not all the goods had reached the far side. The pack animals could have been taken over on the ferry without unloading; horse ferries, large, flat-bottomed boats, were in use by the sixteenth century.[20]

The besiegers at Pontefract were getting at least some of their supplies through both Leeds and York,[21] but wherever they came from it is not easy to see why the route should have been across the Aire at Allerton Boat.

Thornhill

At around the same time, the Pontefract garrison was causing trouble elsewhere for Parliament's forces. There was a rumour from Ferrybridge that the Royalists were to march north in response to a letter from Langdale, but nothing came of it.[22] In the middle of July a

Royalist news sheet announced that they had captured two houses, Thorney and Homely.[23] Homely is probably Honley House,* but no details can be found of the incident. Thorney was Thornhill Hall near Dewsbury,† a moated manor of Lord Savile's.[24] It is about fifteen miles by road from Pontefract, with Honley another eleven miles further west (map 3).

Thornhill is said to be have been occupied by 200 foot from Pontefract, a considerable and slow-moving body of men: a week after their defeat at Willoughby Fields the besieged garrison was still not closely controlled.

A letter from Colonel Fairfax said that he had been ordered to Thornhill with 500 of his foot and 200 horse from Cholmley's. However, he was not able to march at once: 'I intended to have bene there last Saturday night [15 July] but too much of that day was spent in pacification of ye souldiers that exclaimed for pay (and indeed they are gallant men if they were not too ~~mutinous~~ clamerous [)] it was past nine next morninge before we came thither . . .'[25]

They appear to have made an immediate and unsuccessful attack, losing twelve killed and thirty wounded. On Monday 17th they cut off the water supply and began to drain the moat, which was completed the following day. By chance the troops sent north by Cromwell were on hand to assist: '[Horse from Cromwell] joyn'd with such as of that County were intended for Major Gen. Lambert, had faln upon the house of my Lord Savils call'd Thorney House.'[26] Sir Henry Cholmley arrived in person and the Royalist garrison under Captain Thomas Paulden surrendered to Colonel Fairfax on Tuesday 18th. They were allowed to go to Pontefract leaving their arms, ammunition and baggage, and the three officers were each allowed to take a horse and a sword. In return, it was agreed that eleven of the Lord General's horse who had been taken at Allerton Boat would be released from Pontefract. The powder magazine then caught fire by accident, blowing up part of the house and killing five Royalists 'and miserably scorched about seven or eight more', and the subsequent fire destroyed the rest of the Hall. The Pembroke horse then continued their journey north to join Lambert, along with Wastell's and Lascelles' foot, and two companies of the Lord General's foot. Bethell's horse was also ordered north.[27]

---

* Honley, Huddersfield, SE 138122.
† SE 256189.

Chapter 6

APPLEBY, STAINMORE AND BOWES

Penrith to Appleby

THE END OF CHAPTER 4 saw Lambert in Penrith, which he was said to be determined not to leave. But leave he did, after a sharp skirmish near Warwick Bridge followed by the advance of the Scottish army. The precise date of the fighting is unclear. The only report of the action comes in a letter from Penrith, dated 16 July. It also includes a reference to Rose Castle, in which it uses precisely the same wording and orthography as a report dated 'Newcastle 13 July'.[1] The writer seems to have been in or closely connected with the Parliamentary army, which left Penrith on the night of the 14–15th, and the letter is presumably wrongly dated by either the writer or the typesetter. The writer is also bringing the recipient up to date 'since my last of 14th', but then goes on to describe actions that took place before the 14th. On that date he may, of course, simply have been out of touch.

The date of the action is given in the letter as 'upon Sunday morning last' which was 9 July, the day after the Scots invaded, but the title to the printed version says the action was 'on Monday last', that is 10 July. All that can safely be said is that it occurred between the 9th and 13th.

Parliamentary horse guards were stationed about four miles north of Penrith – Plumpton, around five miles north, might have been a suitable place[2] – but scouts were active in advance of this point. They saw some Scottish horse described as 'from Carlisle', and passed word back. The warning was received by Captain Bethell who advanced towards Warwick Bridge with six troops of horse and two of dragoons. Around two o'clock in the morning they surprised a party of Scots horse and four companies of foot who were waiting for orders about two miles short of the bridge, that is, around Wetheral. Bethell was able to surprise them as the Scots horse, whose appearance had occasioned the alarm, retreated 'another way', perhaps continuing up the main road towards Carlisle (map 5).

There was a sharp fight of charge and counter-charge, with the horse well supported by the dragoons. It ended when the dragoons broke a passage for the horse through a breast-high field wall which was sheltering the Scots, who were then pursued over two fields, but were reinforced and made good their retreat.

In the action about eight of Lambert's men were killed while the Royalists, 'who might easily be discovered by their gray shootes [suits] and blew Bonnets', lost above twenty. Apart from the loss of Rose Castle, this seems to have been the first action against the Scots since they had crossed the border, and probably had a lowering effect on their morale. It appears to have been a sharp, successful action by the Parliamentary horse, which were ready and able to fall on the enemy from some distance to their discouragement. It does, however, raise some questions.

First, Captain Bethell was with the horse guards, stationed perhaps at Plumpton, and took with him a total of between 600 and 800 men depending on the troop strength. To ride off on his own initiative would have been to leave the army very poorly guarded. Secondly, it is doubtful that a captain would take that upon himself without definite orders even though he is described as 'a man of known valour and integrity'. And the fact that Bethell knew to turn off towards Warwick Bridge, even though the Scots horse went back another way, suggests very strongly that this was a planned operation based on good intelligence. The account does not say that Bethell was in command, and there will very likely have been a more senior officer in charge. It reads rather as though the correspondent had the account from Bethell and by omission gave him as much credit as he could. A minor point is that there was no moon at two o'clock, and the sun did not rise until about four o'clock. It would probably have been too dark to identify the Scots scouts much before three o'clock, let alone chase them, and the time given could be too early. The intelligence may be related to Hodgson's comment that Lambert had 'spies among their army' at this time, giving information of the Scots numbers and intentions.[3]

There is a further point to be considered. Only one version exists, and without confirmation it is difficult to know how much weight to put on the account, in part as well as in whole. However, there is a good deal of circumstantial information given, including the names of two of the Scots officers, Lieutenant-Colonel Hames and Major Ennis, said to be mortally wounded.

Modern commentaries tend to say that the Scots cavalry fought with Lambert's outside Penrith on Friday 14 July,[4] but the contemporary records do not confirm this. All that happened was that the two armies faced one another. Burnet's account of the meeting of the two armies there is worth quoting at length:

> Duke sent out a Party of some three hundred Horse, who discovered the
> Enemies Main-guard of Horse, and gave the General notice of it; who
> thereupon commanded the whole Cavalry to march purposing to fall upon
> the Enemy that very night, and he sent orders to Baylie to hasten the advance
> of the Infantry. A full discovery being made of the Enemy, our Cavalry was
> drawn up in their view, where expecting the advance of the Foot, we stood in
> Arms till night, but about midnight the Enemy drew off quietly.[5]

A letter from one of Lambert's staff simply says that the enemy forces approached within two miles of Penrith and makes no mention of action.[6] Reade confirms this in a general sense, adding that Lambert's officers were all playing bowls when Hamilton's men approached the town and would have thrown down their arms if the Scots had attacked.[7] It is difficult to believe that Lambert's experienced officers would have seriously considered taking this course; it is more likely that either Reade was denigrating the Parliamentary army or a colonel's jocular remark was taken as truth by an onlooker.

The combined army of Scots and English Royalists, now said to be 3,000 horse and 4,000 foot, had advanced from their quarters in Wigton, Crofton Hall and Thursby, probably down what is now the B5305 to within two miles of Penrith, near the junction of that road with the A6. However, 'by reason of the length of the way . . . and some narrow passages (which much retarded) we were benighted three miles short of Penreth, and therefore quartered in the field that night, not exposing our selves to the disadvantage of making an onset at a time so unseasonable'.[8] The Scots horse, sensibly, were not prepared to risk an engagement without infantry support, and Lambert presumably saw no purpose in engaging unless essential. To oppose the Scots he had around 2,700 horse, and no doubt also had at least some of his 3,000 infantry drawn up with the cavalry.

One reason for the delay in the Scots foot joining with their horse outside Penrith may have been that only a week earlier much of Lambert's army had used the last seven miles or so of the same road when pulling back from Carlisle through Bolton, Sandale, Caldbeck and Sowerby. Several thousand men and horses marching along an unpaved road in pouring rain, as reported by Birch, will have turned it into a quagmire, which would have slowed and exhausted the Scots foot even more than it would the horse. The road is otherwise generally not a difficult route, apart from the steep inclines into and out of the valley of the river Caldew at Sebergham, which would seriously have delayed the passage of foot marching with the supply wagons necessary to the whole army moving south.

That night, 14 July, the sun set at 8.15 p.m. when the moon (waxing crescent) was 20 degrees above the horizon; at nine o'clock the moon was at 14 degrees; at ten o'clock it had dropped to just over 5 degrees and it set before eleven o'clock.[9] Twilight would have lasted until perhaps 9.15 p.m. if the sky were reasonably clear but, bearing in mind that it rained heavily overnight (see below), it is doubtful if it were cloudless. By eleven o'clock. it was probably very dark and it is unlikely that the opposing horse faced each other until midnight. At some time during the night Lambert pulled back to Appleby.

A letter in the Braye manuscripts, which reads as from one who was not there, says that Lambert's forces left Penrith at 'about eleven that night'.[10] Birch, who was there, says: 'We drew out of Penrith and march't all night and the next morning – extremely wet it was – we came about eleven o'clocke to Appleby.' It is difficult to see how it took twelve hours to cover thirteen miles in a straight march, even at night. It may be that the time of leaving was later than 11 p.m., and if the horse did indeed not fall back until midnight the retreat may not have begun for another hour or two. Something like eight or nine hours is more believable given that they may have moved in stages, guarding against an attack on the march, which could have proved fatal. Birch, of course, may have given his time from memory. *Letter from Holland* gives 'about midnight' – a time that the writer presumably heard from the inhabitants of Penrith.

The move seems to have been planned well in advance, for Hodgson says: 'We sent away our carriages for Appleby, and only kept our ammunition with us; and so we retreated by degrees.' This sounds as though all spare equipment and supplies had been sent to the rear, and supports the idea of a planned withdrawal.

Hamilton had intended to attack the following day, Saturday 15 July – *Letter from Holland* says his horse broke camp at five in the morning – but he was too late. 'Next morning betimes a great rain falling, we advanced to a Bridge a mile beyond Penreith, with design to engage the Enemy, but missing our hopes were forced for our accommodation in Quartering to return to Penreith.'[11] *Letter from Holland* gives an alternative view:

> Having advanced two miles beyond the town [Penrith], our horse intending
> to pursue him, the intelligence of the countreymen, did assure his being by
> that time at Appleby, whereto there was about eight miles, and severall waters
> unpassable betwixt us, by means of the great rain that fell in such abundance,
> the which occasioned our quartering that saturday night, and sunday, at and
> about Penreth.

Some at least of the invading army is reported to have camped near Brougham Castle in the area known as the Two Bridges, and remained there for two days.[12]

Starting out early in the morning could have been a productive move for Hamilton, but the sense of the reports is that once Lambert was known to have reached Appleby the energy went out of the Royalists. The heavy rains did not stop Lambert from retreating, and the fact that it was still raining heavily three days later did not prevent Hamilton from eventually resuming his advance. It is as though Hamilton had planned to quarter in Penrith after beating Lambert there, and when it was found that the bird had flown the Scots army sat down and wondered what to do next.

Lambert's retreat from Penrith, however necessary, will not have been good news for Parliament, but there was better news from the south. Cromwell wrote to the Speaker on 11 July to announce the fall of Pembroke Castle, and on the 18th Derby House ordered Cromwell 'with such forces as may be spared with safety to these parts to march into the north, and there use your best endeavours to suppress the enemy in those parts'.[13] On the 20th they advised Lambert of this and brought him up to date with the troubles at Colchester, which they hoped would soon be ended. It was doubtless with this speedy end in mind that they wrote to General Fairfax on the 21st asking him to spare a regiment of horse for Lambert, and on the 25th for a troop to be sent to the Isle of Wight. This, on top of many earlier demands for small packets of troops to be sent to various parts, can only have added to Fairfax's burden as he conducted the bitter siege.

July was a busy time for the Derby House Committee. On the 15th, they wrote to the County Committees of Nottingham, Leicester, Lincoln, Northampton and Derby, and to the Governor of Belvoir, ordering them to send a total of 660 horse to assist in the siege of Pontefract. They were obliged to send a reminder to Leicester, Lincoln, Nottingham, Derby and to the Governor of Belvoir Castle, on the 25th as their horse had not yet appeared. They were given until 3 August, or earlier if possible, to comply, but Northamptonshire and Leicestershire had to be prodded again on 8 August.[14] There was a need for more horse at Pontefract for, as shown in the previous chapter, the garrison was roaming almost at will.

On 27 July Derby House wrote to Cromwell urging him to march with all speed, and confirmed that shoes and stockings would be provided at Northampton and Coventry. The following day they advised the lieutenant of the Tower that there was a design against it which would be executed in the next two or three days. They were also concerned through July about pay for Lambert's forces.[15]

Derby House also found time to deal with another matter. On 11 July the Committee wrote to Lambert: 'We are informed you are about to publish in print a Declaration, but know not the contents thereof . . . We, therefore, desire you upon these considerations to forbear the publishing of anything in print or otherwise, except such things as concern your own army . . .' There are two implications of interest here. First, Derby House once again seems to be showing mistrust or a lack of confidence in Lambert, and, secondly, it appears that someone at his headquarters was keeping Derby House informed of the general's actions – the notion of a political commissar comes to mind. There is no indication of what Lambert was intending to publish.

Appleby

Lambert's men reached Appleby safely on the morning of Saturday 15 July, when Birch's company was put to guarding the magazine. A letter from Lambert's army dated the 17th points out that the Parliamentary and Scots armies were so close that they were both foraging in the same area: 'Our Army are in straits, have for a good while drunk nothing but water, we and they fetch victuals from the same place, about twenty miles in length.'[16]

The proximity of Hamilton's army caused Lambert's horse to be kept in a body until Monday morning in expectation of an attack. In particular, the horse was standing-to all through Sunday night in cold, wet weather.[17] However, there was no further action until the morning of Monday the 17th, when the Scots advanced 'notwithstanding of the great deluge of waters, it continually raining' (*Letter from Holland*).

The geography of the immediate area is of significance (see map 6 and fig. 3). The town and castle of Appleby lie in a loop of the river Eden, half a mile south of the Roman road from Penrith to Brough and Bowes. The only access to the town on the north side was (and is) a single bridge, and a ford which is still in occasional use and negotiable when the river is low (plates 20, 21, 22). The river is typically 95 feet wide, shallow in places but with deep pools, and deep and fast-flowing when in flood. In June 2007 a horse was drowned in one of the pools while being washed in the river when the general water level was quite low. The river can rise by up to three feet within a few hours of heavy rain upstream, and with no further rain will take 10–15 hours to fall to more normal levels. Prolonged heavy rain, such as was the case in 1648, can raise the level by up to six feet. The banks of the river have been significantly altered over the past fifty years as part of flood defence work, but it does not appear ever to have been an easy river to cross.

From its position on a low hill the castle dominates the town (plate 23), which is virtually surrounded by hills. The minor road immediately east of the bridge is more or less at the foot of steeply rising ground; on the plan (fig. 3) the area of reasonably flat or easy ground is hatched, and some of the more obvious high points shaded.

Just west of Appleby the modern road swings southwest in an arc close to Crackenthorpe but the Roman road, 30 feet wide between its ditches, ran westwards in a straight line. It is still in use as a farm road in places (plate 24), and is clearly visible between its walls and hedges. It was sufficiently important in 1876 for a very substantial stone bridge to be provided over the railway to Carlisle, and the road line would certainly have been negotiable in the seventeenth century.

Early on Monday the 17th most of Lambert's foot and six regiments of horse were dismissed 'for refreshment' to quarters four or five miles to the south of Appleby, after their overnight duty.[18] There are few places of any size in the area, although farms as well as villages would have provided provisions. If the direction and distance are taken literally the settlements of Hoff, Drybeck and Great Ormside might have been among those visited. The only three villages marked on the Quartermasters' Map (plate 25) are Great Ormside (3½ miles away), Great Asby (almost five miles) and Crosby Ravensworth (just over seven miles).[19]

One foot regiment from Lancashire[20] was left in the town and Harrison's regiment of horse provided guards 'on a moor beyond the town'.[21] This is a very imprecise location, but it would have been a place where there was a reasonable view along the road towards Penrith.

Burnet says that Lord Levingstoun (brother of the Earl of Callander), with a party of horse, presumably a reconnaissance patrol, discovered Harrison's guards, 300 strong (probably three troops), within a mile of Appleby. Stretching the distance to nearer 1½ miles, guards placed near the old Roman road near 'A' on fig. 3 would, in clear weather, have a view towards Kirkby Thore. However, undulations in the landscape have a limiting effect, and on a visit in July 2010, in low, heavy cloud and a light drizzle, the visibility towards the west was very severely limited.

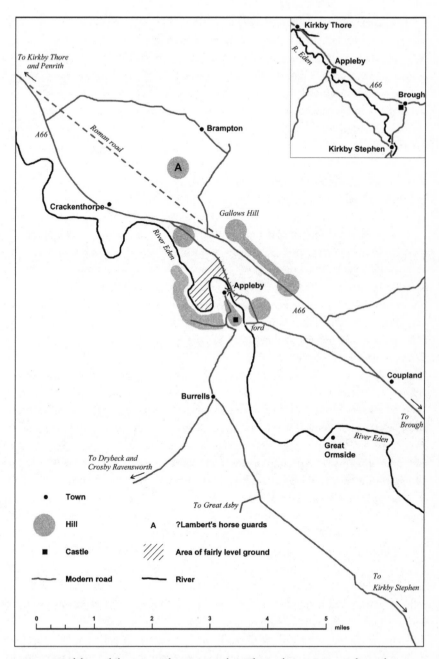

FIG. 3 *Appleby and the surrounding topography. The modern A66 is partly on the Roman road line, but bends south towards Crackenthorpe.*

The Scots were not seen until 'they marched again with their whole body towards us (it being a very dark rainy morning) [and] were within a mile of our horse guards, before they were discovered'.[22] Elsewhere the weather is described as foggy.[23] The reason the enemy came so close to the guards before being seen was said to be because 'we want good Scouts, for want of allowance of pay from the Parliament for a Scout-master-general'.[24] Similar complaints had been made before, without effect (see Introduction, p. xxiii).

The first sighting by Lambert's horse guards is variously given as nine o'clock, eleven o'clock and noon,[25] at which point the enemy scouts were two miles or so from Appleby. Levingstoun's patrol would have reported back to Hamilton. Equally, Harrison's guards would send back a report to Lambert in the castle, perhaps saying no more than that a patrol had been sighted. This may well not have occasioned any great alarm. Soon, however, the situation would be seen to be serious.

It appears from the various reports that Scots scouts were seen first, perhaps mid-morning, followed later by a large body of horse perhaps at noon; one account gives the number of Royalists attacking as 3,000.[26] Whatever the time, all four reports[27] agree that the Scots horse soon appeared in force on three hills within half a mile of Appleby so that the horse guards were forced to retreat. One of the hills occupied by the Royalists was identified as Gallows Hill,* across the Stainmore road half a mile north of the town. The hill is around 610 feet high, 175 feet above the bridge, and the appearance of the enemy there must have caused some alarm.

Hamilton's army was marching from its quarters around Penrith. The distance to Appleby is fourteen miles, and there is no indication at all as to when their march began. If his scouts saw Lambert's guard at nine o'clock, and if it were not until eleven o'clock (or later) that the main body of horse had advanced and formed up on the hills, the much slower foot might have been still quite close to Penrith. At this point, if not before, Lambert's horse and foot regiments which had been sent to the south for quarters would have been recalled, by which time they could well have been two or three hours' march away.

The Scots horse were under the command of Lieutenant-General Middleton, who ordered the captain of the general's troop to charge down the hill. The Parliamentary guards were pushed back to Appleby,[28] whereupon Harrison led the other three troops of his regiment forward. He charged ahead of the rest and seized one of the Royalist horse colours but was badly wounded in his left wrist, back and thigh, and surrounded, along with three of his men. One account says he was obliged to surrender, another that he was refused quarter and continued to fight resolutely. Others of his regiment, outnumbered and not expecting quarter, fell upon the Scots, killed a number and rescued Harrison.[29] This charge also saw the death of Captain Henry Cromwell's lieutenant, and a Lieutenant Sheeres captured.[30] *Letter from Holland* records the return of Sheeres and five others the next

* NY 683214.

day without exchange. *Ane Information*, published in Edinburgh, has a slightly different interpretation, saying that Hamilton's and Middleton's own troops killed some, took some prisoners, and chased the rest back to the bridge. Certainly, Lambert's forces were thrown back in some haste even if only one man was killed rather than many.

The Parliamentary defenders were greatly assisted by the heavy rains of the previous day which had raised the level of the river. Hodgson explains that when the Scots first appeared the river was fordable, 'but in a short time it was risen so high as we had no fords to maintain but only the bridge, where we had our foot placed on a piece of advantageous ground'. Most other reports make the same point. *Letter from Holland* says that nowhere within ten miles was fordable. It is not clear what Hodgson's 'advantageous ground' might have been, as the ground slopes up in every direction within a short distance of the bridge. Almost all sources quoted for the fight mention the infantry coming out of the town after Harrison's repulse, lining hedges and manning barricades, especially on the bridge. The bridge, as described below, was only thirteen feet wide and would have been relatively easy to block.

It is uncertain at what point the Royalist foot came into action. Parliamentary commentaries suggests that it was soon after the horse, but Burnet is clear that it was much later: 'That evening our whole Cavalry made a stand for several hours, expecting the advance of Langdale who being marched up did presently with his Foot engage with the Enemy into the Town till it was dark.'[31] As recorded in *Letter from Holland*, most of the foot were held up at Kirkby Thore by a small river (the Trout Beck, now some twenty feet wide) much swollen by the heavy rains, and it was not until evening that 'some foot came to us, who during the small remnant of the day endeavoured to gain the bridge'.

This, incidentally, implies that the Trout Beck was not effectively bridged at Kirkby Thore, which is a little surprising. The bridge, which was first mentioned in 1358, was said to have been in decay after the Civil War. It is possible that it was of wood, as in 1676 a rate was levied for 'building a stone bridge at K. Thore'. A later stone bridge was badly damaged in a flood in February 1822, and it may be that the heavy rains of 1648 had caused serious damage to a wooden one.[32] It may also have been damaged by Lambert on his retreat.

Ane Information is clear that: 'About night, our commanded party of Musketiers came up, all wet and dragled by a long march in foul weather, and through deep waters.' If, as suggested above, the foot were still quite close to Penrith at nine o'clock, they would have been about five hours' march from Appleby. Add to this the hold-up at Kirkby Thore, and it is clear that they cannot have reached Appleby until late afternoon at best.

When the foot did arrive they were determined, and 'drew out several strong Parties, to break into the Town, every quarter of an hour'.[33] It is not clear in just which area the fighting occurred, but it was probably confined to the more or less level area, shown hatched on fig 3, alongside the river. However, fighting in the bight of the river to the west of the town could have led to one or other party being trapped.

The attacks were all repulsed, and the defenders went onto the attack. At some point unspecified, the main body of the Parliamentary horse and foot returned from the south and the Royalists were forced to retire. A small party under Colonel (or Captain) Hatfield charged 'a great body of the enemies horse' on Gallows Hill and forced them to retreat.[34] One source says the attack was by a party of foot, which seems unlikely. A Captain Hatfield was in Lambert's regiment of horse in 1655,[35] but whether this was the same man is unknown.

The timing of all these events is difficult. Harrison's charge is variously said to have taken place at twelve o'clock and two o'clock, with fighting continuing until nightfall or until nine and ten o'clock at night with 'extream hard service'.[36] Only one source differs, with fighting said to have been between three o'clock and seven o'clock, when the Scots gave way and the Parliamentary force followed up for 'about a mile, until it was very dark. Many of their foot ran away and threw down their arms'.[37] Sanderson says that the fighting went on until nine o'clock, but he was not present.

It was something of a victory for Lambert's army, albeit a defensive one. Six of Parliament's force were reported killed, against sixteen Royalists at Appleby itself, 200 or more afterwards (presumably in the pursuit) and 300 wounded. Up to 300 of them threw down their arms. In addition, sixty (or a hundred) Royalists were discovered in a barn, presumably trying to avoid involvement, and sixty were put to the sword.[38] It may be this action that was referred to thus: 'The Scots army . . . with a resolution to inlarge their Quarters more Southerly, were so gallantly entertained that a hundred of them were slain, many wounded and many taken prisoners.'[39] The Royalist horse and those of the foot who had reached the fight quartered that night in the field near Appleby.[40]

Lambert held a Council of War that evening. In the face of Hamilton's superior numbers, it was decided to retreat to Kirkby Stephen at daybreak on the following day, Tuesday the 18th,[41] leaving a garrison in Appleby Castle as discussed below.

From the town, the Parliamentary army had the choice of heading south to Tebay, which would have meant abandoning the area to Hamilton, southeast to Kirkby Stephen, or regaining the main road leading east over Stainmore, to which they had no direct access apart from the one bridge. If they had left by the latter way they would have been observed and their rear open to attack as they retreated. Instead, after cutting the bridge to discourage pursuit (but see below),[42] they had little alternative but to march 10½ miles to Kirkby Stephen.

Sunset on the evening of the 17th was a little after 8 p.m., with twilight lasting no more than another hour.[43] Accepting that the fighting finished around nine, the troops had to find quarters for the night, to eat if possible, and to get what sleep they could before leaving at daybreak. The sun rose about 4.15 a.m. and it would probably have been light enough to march by 3 a.m.

The army rested at Kirkby Stephen for two hours and then marched 4½ miles north to Brough, whence it was thirteen miles to Bowes at the eastern end of the Stainmore pass, which they reached the same evening. 'At Kirby Stephen wee refresht for an houre or two, and conceiving the enemy might march to Brough, and so prevent us the passe into Yorkshire, wee thought fitt to march to Bowes'.[44] The relatively long halt at Kirkby Stephen may have been due to Lambert awaiting intelligence of Hamilton's movements.

It may be asked why Lambert retreated so far from Hamilton's army after he reached Brough, and indeed why he maintained his advance guard around Bowes, only four miles from his base at Barnard Castle but thirteen miles from Brough and twenty-six from Kirkby Thore. The explanation is a simple one: between Bowes and Brough is the largely rather bleak Stainmore (Stane-moor), with little in the way of arable land and virtually no accommodation. Feeding an army would have been impossible, and the area around Brough had been campaigned over by both armies over several months.

Carlton refers to an ambush at Appleby, killing four or five and wounding others, and says that this so panicked the survivors that they retreated for two days without pausing to eat.[45] This confuses a back reference by Birch on 18 July to the fighting of the day before giving the numbers which his company, or his regiment, had lost in the fighting, with no mention of an ambush on the retreat, and all contemporary writers agree that there was no pursuit: 'without any trouble of the Enemy, who never appeared in our Reer'.[46] Indeed, with the river Eden dividing the two armies, there was no possibility of setting an ambush. Birch, who had been in the rearguard of the foot from Appleby under Major Greenlishe, merely records that he came to Bowes and 'quarterd upon the bare walls of a cottage after long fasting'. There is no suggestion of a two-day retreat with no time to eat, and every source gives one day for the march. But it is no wonder that Lambert described his men as 'very much tired and worn out with continual duty, hard marches and bad weather'.[47] A day of marching to and from quarters at Appleby, then heavy fighting, followed the next day by a march of almost twenty-eight miles beginning at dawn would have been enough to exhaust the most determined troops.

The following day, 19 July, Lambert moved from Bowes to his headquarters at Barnard Castle. He wrote from there to Hesilrige, making a second request for 500–600 foot from the Newcastle garrison; it is not known whether they were sent. He also asked for more ammunition to be sent to Raby as his army was in great want of it.

Sanderson's diary sheds a little light on the retreat from Appleby. On 13 July Sanderson's and Bradford's troops, then in Alnwick, received orders 'from Collo: Lilburne for us to march to the army'. Interestingly, this did not mean that they were to rejoin Lilburne's regiment, then in Penrith with Lambert, but to go south to Bowes, which they reached on the 18th in time to meet the retreating army. It is not likely that such a coincidence of timing was intentional, but rather that Lambert was anticipating a retreat in the face of Hamilton's army and had arranged for what forces he could muster to form a guard at the eastern end of the Stainmore pass.

A letter, referring to Lambert's army's arrival at Bowes on 18 July, mentions meeting only: 'Major Sanderson and Capt Bradfords Troops, out of Northumberland, Colonel

Wrens five Troops, and Captain Harleys, and Captain Persons company, who are grown very thin by their lying at York.'[48] The total may have been somewhere between 500 and 600 horse and foot, a useful reinforcement to Lambert's weary force.

With the benefit of hindsight, Lambert's decision to send most of his men away from Appleby looks unwise. However, not only had all the horse been on duty overnight in foul weather, but for two days had been kept together in readiness after their very wet night march from Penrith. The principal concern for Lambert may not have been refreshment for the men but for the horses, which had been Langdale's problem at Carlisle in June. Appleby is, and was, a small town, and Lambert's 5,700 men and 2,800 horses could not expect to survive long if penned up there surrounded by the Scottish army. Within a week men and horses would have been starving, and the latter fast losing condition. Men who are short of provisions can be coerced by large promises into waiting until tomorrow for a good breakfast, but the demands of horses are not so easily ignored. The fact that so many regiments had been sent south to quarters indicates that the lack of supplies was already becoming dangerous on the day Hamilton attacked and it is doubtful whether Lambert had much choice. At least he ensured that patrols were sufficiently in advance of the town to give just enough warning, although it was a close-run thing.

The heavy rain which raised the river introduced a strong element of luck into the Parliamentary success, and if Hamilton had known of Lambert's situation and made an early attack he would have had a very good chance of victory. A start at daybreak, as he did when advancing on Penrith, could have got them to Appleby when the river was still fordable. An opportunity had been lost, but there was more to come.

Lambert's move to Kirkby Stephen had left the Stainmore route wide open for a few hours, but instead of taking it Hamilton retreated back to Kirkby Thore and sat down. Even Burnet could not disguise what happened: 'Before the next morning, the Enemy marched away both Horse and Foot, leaving only a Garrison in Appleby-Castle; and did cut the Bridge, so that it was impossible to follow, for the rains had fallen in such abundance that the Waters were not to be forded: whereupon we went to Kirby-thure in Cumberland, where we lay three weeks . . .'[49]

The statement that the bridge at Appleby was broken by Lambert is worth examining. The bridge, first mentioned in the fourteenth century, was of stone and a survey of it in 1887 showed it to consist of two segmental arches, each consisting of five sandstone ribs bridged by stone slabs to give an original road width of thirteen feet.[50] The slabs will have been covered with metalling to form a ramp at each end and to fill the spandrel between the two arches (fig. 4).

Such a bridge may be broken in two ways. First, gunpowder charges, well tamped in a trench in the metalling between haunch and crown, would bring an arch down very quickly.[51] Secondly, digging away the metalling and lifting the slabs between the ribs over a distance of a few feet, and tossing them into the river, would effectively close the bridge

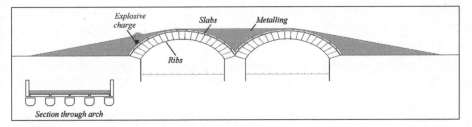

FIG. 4 *The parts of a segmental arch. Either firing a demolition charge or removing some of the slabs would render the bridge unusable.*

except for those willing to walk along the ribs. The ribs would remain stable, and temporary repairs with planks would make the bridge usable within a day or so. Certainly Langdale's men were engaging with the garrison of Appleby very soon – a week later a letter from Barnard Castle gave some details of action there (described below) which seems to have spread over a few days. In 1649 Appleby was one of the bridges in Westmorland 'in great decay'[52] but if Lambert had blown up an arch it would surely have been reported as broken. The likelihood, therefore, is that minor damage such as removing part of the roadway was the limit of any 'breaking down'. Neither Lambert, Hodgson nor Birch mention breaking the bridge.

The excuse that the Scots army was unable to follow Lambert does not stand up to examination, for the broken bridge (if it were indeed so) was little barrier to following Lambert or otherwise prosecuting the war. If Hamilton had been more resolute and proactive, the Scots army could easily have marched the eight or ten miles to Brough from their quarters in the field near Appleby and been there well ahead of Lambert, who would then have had to fight his way out against greatly superior numbers. Lambert had fourteen or fifteen miles to cover, taking perhaps seven hours including the two-hour break. If it had taken Hamilton a couple of hours to gather his army together, the march to Brough at an average of 3 m.p.h. would have been complete in a total of about five hours, putting him two hours ahead of Lambert. The condition of the Stainmore road is not known, but the lanes between Appleby and Kirkby Stephen, still narrow ways between banks and hedges, would almost certainly have given worse conditions for marching, suggesting that Hamilton's advantage could have been greater. With determination he could have been in Bowes up to three hours ahead of Lambert, with the way to Yorkshire open to him. The small guard of a few hundred horse and foot waiting at Bowes[53] was quite inadequate to repel an invading army.

Letter from Holland explains that it was necessary for Hamilton to wait at Kirkby Thore because: 'We still wanted the main materials and sinews of the Army . . . there being in store with us no more than ten barrels of pouder, other ammunition proportionable, no artillery at all, no meal, but a little for the souldiers subsistence some dayes on the way.' While the letter may be an apologia for the Royalist failings, it does appear to be true that they were short of supplies. On 19 July Hamilton wrote to Langdale that most of their ammunition was still at Carlisle for want of transport, and he was able to spare him only one barrel of powder and a case of ball.[54] Perhaps Hamilton had hoped to catch Lambert off-balance, first at Penrith and then at Appleby, and when this failed he did not care to risk moving further from his source of supply.

Another reason that Hamilton did not try to get over Stainmore ahead of Lambert may have been because the latter was said to have marched towards Lancashire from Appleby.[55] The source for that belief is dated in Edinburgh a month later, and it may have been no more than an attempt to put a gloss on Hamilton's failure.

If Hamilton had been able to break through, the history of the second Civil War might have been very different, but the Royalists never did manage to break Lambert's grip on the Stainmore road into Yorkshire.

Stainmore

On his withdrawal to Bowes, Lambert left troops to guard the Stainmore pass. They were attacked almost at once, and the account is worth quoting at length:

> Duke Hamilton . . . thought to have forced his way at Stainmore passage, but was presented [*sic*]; for Major-Generall Lambert having placed a very considerable party to secure the said Bridge and passage, and a Briggade of the Scots comming up, thinking to passe the River, found opposition, and the quarrel disputed for the space of two hours, and had not another Briggade of the Scots come up, we had been Masters of the day; but seeing our selvs over-powred, made an honourable retreat towards Barnard Castle, which was six or seven miles distant from us, the enemy pursued about three miles, but at a distant, they over-powr us exceedingly in Foot, and have great numbers of horse. In this conflict we lost about thirty men, and brought off about twenty which were wounded; the losse of the enemy is thought to be far more.[56]

A second account dated 23 July, briefer and with quite different wording, does not give any indication of place but agrees with the numbers lost and clearly refers to the same action, and gives a more precise date: 'On Wednesday and Thursday last [i.e. 19 and 20 July], several disputes happenned betwene both Armies, on Thursday morning about five of the clock, the forlones of Horce engaged, and had a sharp conflict, and by the overpowring of their Horse, our men were forced to retreat, with the losse of thirty men.'[57]

These accounts sound straightforward enough, but they raise a number of questions. Wanklyn dismisses the first account as fictional and written in London,[58] but it appears to be confirmed by the second, seemingly independent account showing that there was a relatively serious action between elements of the two armies. The precise site and date now have to be identified.

A letter of 21 July from Newcastle says clearly that: 'Major Gen: Lambert by his retreat, to the aforesaid places, is in capacity to make good the passe at Staynmore with a small power, and have the rest of his Army ready in case of other need.'[59] The head of the pass is at Maiden Castle, which he had occupied on the way over to Carlisle in June, and is the obvious, and perhaps the only, defensible point on the road. There, it is possible to halt an attacker from the west as he breasts the steepest hill on the road (map 6, fig. 1 and plate 7). From Brough the road rises 800 feet to 1,400 feet in under 5½ miles in an almost continuous ascent, with a climb of a hundred feet over the last 300 yards. East of Maiden Castle an attacker would be moving gently downhill.

The mention of a bridge suggests that the site of the action was at a river crossing. The most substantial water courses crossing the road are in and close to Brough, the Swindale Beck and Augill Beck respectively, but Brough is over thirteen miles from Bowes which, so far as is known, was where the nearest major elements of Lambert's army kept guard. This would be not only militarily unsound, but does not accord with the distance given. However, Beldoo Moss is drained by a stream that crosses the road about 1,000 yards west of Maiden Castle. When in spate, as the very wet summer suggests, this would have required a bridge, and the countryside immediately around is very broken without other convenient crossing points (plate 9). It is worth looking at the distances given in the first account to see if there is any relation to the locality: '[We] made an honourable retreat towards Barnard Castle, which was six or seven miles distant from us, the enemy pursued about three miles.' Seven miles from Barnard Castle is Spital Park,* a mile east of the modern Bowes Moor Hotel. If the enemy had pursued for three miles east from there, they would have been in Bowes, which sounds most unlikely as this is where forward elements of the Parliamentary army were stationed. Major Sanderson was on guard there on 18 and 23 July.[60] Maiden Castle is 11½ miles from Barnard Castle.

It is not uncommon in seventeenth-century texts for events to be described in what to modern eyes is a reversed order. There may have been a retreat from Maiden Castle with the enemy following for about three miles, that is to somewhere around the modern Bowes Moor Hotel (actually about 3½ miles). From there, a seven-mile retreat (actually nearer eight) to Barnard Castle fits the account as well as can be expected. A revision of the order to 'the enemy pursued for three miles, and then we retreated a further six or seven miles to Barnard Castle' would make more sense as well as fitting the locality. The losses suggest that the fighting was intense.

The first and more detailed account is not itself dated, although it is indexed by Fortescue as the 27th and the printed pamphlet in which the letter appears is dated in manuscript

---

* NY 943127.

31 July, and refers to the fight having taken place 'on Wednesday last'. It has often been accepted that the action took place on the 26th,[61] but if the letter really was written on the 27th 'Wednesday last' is more likely to have been the previous week, Wednesday 19th. However, the second account is more informative. This letter, from Kendal, is dated 23 July,[62] a Sunday, and refers to the action at Appleby (on Monday 17 July) as 'Monday last'. It goes on to say that: 'On Wednesday and Thursday last, several disputes happened betwene both Armies, on Thursday morning about five of the clock . . . our men were forced to retreat', making it clear that the fighting spread over two days and that the retreat was on Thursday 20 July.

Also, a letter from Lambert's headquarters at Barnard Castle dated the 28th makes no mention of an attack two days earlier ('The Scots advance not, nor hath the Major-General given ground these ten days and upwards'), but only of cavalry reinforcements from Cromwell's army, who immediately attacked the Scots scouts and threw them back to Appleby.[63] There is no indication of whether the scouts were still occupying the pass or were around Brough.

Furthermore, a letter from Lambert dated the 25th says that there had been no action between himself and the enemy, since his men had beat up enemy quarters near Appleby.[64] This is relating past events, and sounds rather like the Scots being driven back after an advance some days earlier. The Scots did not come over Stainmore on the 26th, as is often said, but the week before, following closely on Lambert's retreat ten days before the letter of the 28th. The writers of two letters report that they had no knowledge of the enemy following up Lambert's retreat (Tuesday 18th), but there is no reason why detachments should not have advanced the following day.[65] Once Hamilton realised that Lambert was again blocking Stainmore he may have made an immediate effort to open the road.

In summary, the action probably did take place, the accounts fit reasonably well with the locality, and it happened on 19 and 20 July rather than the 26th. It is not known whether the Scots stayed at the head of the pass, or pulled back to Brough, although Lambert's letter of the 28th suggests that they had been thrown back as far as Appleby.

Bowes

The two armies now lay twenty-five miles apart, around Bowes and Kirkby Thore respectively, with little action save disputes between their scouts. The Scots were said to have no choice but to stay where they were or to go back and advance on Newcastle along the river Tyne.[66] A move to Newcastle from Kirkby Thore would have been possible if the Roman road north from there were still negotiable, in which case they could have joined what is now the A686 Penrith to Haydon Bridge road southwest of Alston (map 5). This sixty-mile route to Newcastle is not an easy one, rising to over 2,000 feet, but it would have been possible. But the only practicable time to have decided on Newcastle was after he had

Major-General Lambert.

1 *Major-General John Lambert, from H. Walpole,* Anecdotes of Painting in England *(1762),*
vol. 2, p. 155 (courtesy of the University of St Andrews Library).

Packets of   *Num.* 19

LETTERS

FROM

Scotland, and the North parts of *Eng-land*, to Members of the House of

COMMONS

CONCERNING

The Tranſactions of the Kingdome of Scotland, and the Commiſſioners of the Parliament of *England.*

Brought by the Poſt, on Munday *July* 24. 1648.

The Landing of *Prince Charles*, and 19 Sale of Ships come with him to *Yarmouth.* And the Treaty with the Inhabitants of the Town.   His Declaration, and offer to the Magiſtrates.

And the Fight between the Sea men and the Lord Ge-nralls Forces neer *Yarmouth.*

The great fight between the Scots and the Engliſh at Appleby.

The Scots Letters to the K I N G, and P E E R E S of *England.* And good News from *H V L L.*

July 27

Printed at *London* by *Robert Ibbitſon* in *Smithfield,* neere the Queens-head Tavern. 1648.

3 ABOVE: *Barnard Castle above the river Tees. Lambert had his headquarters here in May and early June, and again at the end of July.*

4 BELOW: *Bowes Castle from the east. It was probably not defensible in 1648, but would have provided shelter for the guards watching the eastern end of the Stainmore road.*

5 ABOVE: *The river at Greta Bridge following a spell of dry weather. It would be impassable after heavy rains without using the bridge.*

6 BELOW: *View from the east of the Maiden Castle area, showing the bleak nature of the countryside on Stainmore. The direction of the Roman fortlet, about 1½ miles away and out of view, is marked with a cross. The gentle nature of the slope from the east can readily be judged, and compared with that on the west side (see plate top right).*

7 ABOVE: *The modern road approaching the head of the Stainmore pass from the west. The Roman and eighteenth-century route is shown by the white line running up the hillside as the modern road bends to the right. Maiden Castle is just beyond the sky line to the right of the Roman road.*

8 BELOW: *Second World War-type FW3/24 pill box built southeast of Maiden Castle in 1940–1, to cover the Stainmore pass.*

9 ABOVE: *The stream draining Beldoo Moss, after a spell of dry weather, as it approaches the modern road at NY 866135, 700 yards from Maiden Castle. The height of the modern bank defences shows the volume of water that can be expected after prolonged wet weather such as was the case in 1648.*

10 BELOW: *Brough Castle from the south. The castle was ruinous in 1648 following a fire in 1521.*

11 ABOVE: *Brougham Castle from the north. It was briefly held by Royalists in 1648, but surrendered on being summoned.*

12 RIGHT: *The ancient pele tower, Greystoke Castle* (by kind permission of N. Howard, Esq.). *The castle was not fought over, but was largely destroyed by Parliament after the Civil War.*

13 ABOVE: *Penrith Castle, a view of part of the interior. It was probably not defensible in 1648, although Lambert may have used it for his headquarters in June and July.*

14 BELOW: *Rose Castle, the seat of the bishops of Carlisle, which was captured in June and garrisoned by Major Cholmley, who burnt it when no longer tenable.*

15 ABOVE: *The bridge at Warwick Bridge, built 1833–5 by John Dobson to replace the bridge fought over in June 1648.*

16 BELOW: *The Priestbeck and Eden bridges in 1790, looking southwest towards Carlisle Castle, from the engraving by Medland. The low-lying island formed by the splitting of the channels can clearly be seen between the two bridges, as can the relationship between the Priestbeck bridge and the castle.*

17 ABOVE: *Scaleby Castle from the air* (reproduced by kind permission of Simon Ledingham). *It was probably in poor condition in June 1648 and was surrendered after the garrison fired a single shot.*

18 BELOW: *Eighteenth-century entrance to the Crofton Hall estate, where Hamilton had his headquarters in July 1648.*

19 ABOVE: *The bridge at Ferrybridge built in 1797, to the design of John Carr, to replace the fourteenth-century one, which was fought over in June 1648.*

20 BELOW: *Appleby Bridge from the north, showing the river Eden at a low level. The mediaeval bridge defended by Lambert in July 1648 was replaced in 1888 by this bridge to a very similar design.*

21 ABOVE: *Appleby from the hill to the southeast. The outer end of the bridge is between the two white houses on the left .*

22 BELOW: *The ford at Appleby, still in occasional use. After comparatively little rain the water level has risen to cover a small weir to the right of the ford.*

23 **ABOVE**: *View over Appleby town and castle from Gallows Hill.*

24 **BELOW**: *The clear route of the Roman road at NY 653238, just under three miles northwest of Appleby.*

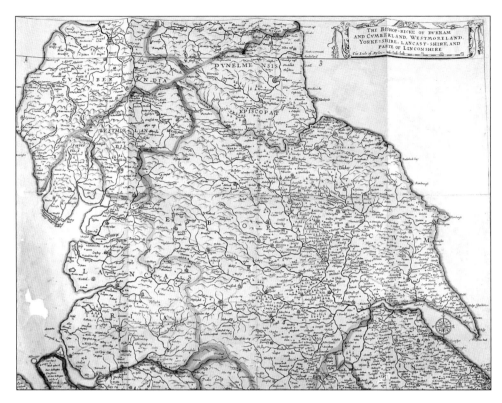

25 ABOVE: *'The Quartermasters' Map'* (SB-0915 Durham, reproduced by permission of Durham University Library).

26 BELOW: *Cockermouth Castle from across the river Derwent, with the rebuilt house alongside an older tower to the right.*

27 ABOVE: *Now almost hidden in the trees, Pontefract Castle seen from Baghill, where Lambert had his main command post.*

28 BELOW: *The base of the keep, Pontefract Castle, from the site of the west gate. This great mass of masonry is little more than cladding to the mound, and the keep proper rose above this.*

29 ABOVE: *Baghill, Pontefract, viewed across the valley from the castle keep.*

30 BELOW: *All Saints Church, Pontefract, from the castle. Following damage in the Civil War the west end is still in ruins.*

forced Lambert's withdrawal from Penrith. Hamilton's foot were then still some way from Penrith, and a quick withdrawal to Warwick Bridge and thence across to Newcastle might have been a possibility, which would have left Lambert wrong-footed and twenty or thirty miles in his rear. Hamilton, however, whatever plans he may have considered, was not that kind of general.

He waited for reinforcements, and Lambert had been ordered to remain on the defensive. A rather strange sentence in a letter to General Fairfax on 21 July from Derby House reads: 'As to Col. Lambert's forbearing to engage till the Lieut.-Genl. be joined with him, and only to retard the Scots' march by keeping on their flank, we shall send to him what is stated in the paper . . .'[67] It is not quite clear whether Derby House initiated the order, or is reluctantly agreeing with Fairfax or Cromwell. It may be that Cromwell had asked for Lambert to be held in check, but no evidence has been found in support of the suggestion.

In any event, the Committee wrote to all militias and commanders in the north on 31 July and 1 August respectively, with an instruction that: 'You are to receive and obey his [Cromwell's] orders and directions.' Also on the 1st they wrote to Cromwell: 'Although we hope, in regard of the place and quality you bear in the army, there will be none in the North who will pretend to a command-in-chief while you are there, yet to take away all colour to any such pretence, we have written to all the commanders of forces there to obey your orders.' These letters should have been unnecessary as, under the reorganisation of the New Model, Cromwell was now not merely Lieutenant-General of the Horse but Lieutenant-General of the Army,[68] indisputably second only to General Fairfax, and clearly outranking Major-General Lambert. Did Derby House, or Fairfax, see the old Northern Association army, even if now part of the New Model, as being a law unto itself? Was it another small indication that Lambert was not wholly trusted by Derby House? Was Cromwell uncertain of Lambert's reaction at being superseded, or was he jealous of the latter's considerable success in holding first Langdale and then Hamilton at bay? These are speculations that space does not permit of discussing here.

A letter from Barnard Castle on 28 July announced that some troops of horse and companies of foot came in from Yorkshire to reinforce Lambert's army, while the Scots stayed around Appleby. There was news that Hamilton intended to take Cockermouth Castle and the Isle (St Herbert's Isle in Derwent Water),[69] which had been recaptured by a Major White for Parliament, but it was hoped that the Parliamentary garrisons would stand firm.[70]

The Yorkshire reinforcements were the foot regiments of Wastell and Lascelles, totalling 1,000 men. With them, and also fresh from the action at Thornhill, were: 'six Troopes from Wales, one of Col. Twistletons, and two of the Lieutenant-Generals and one of M. G. Lamberts', and Col. Bethell's new Regiment (of militia horse) with 'three or four Companies of the old foote'.[71] The six troops from Wales, which had been sent north by Cromwell at the end of June were: three from Scoop's, two of dragoons, and Captain Pennyfeather's.[72]

The total strength of these reinforcements was probably around 2,600. The question of 1,000 foot and thirty troops of horse from Cromwell in south Wales is dealt with, and wholly discounted, in Chapter 1.

Some, at least, of the newly joined horse arrived on the 27th and at once attacked the Scots scouts and drove them back to within two miles of Appleby, that is around Coupland* (about where the road into Appleby leaves the modern A66, fig. 3).[73] The scouts may have been at Brough or still at the summit of Stainmore more than five miles to the east of Brough (map 6).

In one way or another Lambert was clearly keeping himself well informed about Hamilton, for it was recorded on 28 July that the latter was receiving additional forces. At about this time the Commons wrote to Cromwell urging him to expedite his march northwards.[74]

At the end of July, Colonel Boynton, Parliamentary governor of Scarborough Castle, changed sides. Extra supplies had been sent there in the previous months and Lambert had been asked to send assistance, although Derby House said that money for more beds might not be forthcoming but saw this as no great matter as it was summer time.[75]

There had been some suspicion of Boynton, and as late as 28 July a letter from Derby House asked Mr Anlaby (MP for Scarborough and Boynton's brother-in-law) and Richard Darley (a Yorkshire commissioner for compounding and ardent Puritan) to discuss paying his arrears in return for him relinquishing the governorship. However, this letter crossed with one announcing the betrayal of the castle on the 27th. The loss of Scarborough was serious enough for ships to be sent in the middle of August to prevent relief by sea.[76]

At the same time Appleby Castle, where Lambert had left a garrison of 200 foot and sixty horse, surrendered.[77] The castle had been under siege by Langdale, backed by two brigades under Turner sent there in case Lambert attacked the besiegers. These 'brigades' cannot have been large, as they were both quartered in one village half a mile from Appleby.[78] There is today no village within one mile, and it may well have been a collection of houses now part of Appleby. Hodgson gives Captain Atkinson as commander of the garrison, with Lieutenant Elwand of Bright's. A letter from Barnard Castle also gives his name as Atkinson,[79] but a letter from Helmsley refers to the 'lieutenant that commanded', and gives him as lieutenant to Captain Cotes. There was a Coates who was a captain in Bright's;[80] his lieutenant could have been Atkinson, later promoted captain or perhaps had the title as 'Captain of the castle' while acting as governor.[81]

Whatever his rank, he was a spirited defender. He sallied out of the castle, beat the besiegers out of the town, killing some, blocked the way with carts and furniture which he fired to cover his retreat, and got back to the castle without loss of a man. Langdale pulled back, the Scots called the English cowards, and in a brawl a Scots captain was killed.

---

* NY 713187.

Langdale restored order and drew his men up to a defensive breastwork. The lieutenant sallied out again, beat off Langdale's men and returned to the castle with forty prisoners for no loss. Langdale thereupon began a mine which got within three or four yards of the castle, at which point terms were accepted on Saturday 29 July.[82] A somewhat partial report appeared in *The Moderate Intelligencer*: 'Appleby Castle was surrendred [*sic*] upon Saturday last, to Major Gen. Langdale, but upon honourable conditions, (it cannot be) to march away with all their arms and ammunition, with Colours flying, Drums beating, all their baggage, and to have a safe convoy to Major Gen. Lamberts Quarters, who were as welcome to him as water in his shoos.'[83]

Meanwhile, the Scots were foraging and looting around their quarters, with little respect for allegiances. A letter from Durham dated 3 August referred to the plundering of the Royalist Sir Philip Musgrave's house, near Kirkby Stephen.[84]

At about this time there was a rumour that Lambert had been routed and lost twenty-six colours, but this was declared to be a false account of a little skirmishing.[85]

While Hamilton lay at Kirkby Thore his promised reinforcements reached him, mostly ill-trained foot, which Burnet says gave him about 10,000 foot and 4,000 horse. This accords with Turner's statement that the Scots never amounted to more than 14,000 horse and foot.[86] With Appleby taken and his army re-supplied there was no barrier to Hamilton's advance. A letter dated 4 August from Newcastle said that Westmorland and Cumberland were said to be: 'so harassed, that neither the Scots nor Langdale's can subsist, but will be forced to seek other Quarters in Lancashire, or elsewhere'.

Chapter 7 .

TO PRESTON AND BACK

<u>**August 1648**</u>

Lambert's and Cromwell's progress

AT THE BEGINNING OF August it was reported that Hamilton was advancing to Brough, whereupon Lambert blocked: 'all Passages towards Stanemore; casts up Ditches and Trenches to hinder their Passage'.[1] This possibly took the form of digging up the road on the summit of Stainmore to form defensible ramparts, but the location is not given. The report adds that if the Scots came on, the army was ready to fight 'from which the Major-General hath hitherto, with much difficulty detained them'. Despite the long retreats and the fighting, Lambert's army was clearly in good heart.

On the heels of this report came intelligence that: 'Upon Tuesday [1 August] the enemy marched from Appleby to Kendall, and probably intend for Lancashire, or rather for Pontefract by the way of Craven' (maps 5, 4 and 3). On Wednesday 2 August Lambert withdrew his army from Barnard Castle and began to march south, as he announced in a letter from Richmond to Hesilrige on 3 August.[2]

Birch and Sanderson both record leaving the Barnard Castle area for Richmond on Wednesday 2 August and on to Ripon on Thursday 3rd.

A reworded version of Lambert's letter from Richmond also announced that Royalist forces were believed to have reached Settle on the evening of the 2nd,[3] but unless Langdale had pressed thirty miles ahead of Hamilton this is unlikely. This letter also reports that Hamilton marched to Kendal on Monday [31st], which probably indicates the day he began his march from Kirkby Thore to Brough, a distance of around thirteen miles or about a day's march for an army.

A letter of 4 August from York spoke of a report of the Scots marching within ten miles of Skipton and aiming for Pontefract, saying that it was for this reason that Lambert withdrew to the south. Lambert's scouts were more restrained in their report, and only: 'certified the Scots march to Kendal, they feare our army much, though we are not yet compleat 10,000. But when the Lieu. Gen. is joined, they shall Fight or Runne for't [*sic*]'.[4]

A letter from Preston of the 5th reported the Scots at Kendal, and also raiding horses and provision within four miles of Lancaster. A captain from Preston retaliated by taking sixty horses from the Royalists.[5]

On 7 August Birch reached Knaresborough, and stayed there until the 14th, while Sanderson, who noted that the army marched beyond Knaresborough on the 7th, remained near Ripon until 12 August.

Royle suggests that Lambert withdrew to Richmond because he was alarmed by Langdale's cavalry patrols.[6] He is probably referring to the report of the Scots approaching Skipton, but according to Lambert's letter this was not what influenced his decision, and in any case the information cannot have reached him by the time he began his march to the south.

Rogers[7] says that Lambert had lost contact with the enemy and did not know whether Hamilton was going to go south to Lancashire or across to Yorkshire through Wensleydale or via Skipton, but this is a misreading of the situation. First, Lambert clearly had scouts well forward to know that the Scots had advanced to Brough and then turned south to Kirkby Stephen and Kendal, and he made his own move as a result. Secondly, as to where the Scots would go next Lambert was no worse off than Hamilton himself, who did not yet seem to know where he was headed after Kendal. The point is that the Scots and Langdale were marching in a southerly direction on the west side of the Pennines, and it was sensible for Lambert to parallel their route on the east to block whichever road they might take to cross towards Pontefract. He was not, as many modern works suggest, retreating (one writer even says 'retreated in the face of Hamilton's advance'), but rather keeping pace with an enemy who, should he choose to cross the Pennines by whatever route, was thus likely to find a Parliamentary army waiting for him: 'the Enemy drawing to Kendall, made us draw off from Barnard Castle to prevent their falling in upon Skipton, into Yorkshire'.[8]

Although Hamilton was expecting support in the west, his plans as evolved included the taking of Manchester, which had been held solidly for Parliament throughout the Civil War, and its surrender was unlikely. The major danger for the government was that the Scots would cross the Pennines through Skipton into Yorkshire, where there was believed to be definite support,[9] to relieve Pontefract and find an easier route to London.

Cromwell was also clearly nervous of this move as he took the longer route around the south of the Pennines so as to intercept any invasion down the east side of the country, although Derby House had some reservations about moving too many regiments from the west to the midlands. They also urged Cromwell to hasten his march.[10] He appears to have left Pembroke on 14 July, and was in Gloucester, 150 miles away, by the 24th and the Commons believed that he was still there on the 26th.[11] This is unlikely as the Commons also reported that he was in Warwick, over forty-five miles away, on the 27th.

By Thursday 3 August he had covered another sixty miles to Nottingham.* On the way he picked up shoes and stockings for his 'poor wearied Soldiers' at Leicester.[12] He sent the

---

* It took him no more than twenty-one days to cover almost 260 miles from Pembroke to Nottingham, with around 3,000 foot, a rate of over twelve miles a day without rest days. Assuming only four rest days, the rate of

militia of Nottinghamshire and Derbyshire to Pontefract in order to release troops there who on 15 July[13] had already been ordered by Derby House to join Lambert. Cromwell left imprisoned at Nottingham the Welsh rebels who had surrendered at mercy – Poyer, Laugharne and Powell. He also wrote to Lambert: 'to desire him to forbear engaging before he comes up'. He was in Mansfield on the 6th, and reached Doncaster on the 7th, where he remained until Wednesday 9th, when he went on to Pontefract.[14]

There he took the town on 10 August in what seems to have been a remarkably hard fight. His forces and the Royalist cavalry were said to be charging each other in the streets, which sounds as though Cromwell was attacking horse with horse. The use of cavalry for street fighting was not uncommon in the Civil Wars, although it is far from ideal and very likely to be dangerous. The Royalists were reported to have lost twenty dead and forty taken prisoner, although another source gives thirty and a hundred respectively. Cromwell lost ten dead. The castle garrison took in some of their horse after they were pushed back to the castle gates, but shut out their foot as they already had enough.[15] Cromwell left Pontefract on the 11th leaving eleven troops of horse there as he marched towards Lambert. The source of these troops and the question of whether Cromwell took any of them with him are discussed in Chapter 1.

At about this time White's and Hacker's were said to be at Ackworth, Colonel Fairfax's and Rhodes' at Featherstone, and Cholmley's at Ferrybridge (map 2). All these are about three miles from the castle covering east, west and south, but not the north.[16]

On 9 August Colonel Robert Lilburne's brother, Colonel Henry Lilburne, governor of Tynemouth Castle (map 9), declared for the king, but the castle was retaken by Hesilrige on 11th and did not prove to be any distraction to either Cromwell or Lambert.

By this time Lambert had reached Aberford, fifteen miles north of Pontefract, from where he went on 10 August, with some of his officers, to Leeds in the hope of meeting Cromwell there. When this failed he went down to Pontefract on the 11th, the date on which Cromwell left the town.[17]

Some of their forces joined up about three miles from Leeds, when Lambert addressed the army. The two generals 'shewed themselves at the head of each Regiment and the Maj. Gen. as well by way of entertainment as favourable reception made a speech Declaratory to the same effect as also by way of incouragement to the souldiers which was recented [responded to] with great applause echoing a forwardnesse in the service'.[18]

Dawson suggests that Lambert's ovation may have been one reason for a coolness existing for a time between himself and Cromwell.[19] The only contemporary record of this occurs two weeks later in a Royalist news sheet – 'Some Disagreement is at present betwixt him and Lambert' – and may not be trustworthy.[20] But certainly Cromwell omitted the

---

march would have been around fifteen miles a day. Three rest days would give over fourteen miles a day, still a remarkably good rate for a large body of infantry over a prolonged period.

names of Lambert and his close associate Colonel Lilburne from his accounts of the battle of Preston, despite the fact that both had taken a very prominent part in the fighting and also that Cromwell took care to mention all other regiments there.[21] Margetts referred to this a month later, saying that in the accounts of the battle of Preston: 'more is attributed to some and less to others than they deserved'.[22]

At the time Cromwell and Lambert met it was believed[23] that Hamilton's army 'still lye upon the confines of Yorkshire, Westmoreland and Lancashire', which, given that Hamilton was then at Hornby and Langdale was around Settle, shows that Parliamentary intelligence was not wholly inadequate.

On the 13th the army quartered around Otley, where Sanderson was met by Cromwell with three regiments of foot and one of horse, and Birch marched through on his way to Skipton.[24] On the 14th the army was at Skipton, in the Gisburn area on the 15th, and by the 16th had concentrated at Stonyhurst, a few miles from Preston. They had covered forty miles in three days, a good rate of march for an army of some 12,000 men, which must have had baggage wagons, although the artillery had been left at Knaresborough to allow for a rapid march.[25]

Hamilton's route

Hamilton's march from his headquarters at Kirkby Thore to Kendal and Preston has been well described as meandering, and repays close examination. The shortest route is the modern road marked 'A' on fig. 5, a distance of twenty-eight miles, but it may then not have been possible to cross the Eden near Kirkby Thore. The next choice, 'B', depends on the state of the bridge at Appleby as described above and, while small numbers may have been able to cross, it could have been a problem for the whole army. The report from Lambert's scouts that the Scots had gone to Brough suggest that route C, a march of forty miles to Kendal was the best available to him. An alternative of similar length was route D, taking the Sedbergh road from Kirkby Stephen. Both routes rise to well over 1,000 feet, through countryside not ideal for supporting an army on what even today are not major roads. There is another route, marked E, through Mallerstang, alongside the river Eden. It is seven or eight miles longer but is at least well watered with grazing for cavalry on the narrow but flat-bottomed valley, although at the southern end the road climbs to over 1,100 feet at the head of the valley. It is possible that the army used more than one route in order to increase the chance of finding supplies. Whatever route was taken, the thirty-mile march from Brough took two days and Kendal was reached on 2 August.[26]

Hamilton stayed for a week at Kendal, partly to wait for Monro's reinforcements. On 9 August he made the day's march to Hornby, where he remained until the 14th, and it was while there that the decision was taken to go south rather than east to Yorkshire.[27] Whilst

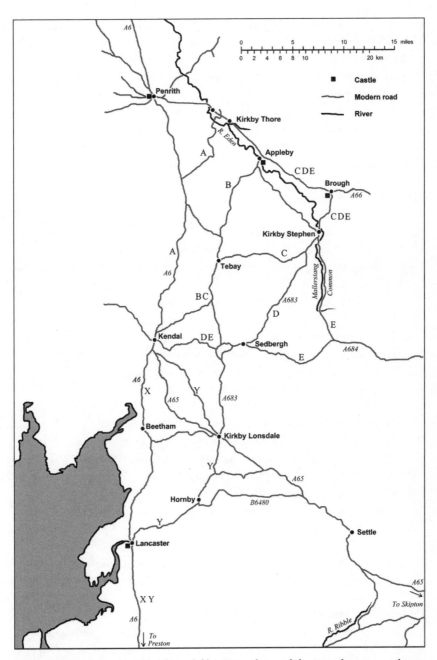

FIG. 5 *The various routes (A–E) available to Hamilton and the Scottish army marching from Kirkby Thore to Kendal, and on to Lancaster and Preston (X, Y).*

the correctness or otherwise of this decision has been argued over many times in print, the question of why he was at Hornby in the first place does not seem to have been asked.

From Kendal to Lancaster, where Hamilton later stayed on the way to Preston, is a simple long day's march of twenty-two miles down the old Roman road, now A6 (fig. 5, route X, and map 4).[28] Instead, Hamilton covered a similar distance to Hornby by marching twelve miles southeast from Kendal to Kirby Lonsdale, then eight miles to Hornby, where he was still nine miles from Lancaster (route Y). The road from Kendal to Kirkby Lonsdale, now A65, continues through Settle to Skipton, from where there is a choice of going east to Knaresborough or southeast to Pontefract, very much as Lambert's intelligence had given on the 2nd. However, at Kirkby Lonsdale they turned southwest to stop at Hornby. This was planned in advance, for Hamilton had announced it to Langdale in the letter the day before,[29] but gives no reason for the strange route. The significance of Hornby, and of the discussions that were held there, is that from there runs the last remotely practicable road towards Settle, now the B6480: Hornby was the final point at which there was a choice of route.

Letter from Holland says that the Lancashire route was decided upon at Kirkby Thore, but if so the argument between Yorkshire or Lancashire continued during the march, and Turner is quite definite that the final decision was made at Hornby. Hamilton himself was considering the Yorkshire route, see below, and yet chose to march to Hornby via Kirkby Lonsdale, an indication perhaps of a vacillating nature. Turner was quite right to describe the army of which he was a part as 'ill equipd and ill ordered', although he did add that 'our march was much retarded by most rainie and tempestuous weather . . . the elements fighting against us; and by staying for countrey horses to carry our little ammunition'.[30]

Meanwhile, Monro had brought his 1,500 foot and 400 horse, all experienced men, across from Ireland to support Hamilton, but his refusal to serve under either Callander or Baillie meant that in the end he was left at Kirkby Lonsdale, ostensibly to await the artillery train, and took no part in the Preston campaign. Sir Philip Musgrave's and Sir Thomas Tyldesley's regiments remained there with him, although Tyldesley very soon moved down to join the force besieging Lancaster Castle.[31]

Langdale marched ahead of Hamilton's army, with a very specific role: 'The vanguard is constantlie given to Sir Marmaduke, upon condition he should constantlie furnish guides, pioneers for clearing the ways, and which was more than both these, to have good and certaine intelligence of all the enemies motions.'[32] His route sheds light on the possible intentions of the Scots army, for with 3,000 foot and 600 horse he went as far east as Settle, nearly twenty miles southeast of the army's eventual easternmost point at Kirkby Lonsdale.[33] He would not have taken so many foot so far merely to collect intelligence, and he must have been prospecting and clearing the planned route with his pioneers in anticipation of the arrival of the army. It is often said that Langdale's role was to guard the left flank of the Royalist army, but, while that was the position in which he ultimately found himself, it was not the one initially given to him.

Langdale was also hoping to persuade the governor of Skipton to betray the castle, which would make an advance along that road rather easier. Hamilton supported him in this enterprise – 'I approve of yoᵣ Resolution in the way of yoᵣ march and heartily wish Skipton were yoᵣˢ' – but did not sound optimistic: 'God increase the Distraction at London and send you Skipton and preserve our friends at Colchester. I shall stay here but I have small hopes.'[34] He was certainly leaning towards a march through Skipton for, announcing his march to Hornby on the morrow, he explained: 'Where I intend to Quarter my self if the Lancashire men continue in their bad disposition to us . . . itt will bee fittest to mark through the County to goe into Yorkshire.'

Hamilton also wrote to the governor of Skipton, encouraging him to accept Langdale's advances.[35] Hodgson was convinced that Captain Currer, whom he describes as the 'dreaping commander' of Skipton, would have handed the castle to Langdale if he had advanced that far.[36] There seems to be some foundation for this belief, as Hamilton wrote to Langdale: 'It is now time to putt the Governoᵤᵣ of Skipton to itt by which you will finde whether hee bee soe really honest or a Knave.' This does sound as though there was an expectation that he would join the Royalist cause. However, a week later he wrote: 'I am sorry the Governoᵤᵣ of Skipton is soe notorious a Knave.'[37] It must not be forgotten, however, that the garrison of a castle could not do more than harass a large army whenever it was safe so to do, although properly handled this could certainly be an irritant. A comparatively small detachment from Hamilton's army could have kept the garrison bottled up. On 14 August, Hamilton stayed only four miles from Lancaster and its Parliamentary garrison without any problem, and at Appleby in June Lambert had no problem with leaving a detachment to contain Appleby, a much larger castle than Skipton.

At Settle on 13 August Langdale heard that: 'the Parliament forces were gathered together and marching towards me'. Cromwell's army was then at Otley, just over thirty miles away. Langdale rode to Hornby to inform Hamilton of an enemy presence, the decision for Lancashire was finally made, and Langdale brought his men to Preston through Clitheroe by way of the Ribble valley.[38] Langdale and Hamilton were now separated by twenty-five miles of small tracks over moor land between Clitheroe and Lancaster, and communication between them must have been difficult (map 4).

There is a choice of two routes from Clitheroe to Preston: one through Whalley on the south side of the Ribble; the other, which Langdale chose, on the north bank through Longridge. The distance is the same in either case, about eighteen miles.

Langdale did not turn back at once. On the 14th Cromwell's army quartered around Skipton with a cavalry screen, which according to Sanderson consisted of part of Lilburne's and Twistleton's, at Gargrave, four miles to the west and eleven miles east of Langdale's base at Settle. There, some of Langdale's horse clashed with Captain Henry Cromwell of Harrison's (part of whose regiment must therefore have been there as well), but, although they overran him, Hodgson says that they did not come further. He adds that Langdale's troops had already taken men and money, and behaved as though never intending to come there again, perhaps an indication that they knew that the route had been abandoned.

Hamilton left Hornby on the 14th,[39] the day after Langdale's report, and stayed overnight at Ashton Hall,* four miles south of Lancaster.[40] On the 16th his cavalry had got as far south as Wigan in search of forage, but the foot were still coming into Preston almost twenty miles to the north (map 4).[41] On the 17th, they were beginning their march south across the Ribble when Cromwell caught up with them.

Preston

At Clitheroe Cromwell made the decision to interpose his army between the invaders and their line of retreat. He accordingly crossed to the north bank of the Ribble, in Langdale's footsteps, and stayed overnight at Stonyhurst, the house of Mr Sherburn. If he had stayed on the left bank he would have faced Hamilton's oncoming infantry to the north with Middleton's cavalry to the south. The fact that he was able to choose the appropriate route shows that he was receiving sufficient intelligence to enable him to locate the enemy with reasonable precision.

The three-day running fight that constitutes the battle of Preston has been discussed at length elsewhere, and a brief summary will suffice here.[42] Langdale was moving towards Preston early on Thursday 17 August when he became aware that Parliamentary forces were close behind (see map 4). From Longridge onwards there was skirmishing between Cromwell's forlorn, under Major Smithson of Lilburne's and Major Pownall of Bright's, and Langdale's rearguard until the Royalist force made a stand. Langdale gives no description of, or location for, this point. It is accepted here as being on the line of the Eaves brook, which crossed the road from Longridge about two miles from Preston and made a suitable defensive line.[43]

The rain had probably swollen the brook, making it difficult to cross except by the bridge which carried the Longridge–Preston road. That would certainly explain why the defence of the bridge was so important to the attackers, and why Dean's and Pride's on the right of Cromwell's line, which extended beyond Langdale's left, were unable to take much part in the fighting. If the brook had been easily fordable these two regiments could have taken the enemy in flank.

In addition to the stream there were also many hedged enclosures, which limited free movement. It appears, although his narrative is not clear, that Hodgson's part of the forlorn managed to get behind some of the enemy who were in advance of the stream and used the cover of hedges to ambush the forlorn of horse as they charged the bridge.

Langdale reported the news to Hamilton. There was a disagreement as to tactics among the command of the Scottish army, and after some delay the Scots infantry continued their

---

* SD 461573.

withdrawal southwards across the Ribble, leaving Langdale to his fate with only minimal assistance and seriously outnumbered.

There was a stiff fight at the bridge over the brook, during which Smithson had two horses shot under him as the forlorn fought with Langdale's infantry and some Scottish lancers. Hodgson's men were much encouraged when a newly raised company of Langdale's foot fired over their heads, a common fault in untrained troops who do not allow for the upward kick of a firearm. This is not of itself an indication of a loss of heart for the battle but is simply an encouraging sign of inexperience. Langdale's troops in fact put up an extremely determined resistance.

The main body of Cromwell's infantry was four miles behind the forlorn, and it was not until four o'clock that they came up in strength.[44] It then took something like four hours to drive Langdale back to Preston, a tribute to the stubbornness of the English Royalists. Lilburne's regiment, at least, gave no quarter for the first hour, typical of the relative bitterness of the second Civil War. Langdale's men were totally defeated (Sanderson says: 'his foot were most slain and taken'), and his cavalry fled northwards pursued by Twistleton's and Thornhaugh's regiments, when 'many are slaine . . . from *Preston* six miles towards *Lancaster*'.

According to Hodgson it seems to have been Lambert who encouraged the Lancashire foot to move down a lane on the Parliamentary left, a move that both turned Langdale's flank and blocked his retreat to the river. Towards nightfall the Ribble Bridge was forced by the Lancashire foot led by their forlorn hope under Captain Birch, along with part of the Lord General's foot, and the Scots army retreated under cover of darkness with no supplies except what could be carried on the man. Cromwell's men were also suffering shortages, and stripped the lead from the chancel of Preston church to make bullets.[45]

The Royalist cavalry returned from Wigan on the following day, Friday 18th, but came through Standish and Euxton, while the retreating infantry took the road through Chorley (map 4). Colonel Thornhaugh was killed when he led his regiment and part of Lambert's against the Royalist horse. Lilburne's was in the van as they pursued the Scots infantry to Wigan, where the horse fought their way in until midnight, and again the following day, 19th. A few miles short of Warrington Cromwell's army was held up for perhaps three hours at Winwick Wood where the Scots made a determined stand. When they eventually broke, four troops from Lilburne's and Twistleton's 'carreered up to Winwicke', as Sanderson described it, ahead of the Scots and hindered their retreat so successfully that many were killed and 1,500 taken prisoner. They then charged on to Warrington, where the infantry that had escaped from Winwick, and who were now abandoned by Hamilton and the cavalry, surrendered.[46]

Parliamentary losses were very light, but Langdale and the Scots lost at least 2,000 by Cromwell's reckoning, and Sanderson describes how from Preston towards Lancaster and down to Warrington: 'all the high wayes, Corne Fields, Meddows, Woods and ditches strewed with dead bodies'.

From Warrington, probably on the 22nd, Lambert was ordered south with over 2,000 horse and dragoons and 1,400 foot[47] to follow Hamilton, and brought him to bay fifty-five miles away at Uttoxeter on the 24th. The four horse regiments with Lambert are not all identified, but Sanderson's diary makes it clear that Lilburne's was certainly one, and Lambert's own was probably another; the other two were Cromwell's, Harrison's, or Thornhaugh's.[48] Within two more days, Lambert's force, including foot, was marching north on Cromwell's orders.

Chapter 8

TO SCOTLAND AND PONTEFRACT

B Y THE TIME HAMILTON surrendered to Lambert, Cromwell had turned north to seek out Sir George Monro, who had retreated at news of Hamilton's defeat and had been joined by fugitives from Preston.[1] Munro went up towards Penrith and crossed to the east over Stainmore, while Cromwell returned the way he had come, through Skipton and Knaresborough which he reached on 2 September: 'being upon a speedy advance into Northumberland'.[2] He chose this route owing to the scarcity of provisions and the state of the roads further north. Two armies had quartered and skirmished between Brough and Bowes for some two months, demanding food and churning up the roads with the constant passage.[3]

These last two letters show that Cromwell was actually making slow progress. He was at Skipton on 28 August when he wrote to William Pierrepont, was understood to be at Otley on the 29th, and came to Knaresborough on 2 September. The distance is only twenty-five miles, no more than a two-day march, and he had been expected in Knaresborough on 30 August.[4] Although the letter from Skipton reads as though the army was in process of passing through the town, it appears that they rested there for three days. He was in fact letting Lambert catch up: 'Wee march slowly, because, wee wait the comming of Lambert with his four Regiments.' The letter from Knaresborough of 2nd also says that Lambert was on his way with four regiments. It is not known just when Cromwell left Knaresborough but he reached Durham, sixty miles away, on the 7th.[5]

It is sometimes accepted that, on leaving Uttoxeter, Lambert went up to Carlisle, as two contemporary reports suggest: 'Lambert lately blocked up Carlisle but upon a letter from Cromwell drew off and now marching towards the Borders of Scotland'[6] and 'Major-General Lambert goes by way of Carlisle, many Countrymen go with him, and the Lieutenant-General likewise . . .'[7] It is clear from the preceding paragraph that Cromwell went through Skipton and did not go to Carlisle, and the same is true of Lambert. The troops going to invest Carlisle were probably some that had been under Lambert's command before Preston, and this may be where the confusion arose.

The date of Lambert's move from Uttoxeter is not recorded. It was probably on 26 August, when Major Sanderson's troop began its march north from there, although, typically, he does not mention the rest of his own regiment let alone any other. They travelled northeast to the west of Derby, skirted Leeds and so up the Great North Road (A1) to Durham (see frontispiece map).[8] They quartered in Horsforth, then a village five miles northwest of Leeds, on 4 September, and arrived in Killinghall, five miles west of Knaresborough on the 5th and stayed there until the 7th.

Lambert was in Leeds on the same day that Sanderson was in Horsforth, showing that he was following roughly the same route but that his four regiments were not travelling in a single body.[9] One would expect them to travel as widely spaced as practicable, while still in contact with each other, for reasons of easier quartering. At Knaresborough on the 7th Lambert's force was said to be two days' march behind Cromwell, and he himself made a visit to York on that date, perhaps from Knaresborough. It was reported on 11 September that a hundred Scots prisoners taken by local people were sent from Knaresborough to York.[10]

Lambert took thirteen days to march about 105 miles from Uttoxeter to Knaresborough. This is a slow rate of progress, but no troops are able to march every day and Cromwell had noted that all the horse was exhausted after the fighting. Furthermore, many horses had been lost in the fighting, and 'abundance of our Horse-soldiers are on foot'.[11] Sanderson travelled an average of thirteen miles on eight out of the thirteen days.

Colonel Lascelles' regiment was detached from the march to assist with the siege of Scarborough, which was under the command of Colonel Hugh Bethell with his regiment of horse, Legard's foot, and a commanded party of 160 musketeers from Hull under Captain Smith. The governor of the castle, Colonel Matthew Boynton, had eighty foot, and twenty horse – thirty foot and twenty horse having deserted him.[12] But on 11 September it was reported that 300 Walloons were landed from four ships sent north by the Prince of Wales, about which Derby House sent warning to Scarborough and elsewhere on 24 August.[13]

Derby House wrote to the York Committee arguing against the decision to divert both Lascelles' and Wastell's foot regiments, on the grounds that Cromwell needed all the numbers he could muster.[14] In the event Lascelles' did go to Scarborough and remained there until the siege ended. Where Wastell's went is unclear, but it was expected at Pontefract late in November 1648, perhaps from Scarborough where the siege was drawing towards a close.[15]

Bright's regiment made it known that they would prefer to join the siege of Pontefract rather than go north to Scotland with Lambert and Cromwell, but Derby House wrote to Colonel Bright 'desiring' him to join Cromwell.[16] On the same day they also wrote to the Deputy Lieutenants and Committee of Lancashire and to Colonel Ashton urging that the Lancashire forces join Cromwell rather than remain in the county. This was clearly at Cromwell's request as they confirmed to him that they had written to all the forces named by him in a letter which does not seem to have survived.

Derby House also assured Cromwell that they would do what they could to provide supplies for him and his men. Money seems to have been short, as usual, for three days later they pointed out to the Commons: 'That this Committee has had no money at all for near two months.' In this case they were principally concerned with seeking intelligence abroad of the enemy's designs, and had no money even to send a letter to those agents concerned. They must have found a little money from somewhere, however, for on the 8th they paid £20: 'to a person not to be named, who is to be employed on secret service abroad'. This is no doubt why a pass was issued to: 'a certain man . . . to be employed on special service'.[17]

While the two divisions of the army were marching north there were other disturbances. Late in August Fenwick's Northumberland militia horse went with some dragoons to relieve Holy Island (map 9). They stormed Fenham Castle,* killing some of the Scots garrison and capturing others, and summoned Haggerston Tower.[18] They were driven off by Royalists approaching from Berwick, but they did succeed in passing some necessities into Holy Island. The governor, Captain Batten, had made previous calls for supplies and now sent his wife to Newcastle to explain that if he did not receive them he might be forced to surrender. Hesilrige sent with all possible speed a Major John Mayer, who said that he beat off the enemy guards and sent in provisions for six months. When he got there he found 200 sheep, a large warren of rabbits, and cobles bringing in fish; furthermore, two months earlier (actually 7 June) Major Sanderson had provisioned the island for at least six months.[19] Mayer seems to have been left in charge of the Holy Island garrison, under Batten, as he received pay for them in March 1649.[20]

The precise date of these actions is uncertain. The first report was in a letter from Newcastle of 1 September, and Mayer places it after Preston and while Cromwell was still on his way north. Allowing time for the news of the action to reach Newcastle, fifty-five miles away, the likely date is around 28–30 August.

While on his march north from Preston, Monro 'burnt eighty of my Lord Whartons Tenants Houses as they marched over Stainmore' and was reported to 'excercise the same cruelty as the *Hambletonian Army*, deflouring women, burning and plundering of houses, driving away all sorts of cattell . . .' His strength was said to equal almost fifteen regiments or around 7,000 men and twenty pieces of ordnance, with 2,500 men remaining at Appleby. The Scots forces were to pull back to Penrith, the English to go into the Bishopric, and all were to rendezvous with Musgrave at Hexham.[21]

At the same time, Sir Philip Musgrave had been active in Appleby, issuing orders on all manner of things pertaining to the support of the Royalist cause. Assessments were to be levied for the maintenance of the Appleby garrison, houses and land belonging to those fighting for Parliament were to be seized, and those disaffected to the king were to be examined.[22]

---

* Probably Fenham Grange, NU 087408.

It was probably at the end of August that Musgrave, Sir Robert Strickland and Sir William Blackstone moved eastwards into Cleveland with 500 horse, in an attempt to relieve the siege of Scarborough and to raise men from the Trained Bands, but they found the enemy and the local population too strong for them. After taking horses and other plunder they were ambushed and fired on by men of the Middle Dale (not located), whereupon Musgrave effectively surrendered, ordered that all property was to be restored, threatened death for future plunderers, and his force was escorted out of the area.[23] This seems to have taken place just before Cromwell reached Knaresborough on 2 September.

A few days later, Cromwell may have sent forces to the west over Stainmore as he marched north, for it was reported that some of his horse had clashed with the enemy, in particular the Irish (from Monro's force), and had killed or taken around thirty of them. Five thousand Scots were reported to have invaded across the Tweed, but this was no more than a rumour.[24]

On 28 August General Fairfax finally starved Colchester into surrender after a long and bitter siege. Typical of the harshness of the second Civil War, two of the leaders – Sir Charles Lucas and Sir George Lisle – were shot on the day of surrender after they were condemned by a Council of War.

The correctness or otherwise of the decision has been argued over at length, but it was certainly in accord with the laws of war as then in force. It is worth noting that in June Derby House had taken note of Lord Goring and Sir Charles Lucas acting 'by violence and ways unusual to soldiers and men of honour' and asked Colonel Whalley to inform them: 'that if they shall so depart from the rules of war and the customs and practice of all nations they must expect a retaliation . . .' Such views may have contributed to Fairfax's decision to execute Lucas.[25]

SEPTEMBER 1648

The Royalists caused further problems for Parliament in the northwest at around this time, and it will be convenient to deal with the actions and their outcome before returning to the progress of the Parliamentary army.

At the end of August Sir William Huddlestone, a committed Royalist from Millom Castle in the extreme south of Cumberland, besieged the castle at Cockermouth (frontispiece map and plate 26) with 500 men, a somewhat inexplicable move. The Lancashire forces under Ashton, with Bright's regiment of foot and the Westmorland horse were sent to relieve the siege.[26] Birch records that Ashton's regiment left Blackburn on 18 September to march the 120 miles to Cockermouth. The thirteen-day journey included three rest days, an average of twelve miles per marching day. On 25 September Hacker's regiment of horse and White's foot, who had been besieging Pontefract but were now rapidly marching north to join Cromwell, were diverted to assist with the relief of Cockermouth.[27]

The small garrison of Cockermouth was commanded by Lieutenant Bird, who seems to have been as pro-active as Captain Atkinson at Appleby in July. 'The Enemy had mined very near the Wall; he sallied out, killed and took them all that were at work, and brought away their Tools, and burnt the Barn that sheltered them.'[28] In this report, received in London on 2 October, he was said to have a fortnight's provisions left. Ten of the besiegers were killed, but only one of the garrison.[29]

The siege was lifted on 29 September, although Birch's company did not get there until the 30th. There were negotiations between the two sides, but the major part of the Royalist horse fled to Carlisle, and after being refused entry there took refuge in Appleby Castle. It will be convenient to deal with the results at this point.

Colonel-General Ashton, as he was now referred to, pursued them to Appleby. On 7 October Birch left his quarters at Torpenhow, where he had waited during two cold, miserable days of negotiation, and marched back to Caldbeck. The next day he was at Penrith, and on the 9th went to Appleby, which surrendered to Ashton at once. The terms were lenient: the senior officers, Sir Philip Musgrave, Sir Thomas Tyldesley, Sir Robert Strickland, Sir William Huddlestone, Sir Thomas Dacres and Sir William Blackstone, were ordered to go abroad within six months, and their juniors allowed to go home. The latter included twenty-five colonels, nine lieutenant-colonels, six majors, forty-six captains, seventeen lieutenants, ten cornets, three ensigns, about 1,000 men, and all their baggage along with five pieces of ordnance and a hundred arms. There were also 1,200 horses, but these were bought at knock-down prices by individual Parliamentary soldiers before the surrender was agreed, rather than them being claimed by the army as would have happened if they were taken after the siege.[30]

The castles of Cockermouth and Appleby were ordered to be slighted, but a month later the garrison of the former was given as thirty men, suggesting that it was still defensible. There was no garrison shown for Appleby, but Birch was certainly there until the middle of December in his role as governor of the castle.[31]

On 15 September there was trouble around Carlisle which was still under Royalist control. A party of horse and dragoons went out and stole a large herd of cattle, but were caught by 'a party of Major Gen. Lambert's horse', which recovered the cattle and killed thirty men for the loss of five killed and six wounded. The rest escaped owing to the difficult roads and the tiredness of the Parliamentary horses, which then marched off towards Cromwell. 'Lambert's horse' must be a reference to horse under Lambert's control, rather than his own regiment. The same report, from Richmond seventy miles from the scene of the action, also says that Hacker's and White's were marching after Cromwell, whereas in fact they were now going to Cockermouth.[32]

The Richmond letter (and one from York) reports another action, this time towards Berwick, sometime before 10 September. The two reports conflict at several points, and the following account conflates the two. There was intelligence of a party of English horse accompanying Monro under Sir Thomas Tyldesley heading for the town, and Cromwell ordered out a Major Sanderson with the Bishopric (i.e. Durham militia) horse and some of his own horse in one account, or simply a party of 500 horse according to the other. After five hours' pursuit they caught up with the enemy somewhere between Alnwick and Chillingham and most of the rearguard were killed or taken prisoner. The major lost eleven men against a hundred Scots, as well as the prisoners, or, alternatively, he killed some and took some prisoners. The rest of the force escaped either to Berwick or to the west. The remainder of these English supporters of Monro were refused entry to Scotland and had to make their escape as best they could. About eighty left Berwick by sea and the rest made their way towards Carlisle, where it was hoped that Lambert's force would intercept them. Tyldesley himself ultimately made his way to Appleby, where the castle was held as described above.[33]

The Major Sanderson in this account is not John, for he was still on the road from Preston and had got no further north than Scotch Corner on 10 September. It was possibly John Sanderson's brother Henry, who had no known employment at this time and as a County Durham resident may well have joined the militia horse. However, he had previously held a colonel's commission and was invariably so referred to, and it could have been some other Sanderson not closely related to the two brothers.[34] Given the uncertain orthography and frequent carelessness over names it may have been Major Saunders of Thornhaugh's. The colonel of the Bishopric horse, Colonel Wren, was presumably elsewhere at the time.

While the Parliamentary army was harassing the Royalists in Northumberland, progress was also being made in Scarborough. Despite the siege, the Prince of Wales was managing to get men, supplies and ammunition through the siege lines, and to counter this the besiegers stormed the town. Lascelles' foot and Bethell's horse were joined by 400 horse and the town was taken, probably on 15 September, with the loss of four men. The Royalists lost eighteen, and up to 200 prisoners were reported taken, including thirty of the Walloons who were thought to be Irish and so put to the sword. On 25 September the Commons voted £50 to the messenger who brought the news, ordered the sending of a hundred barrels of powder, with match and bullet, and asked the Lord Admiral to ensure that the coast was blockaded to prevent relief of the castle by sea. Rather ominously, they ordered that the prisoners be examined and any who had fought for Parliament in the past, or who had previously undertaken not to fight against Parliament, should be proceeded against by martial law.[35]

Cromwell's and Lambert's march north

Cromwell, in Knaresborough on 2 September, was in Durham on the 7th, left Newcastle for Morpeth on the 11th and arrived in Alnwick on the 12th.[36] En route to the north he must have collected the artillery, which he left behind at Knaresborough on the march to Preston,[37] for he now left it at either Newcastle or Morpeth.[38]

Monro, meanwhile, who was at this point no more than thirty miles ahead of Cromwell, held a Council of War at Morpeth on Saturday 9 September. There it was resolved to march back and fire the coal pits, but on Sunday he was called back to Scotland, where the Kirk party was in the ascendant and had made the Marquis of Argyll their general with an army variously reported as between 6,000 and 10,000, although with few horse.[39]

It was perhaps as a result of Monro's passage through the county that the people of Northumberland: 'put themselves into a posture of defence, and upon the 6th of this instant made proclamation at Morpeth, declaring their resolution to live and die with Lieutenant-General Cromwell', referring to the 'perfidious Scot . . . [and] their barbarous and inhumane actions . . .' Northumberland tended to be Royalist in sympathy but there was certainly an aversion to the Scots, and their resolution may have been encouraged by the knowledge that a large, and perhaps unforgiving, Parliamentary army was about to enter the county.[40]

When Cromwell was at Alnwick, Lambert was at Brancepeth near Durham, some fifty miles behind. A letter from there describes the Royalist forces in Cumberland, Westmorland and Northumberland as not knowing what to do and deserting daily. This may have been cheering news, but the letter also describes Lambert's army in forceful terms worth quoting at length:

> This Army's much discontented for want of Pay, having received none a long
> time . . . they have not a Penny to shoe their Horses, and have lost so many,
> slain, lamed or tired out . . . abundance of our Horse-soldiers are on foot, and
> they see no Course taken to recruit them. They are very much troubled, that
> the Parliament hath . . . taken no Care for their Supply, after all their Service
> and miserable Sufferings . . .[41]

The fact that a number of the horse was marching on foot explains the relatively slow progress made on the march north, especially by Sanderson's troop for which we have a detailed itinerary.* Cromwell's letter from Alnwick also mentions the lack of bread until the plentiful new corn had been brought in. The latter point is somewhat surprising in view of the very poor summer. A letter from Cromwell's headquarters at Norham a few days latter is even more explicit: 'The Sad Condition of the County of Northumberland, and our Army in it, would make a Heart of Flint to melt. Neither Corn nor Cattel did the wretched Army of Monroe leave; insomuch that in the Head Quarters, for divers days, neither Bread nor Drink was to be had, only a little Biskit.'[42] If even headquarters had only biscuit, one may imagine the condition of the troops.

Before Cromwell left Alnwick he ordered Lambert and a strong party of horse to move from the Durham area to Belford, with instructions to summon Berwick, fifteen miles to the north.[43] To cover the sixty-five miles to Belford will have taken at least three days

---

* They took twenty days to cover 225 miles from 28 August to 17 September.

and probably four, unless the horse had very much recovered from their exertions and remounts had been found. Sanderson's troop took five days to march seventy-five miles on a roundabout route from Durham to Lesbury, that is fifteen miles a day (map 9).

The summons to Berwick delivered by Lambert appears to have been in the form of a letter from Cromwell dated 15 September at Alnwick. Cromwell himself went up towards Berwick, and wrote to the Committee of Estates for Scotland from near there on the 16th, demanding the return of Berwick and Carlisle, backed by a clear threat of an invasion by a hostile army. The Committee had by now been superseded by the change of regime, and on the 18th he wrote from Cheswick to the Earl of Loudon as Chancellor of Scotland, announcing his intention of marching into Scotland to give assistance to the new government. Another reason given for moving into Scotland was the shortage of food in Northumberland, in part due to the depredations of Monro.[44] The invasion was now to be a peaceful one.

Sanderson's diary shows that he was sent up to Cheswick to see Cromwell on 18 September, returning the next day, and he adds the note that: 'pt of his [Cromwell's] horse marcht into Scotland'. This was not the start of the invasion, but an unauthorised plundering venture by some of Wren's militia regiment of Durham horse. It had happened on Sunday 17th as Cromwell explained to the Committee of Estates in a letter from Norham of the 21st, saying that he had sent the regiment back to England. The offenders were cashiered, a lieutenant who had allowed it was handed over to the [Provost] Marshall, and Wren, who had taken no action on complaints, was suspended from duty to face a Council of War with the expectation of being cashiered. Cromwell's explanation for the lack of discipline was that the Durham horse had only just come under his command, perhaps an implied criticism of Lambert under whose orders they had formerly been. Or it may just have been an understandable excuse. Cromwell put out a proclamation on 20 September threatening the death penalty against any officer or soldier taking money, horses or food, or abusing the people.[45] On 23 October, following a Council of War, a soldier was shot in Durham for plundering in Scotland.[46]

The fate of Wren's regiment is not clear, as it was reported in mid-October that: 'the Bishopricks Regiment of Horse is left at Carlisle', as though it either had in the event accompanied Cromwell into Scotland and been left at Carlisle on his way back or, after being sent back from Scotland in disgrace, had been ordered to Carlisle to contain the Royalist garrison pending its surrender.[47]

Cromwell further reported from Norham that he had sent Colonel Bright and Scout-Master-General Roe to the marquis of Argyll to find out how Parliament's forces could assist him.[48] Berwick was still holding out, but Cromwell expected that it would be handed over before long.

Lambert was quartered at Haggerston on 16 September, and on 19 September he crossed the Tweed with three regiments of horse. The foot and the rest of the horse and carriages were to follow the next day, apart from two regiments of foot and Cromwell's regiment of horse, which were left to block Berwick on the English side. Cromwell explained the move into Scotland as being partly to assist the new government there and partly to prevent the governor of Berwick from bringing in provisions from the Scottish side.[49]

Lilburne's regiment was not one of those that crossed on the 19th. Sanderson says that he was ordered over the Twizel ford on the 22nd, but the water was too deep (map 9). They finally crossed at Coldstream on the 26th, but not before Sanderson had been sent to Mordington (by then Cromwell's and Lambert's headquarters, four miles northwest of Berwick on the other side of the Tweed) for orders on the previous day. Presumably the river was fordable by one man on a large horse, such as Sanderson seems to have ridden,[50] but not for larger numbers on smaller horses. If cavalry were unable to cross it must be assumed that the foot and carriages (i.e. supply wagons) were also detained on the English side. All crossings of the Tweed above Berwick were fords: the bridge at Coldstream was built in 1766, and that at Norham not until 1840 (map 10).

It was reported that Monro had joined forces with the Earl of Lanark and with 8,000 horse and foot was within twenty miles of the border. Elements of this army clashed with part of Cromwell's horse, and after three charges the Scots retreated with the loss of five against two of Parliament's men.[51] Monro and Lanark then took Stirling bridge as a move to divide the country, and there was some fighting between Monro's and Argyll's forces.

Cromwell had crossed over on 21 September, and made his headquarters at Mordington. There he was joined on Friday 22nd by the Marquis of Argyll and others as Commissioners from the Kirk, which favoured peace. There were negotiations between the Commissioners and the governor of Berwick, which resulted in messengers being sent to Monro and the Earl of Lanark to obtain their views. On Sunday 24th Colonel Pride took possession of Tweedmouth (on the south side of the Tweed opposite Berwick), and blew up the guard house ('an exceeding strong wooden Fort'), which had been built on the bridge. Cromwell meanwhile drove away sheep from the north side of Berwick to deprive the garrison of supplies. On 29 September, Lanark ordered Berwick and Carlisle to be handed over, and Colonel Bright was sent to take possession of the latter. The two Scottish armies were to be disbanded in favour of a new one supporting the Kirk and the Covenanters. Cromwell had achieved his objectives without a battle, and much of his army was beginning to march away towards Carlisle by 3 October.[52]

In part, at least, the surrender of the two towns was due to the pressure exerted by the presence of the Parliamentary army. On Wednesday 27 September Lambert had been sent with six regiments of horse and one of dragoons towards Edinburgh, with foot following behind him. He was at Broxmouth near Dunbar, twenty-four miles from Mordington, on the 28th, where Sanderson reported to him, probably before he left in the morning. That day the vanguard came within five or six miles of Edinburgh, but Lambert himself quartered at Seton House,* the home of the Earl of Winton, twenty miles from Broxmouth and about eleven miles from Edinburgh.[53] Sanderson's diary shows that at least some of Lambert's force was widely scattered, for Lilburne's was quartered around Abbey St Bathans on the 29th, thirty miles from Seton, but this may simply be because of their delay in crossing the Tweed.

OCTOBER 1648

Cromwell and Lambert went to Edinburgh on 4 October. Referring to their reception there, Margetts took the trouble (or perhaps the pleasure) to draw distinctions between Cromwell and Lambert, as quoted at the head of the Introduction: 'Cromwell hath the honor, but Lambert's discreet, humble, ingenious, sweet and civil deportment gains him more hugs and ingenious respect . . .' Margetts went on the say that: 'The well-affected rejoiced at our being there; the malignants gnashed their teeth, and some of them threatened to be the death of Cromwell and Lambert.' Officers and soldiers were abused and attacked in the street, specifically including six from Lambert's regiment under Quartermaster Dimond, horses were stolen, and they were afraid either to walk the streets or to lie in bed.[54] Towards the end of October, Lambert issued an order that offenders would have their goods seized, and suffer imprisonment or death, as appropriate. Any complaints against soldiers were to be made to the Committee or to Lambert, from whom due satisfaction would be received.[55]

At the request of the Committee of Estates, Lambert was to remain behind with his own, Lilburne's and Twistleton's regiments of horse and two troops of dragoons for their security after the rest of the army had left, until a supportive Scottish army was recruited.

Cromwell did not stay long in Scotland. He left Edinburgh on 7 October to stay at Dalhousie, together with Lambert, and left there on the 9th for Carlisle with the horse, apart from Lambert's force who expected to remain in Scotland for fourteen days.[56] On the 14th Cromwell was able to inform Parliament that the city and castle of Carlisle had been delivered up to him.[57]

From Carlisle he reached Newcastle on the 16th, where they stayed for three days, partly to rest the troops and also to wait for the train to arrive from Berwick. 'The train' was probably heavy baggage wagons, unless the artillery had been moved up to Berwick from Newcastle or Morpeth while Cromwell was in Scotland. Cromwell was given a lavish feast by the Mayor of Newcastle on the 19th, and moved on to Durham, fifteen miles away, on the 20th, arriving there 'late in the night'.[58] There he received a request from the York Committee to assist with the siege of Pontefract, which was not going well, and he assured them that he was on his way with two regiments of horse and two of foot.[59] On 24 October he went to Barnard Castle, where he held discussions with the 'well-affected' gentlemen of the four Northern counties, as a result of which a petition was sent to Parliament asking for

---

* NT 417751.

both military and legal assistance in dealing with moss troopers and 'many Delinquents late in Arms' who were likely to cause renewed fighting.[60]

Cromwell left Barnard Castle for Richmond, a march of fourteen miles, on the 25th (maps 7 and 3). He was at Boroughbridge, twenty-eight miles away, on the 28th, a total of four days to cover forty-two miles. This was not a quick march, but he had foot as well as horse, and was probably marching fourteen miles a day on three days out of the four. It is likely, then, that he took another two days to cover the twenty-nine miles from Boroughbridge to his temporary headquarters at Byram Hall* near Pontefract. A report that he had a meeting at Wetherby on 'Fruday last' [27th] cannot be reconciled with the date of his letter, 28 October, from Boroughbridge thirteen miles north of Wetherby. Sunday 29th is a more likely date for the meeting, with one more sixteen-mile march to Byram, where he probably arrived on Monday 30 October.[61] It does, however, seem likely that at some indeterminate point he went on ahead of the foot, as the Lord General's and Bright's did not arrive at the siege of Pontefract until 7 November.[62]

In Scotland, Lambert's force remained around Edinburgh expecting, on 27 October, to remain for a further ten days. They were quartered on the houses of those opposed to the settlement: 'We are no burden at all to the well affected, who were against the Engagement, quartering all together upon the Contrary Party, and have all this while lain in the County of Lothian till now.' As an example of this quartering policy, Sanderson's troop was quartered on (amongst others) the Earl of Roxborough on 26 September and 4 November, Lord Hay of Yester on 1 October, and the Earl of Dalhousie on 4 October. Towards the end of October, Twistleton's regiment moved south into the Merse, the area below the Lammermuir Hills and centred on Duns (map 10).[63]

The Committee of Estates of Scotland probably gave Lambert leave to withdraw on 6 November, when Sanderson escorted him to Edinburgh from his headquarters at Seton. The Committee expressed their thanks for Cromwell's and Lambert's service, and gave a ten-gun salute from the castle. On the 8th Twistleton's crossed the Tweed, with Lambert's and Lilburne's following on the 9th. Sanderson (of Lilburne's) actually crossed over on the 8th, probably somewhere near Norham as he quartered at Grindon that night (map 9).[64] The progress of the dragoons is not recorded.

It was reported from Pontefract on 18 November that Lambert was already twenty miles south of Berwick, perhaps in the neighbourhood of Belford.[65] Pontefract is 150 miles from Belford, so the news could have been at least three days old. Sanderson was at Newcastle on the 15th, but he had left Scotland at least one day earlier than Lambert.

Lambert himself was in Newcastle on the 16th, on the way to Pontefract, but the correspondent was not optimistic about progress: 'We are marching into Yorkshire toward Pontefract, that our march is exceeding bad be [sic] reason of the ill way, and ill weather.'[66]

---

* SE 498261, just over a mile northeast of Ferrybridge.

The rain was clearly still falling, with the passage of troops turning the roads to mud. On Friday 17th Lambert left Newcastle ahead of his troops and rode post the hundred miles to Pontefract, arriving there on Monday 20 November. If he took the whole of the four days to make the journey, he travelled at twenty-five miles a day; this sounds slow for someone riding post, but was probably all that the weather and roads would allow.[67]

Chapter 9

THE SIEGE OF PONTEFRACT

A T PONTEFRACT THE SIEGE had not been going well. At first there was not a proper besieging force but rather a number of Parliamentary units based in the vicinity, leaving the garrison considerable freedom of movement especially in the first three or four months. The man charged by Parliament with the conduct of operations against the castle was Sir Henry Cholmley, who does not seem to have pursued the task with any real vigour. A letter written in the middle of June summarises the situation: the garrison was so strong that they came and went as they pleased, and Colonel Fairfax, at Ferrybridge with 600 foot and six troops of horse, remained guarding the bridge and did not leave that town.[1] In addition to the castle the Royalists had also fortified New Hall, an Elizabethan mansion about 800 yards to the northeast, the possession of which helped with their raids and foraging (plates 27, 28, map 3 and fig. 6).

Some of the major events – the raid on Axholme and Lincoln, which culminated in the fight at Willoughby, the attack on Ferrybridge, and the ambush at Allerton Boat – have already been reviewed in Chapter 5, but in addition there had been many skirmishes between the garrison and the besiegers. This is not the place to give a full history of the third siege, but a short review of some of these actions will give a background to the situation facing Cromwell and Lambert, although the record is intermittent and at times obscure.

Paulden refers to two night raids in each of which they took 300 head of cattle, both without loss to themselves.[2] One, at Knottingley, was in early June immediately after the capture of the castle, the other at Wentbridge after the death of Rainsborough at the end of October. A letter written at the end of October confirms that 200 head of cattle and a hundred oxen had been taken and, shortly after his arrival at Pontefract, Cromwell wrote that 220–240 fat beasts and sufficient salt had been taken, and that they had provisions for twelve months.[3] Although Paulden can be wrong on some dates by a month or so, as will be seen, here he ties in the raids very closely to the capture of the castle and the death of Rainsborough respectively.[4]

On 9 June a raid was made on Doncaster, fifteen miles away, in which three horses were stolen from the Post House and an attempt made to seize someone they thought to be the

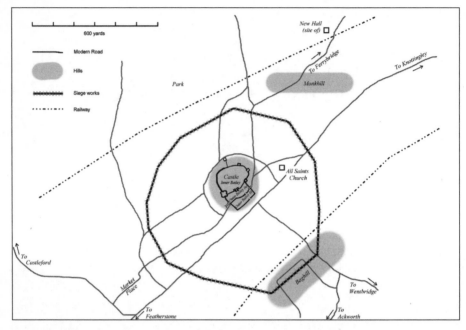

FIG. 6 *Pontefract, showing the original form of the castle with two outer baileys (now lost), and the approximate line of the siege works.*

wife of the Lord General. It was, however, probably the Royalist Alethea, Lady Fairfax, and the raiders eventually left with apologies. The tone of the report is very much of Parliamentary propaganda, with the raiders said to refer to the women as 'whore', 'bitch' or 'jade', threats to cut the Post Master 'as small as herbs for the pot', and telling Lady Fairfax that if she had been the General's wife they would have 'cut her up for the fowls to gaze upon'.[5] However, the fact that the account gives the names both of some of the raiders and of the attacked suggests at least a basis of evidence.

The raid may possibly be linked to another at much the same time – a reported attempt to take the castle of Tickhill about seven miles south of Doncaster.[6]

In August and September there was generally polite correspondence between the garrison and the besiegers at Pontefract about the exchange of prisoners and the granting of passes for the members of the garrison.[7] Some of the letters were addressed to 'Sr John Digby Knt, Comder in cheife att Pontefract' rather than to Morris. On 29 August Colonel Fairfax issued a pass for Captain Thomas Paulden's drum to fetch medicines for his brother William.[8]

The tone of the letters deteriorated in October, when Colonel Fairfax imprisoned the fathers of Thimbleby and Morris and in retaliation Morris put his prisoners in the dungeon. The correspondence became acrimonious, with Fairfax addressing a letter to 'the unworthy

Governor of Pontefract Castle' in which he shrugs off Morris's insults with: 'Your aspersions upon my family are easily wip't off they trouble me no more than the barking of a curre.'[9]

In the middle of October Royalist raiders snatched Sir Arthur Ingram from his house at Temple Newsam, twelve miles away, and took him into the castle, from where he was ransomed at a cost of £1,500. A little later, they took General Fairfax's steward from his manor at Denton near Otley.[10]

In October General Fairfax decided to replace Cholmley with Colonel Thomas Rainsborough.[11] Despite having received orders from the general, Cholmley refused to accept the change of command unless the order came from Parliament, and complained to the Commons that his honour was affected. General Fairfax promised that he would be very tender of Cholmley's honour, but there is no suggestion that Rainsborough's orders were changed.[12]

Rainsborough was delayed in London waiting for pay for his regiment, and when he did reach Pontefract on 15 October Cholmley refused to hand over command. He did offer to allow Rainsborough his own posts on the New Hall side, with each of them commanding their own men but Rainsborough had no horse without which he was unable to protect his men as they dug their entrenchments. He therefore retired to Doncaster until he heard from General Fairfax or received some promised horse and a supply of ammunition. His regiment, which appears to have preceded him, lay in the Isle of Axholme as they were short of provisions and saw no immediate hope of alleviation. Rainsborough wrote that some of his men had committed 'high and crying' offences on their march, and he looked for 'extraordinary justice' to bring the regiment to order.[13]

Despite the Parliamentary forces falling out amongst themselves, there was some action being undertaken. Paulden says that after the news came of the battle of Preston there were more attacks on the town, where many Royalists were still quartered. As there was neither room nor provisions for them in the castle, the Parliamentary forces were asked to give them passes to return to their homes. According to Paulden's Account,[14] this was granted and those from the town departed, leaving 500 foot and sixty horse in the castle. He says that on 9 September (actually October, see below) Parliament's army quietly entered the town. There was at least one raid on the town in mid-September, but this does not seem to have been a permanent occupation.[15]

Cholmley had written to Colonel Fairfax late in September asking that, when the town was taken, work (i.e. siege works) should begin on Baghill, a long, low escarpment some 350 yards from the southeast face of the castle (fig. 6 and plate 29).[16]

As soon as they were in the town, Parliament did indeed establish a guard post on Baghill. If Paulden is correct, it seems to have consisted of three companies of foot with a horse guard, which a party of a hundred foot and forty horse from the castle attacked the following night. They killed some, took prisoners and three colours, and chased the rest to the market place half a mile to the west. There is confirmation of the event in a letter of 20 October, which gives a date of 'Friday last' or 13 October, and corrects Paulden's 'September' for the occupation of the town.[17] Further support that this took place in October comes from the continuation of this account, which describes the arrival on the scene of Colonel Rainsborough just in time to save the day. The Royalists were pursued to the gate of the castle where they fired a mortar loaded with grenades. They were prevented from making another sally, but Parliamentary losses were not inconsiderable.[18] As Rainsborough did not reach Pontefract until Sunday 15th, it would appear that fighting continued over several days.

The following day (16th?) another troop was attacked by the garrison, with ten killed and many prisoners and horse taken. Rainsborough was greatly concerned about the lack of good horse, as those available were on duty almost constantly, which was wearing them down. The horse in the garrison had increased from sixty to 120, and the militia horse were becoming demoralised. This chimes with a comment from Paulden that the garrison 'resolved to weeary the horse', a tactic that was clearly successful. Two more attacks were made on Baghill and, according to Paulden, the position was abandoned and the guards were put in the park to the northwest at about this time. These guards were also attacked with loss to both sides.

It is clear that the garrison was reasonably free to cause considerable problems to the besiegers. A letter at the end of October says that the besiegers bought horses from the garrison and drank with them, although the garrison was preparing for a closer siege as Cromwell approached. The writer himself was attacked on the way to York, and disarmed by Pontefract men.[19]

However, although Rainsborough remained in Doncaster, his arrival was said to have had some effect as the garrison 'dare not take their progresse as formerly, being limited to a narrower distance, since the connjunction [sic] of our Force with Colonell Rainsborough'.[20]

This was wishful thinking, as a party of twenty-two men, under Captain William Paulden, slipped out of the castle on the night of Friday 27 October in an attempt to capture Rainsborough to exchange for Langdale, who had in fact escaped from Nottingham Castle at just this time.

The raiders first rode seventeen miles south to Mexborough, probably using an old pack horse track through Barnbrough to avoid main roads (map 2). They lay up in Mexborough on Saturday morning before crossing the river Don by the ferry on the south side of the town.[21] They sent in a man to spy out the defences and waited at Conisbrough on Saturday night. In the early hours of the next morning, Sunday 29th, they went on to Doncaster nine miles away, where they seized Rainsborough from his lodgings after entering by claiming to have a despatch from Cromwell. Rainsborough was killed when he tried to escape in the street outside his lodgings, and the raiders returned unscathed to Pontefract with, it is said, forty or fifty prisoners.[22]

Cholmley's lax control of the siege was blamed, some even suspecting him of complicity, and the outraged army gave Rainsborough a lavish funeral in London. Letters from Pontefract spoke of the discontent with Cholmley's management of the siege, and some of his officers were said to be going to petition the House about him.[23]

The situation at Pontefract had perhaps not been helped by moves to disband the newly raised militia forces of Yorkshire and Lancashire. On 17 October General Fairfax reported to Derby House that the York Committee wanted to have their forces at Scarborough and Pontefract replaced by three regiments of foot and 600 horse of the New Model. Over the following few days Parliament ordered the disbanding of the Lancashire militia, and those in Yorkshire as soon as the army could be substituted for them. The County Committees, rather than Parliament, were to be responsible for paying-off the men. One of the first to be nominated for disbanding seems to have been Cholmley's horse, in November, but this may have been delayed until January.[24]

NOVEMBER 1648

Three days after his arrival at Pontefract on 30 October, Cromwell sent a note to Colonel Fairfax asking him to reinforce the horse guard in the Park with musketeers against a possible attack, to: 'give them time to mount their horses if the enemy shall attempt upon them . . .'[25] Mounting would itself take no time at all, and the implication is that the horse guards were, very sensibly, not keeping their horses saddled all the time.

A few days later Cromwell was obliged to move guards around, and expressed the hope that now tools (presumably for entrenchments) were available there would be fewer such movements in the future.[26] Fixed defences would allow the guards to operate from prepared, defended positions.

On 5 November Cromwell wrote to Derby House in some detail, asking for supplies and ammunition for both Pontefract and Scarborough.[27] He also explained the strength of Pontefract, founded on rock with thick, high walls and towers, with an internal water supply, and said to be provisioned for a year (plates 27, 28). Furthermore the countryside was very impoverished and not able to provide quarter or provisions – even if the army had any money, which it had not. Also, the weather was cold and wet, and troops were without shelter. For the latter reason only two regiments of foot (Colonel Fairfax's and Colonel John Mauleverer's) were around the castle, and horse was being used for most of the guards, perhaps because they could retire after their duties to a greater distance where food and accommodation were to be found. Some troops were quartered as far away as Lincolnshire and Nottinghamshire. He asked for money for two regiments of horse and three of foot and for many other contingencies, for 500 barrels of powder, with bullet and match, six large guns with shot, and two or three large mortars with shells. Also he urgently wanted shoes and clothes, and boards to make courts-of-guard to shelter the men. On 15 and 18

November the Commons ordered that rather less than half the requested munitions, a total
of 250 barrels of powder, with cannon shot and bullet, and two large cannon, should be sent
to Pontefract.[28]

The courts-of-guard were a part of the intensification of the siege, forts set in a
circumvallation which was now being drawn around the castle on a similar line to that used
in the siege of 1645. The work had been under way since at least mid-October when shots
from the garrison artillery were killing men in their forts and trenches.[29] Rainsborough,
in his letter of 15 October,[30] had complained of the lack of tools for entrenchments. On 3
November the York Committee told Colonel Fairfax that they had ordered boards and spars
and that the Master Carpenter would provide tools and workmen.[31]

The contravallation was continued by Cromwell during November: 'Col. Bright, Col.
Dean, Col. Overton and Col. Okey watch by turn so that the souldiers are kept close at their
work.'[32] It was completed by Lambert.

On 9 November Cromwell summoned the castle, but Morris declared himself unable to
answer as 'the dispute betwixt yourself and Sir Henry Cholmley, Commander in chief by
Commission of the Committee of the Militia of Yorkshire' meant that he did not know to
whom he should reply. He seems not to have informed the garrison of the summons, as they
called over the wall to the besiegers asking why they had not been summoned. Cholmley's
militia horse had now been removed from the siege, their place taken by Cromwell's and
Harrison's horse and the dragoons.[33] As Colonel Okey was himself now at the siege, it
may be that most, if not all, of his dragoon regiment was there also, but its movements are
little documented.

On 10 November the Royalists abandoned their occupation of New Hall and set it on
fire. Cromwell's men quickly quenched the fire and occupied it themselves. At the same
time, in order to limit egress from the castle, the besiegers took a strong house near All
Saints church, the latter no more than a hundred yards from the castle (plate 30) and which
had been badly damaged in the previous sieges and is still partly ruined. This occupation is
confirmed by a second report, that there had been no sallies since Cromwell's arrival.[34] At
the same time Cromwell promised Colonel Fairfax that he would ask the Committee for
money for his regiment, and that he would explain that 'present money and nothing else
will keep the men together'.[35] The army's fervour seems to have been fading somewhat in
the face of shortages of clothes, food, shelter and money.

The Lord General's and Bright's foot, who both came into quarters on the 7th, and
Colonel Fairfax's and Mauleverer's militia foot, were all on duty in and around the town by
11 November. The besiegers 'great guns' were said to have come from Hull on the 6th, but
these must have been large artillery pieces rather than the heavier siege guns, which did not
arrive until January.[36]

During November Morris was again keen to exchange prisoners because, it was said,
there were many desertions and gentlemen were securing passes to leave the castle.[37]

Cromwell himself issued a pass to Sir John Digby and his servant to go into the town and return. This, as Abbott points out, was in sharp contrast to a letter he wrote two days earlier inveighing against the lenient manner in which some prisoners from Preston were being dealt with.[38]

Derby House was still nervous of plots in the north and asked the Committee of Westmorland to ensure that the withdrawal of Lancashire forces from Appleby would not allow that castle to be surprised by the disaffected.[39] There were also difficulties in Lancashire, where Colonel Ashton's forces were said to be showing enmity, and the County Committee imprisoned a Captain Ashton, who was to join Harrison's as a lieutenant, along with some of his thirty men.[40] Towards the end of November it was reported that Colonel Ashton's men would fight the New Model rather than disband.[41]

When Lambert left Newcastle for Pontefract on 17 November, Colonel Lilburne followed in command of the three regiments of horse and the dragoons from Scotland, who were said to be expected in Northallerton, fifty miles away, by the 24th. Sanderson, presumably with the rest of Lilburne's, reached Danby Wiske, less than five miles short of Northallerton on the 23rd and rested for a day. Even if Sanderson did not leave Newcastle until the 18th, he took six days to cover forty-five miles. He, and perhaps all of Lambert's three regiments, reached Aberford, fifteen miles north of Pontefract, on 28 November, from where his troop went to quarter at Rothwell near Leeds on the 29th, ten miles from Pontefract. Lambert's force had travelled 155 miles from the border in about twenty days which, including at least four rest days, gave an average speed of just under ten miles a day.

Politics, Cromwell and Pride's Purge

The date of arrival of both Lambert and his troops is important in relation to events that had been unfolding in London over the previous four months. On 2 August, as Cromwell was marching north from Pembroke and Lambert began his march south from Barnard Castle, Parliament decided to treat with the king. On the opening day of the battle of Preston the Commons had repealed the Vote of No Addresses passed at the beginning of the year,[42] and two days later, on the last day of the battle against the invading Scottish army at Winwick and Warrington, they agreed that the king could have Scots to advise him.[43]

The army, not well-pleased at the idea of talking to the man whom they rightly held responsible for the renewed fighting, prepared a Remonstrance to present their case. This called for Parliament: 'to return to their Votes of Non addresses, and settle with or against the King, that he may come no more to Government' and 'That the King be brought to Justice as the capital cause of all'. On 20 November General Fairfax sent this to be read to the Commons who postponed discussion, first until the 27th, and then 30 November, on which date they rejected it by a substantial majority.[44]

Meanwhile, the army had been taking action on its own account. On 21 November General Fairfax ordered Colonel Robert Hammond, governor of the Isle of Wight, to report to him. The Commons told Fairfax that the order should be withdrawn, and they sent ships to the island to come under Hammond's command. Hammond, however, felt that he should obey his general's order, and set off for Windsor leaving Colonel Ewers in charge of the king at Carisbrooke. On the 30th the army, clearly despairing of Parliament, began to march on London and General Fairfax advised the City authorities that they required £40,000 out of their arrears by the following evening. The following day, in a repeat of the events of 1647, the Commons asked Fairfax not to bring the army any closer to London, but to no greater effect than previously, and troops began their occupation.[45]

On 30 November the army removed the king to Hurst Castle, a remote location on a spit of land opposite the west end of the Isle of Wight, once more taking his person out of the control of Parliament 'without the knowledge or consent of the House', but on 5 December the Commons voted to accept the king's concessions as 'sufficient grounds for settling the Peace of the Kingdom'.[46] This may have been the last straw for the army, and on the 6th Colonel Pride's foot and Colonel Rich's horse prevented the entry of 140 Members who had voted for the treaty with the king, an event known as Pride's Purge. The army had once more taken control of the government, and at the same time took steps to ensure their own financial support, for two days later Fairfax wrote to the Lord Mayor announcing that he had authorised the seizure of the treasuries of Goldsmiths Hall and Weavers Hall, albeit with proper receipts given, in order to pay for quarters.[47]

On 13 December the purged Commons declared that any approach to the king other than by Parliament was to be High Treason. On the same day they approved supplies for Hurst Castle including large quantities of powder and shot for cannon, presumably to provide against attempts to rescue the king. The following day, rather oddly, the purged Commons sent a committee to ask General Fairfax why Members had been excluded.[48]

Cromwell, a major political influence in the army as well as its lieutenant-general, had been absent from London during these events; a letter of 23 November said that he was expected shortly but it was another two weeks before he arrived.[49] He has been accused by many commentators of waiting in Pontefract to avoid being in London at the time of Pride's Purge, and for travelling very slowly when he did start south. These points are worth examining.

It has been said that the siege of Pontefract was unimportant, used by Cromwell as an excuse to remain in the north. The events of the previous months had shown that this was not the case, and that with a half-hearted siege the garrison could roam almost at will and be a focus for Royalist hope. There was much to do in formalising the siege and this was given as a reason for delay.[50] A strong leader and a substantial besieging force was the only way to contain the garrison, and to that extent Cromwell was entirely justified in a military sense.

Also, as already mentioned, there were problems with the militia to be dealt with: 'It's much desired the Lieutenant Gen. stay a little longer here to have seen their disbanded.'[51]

The date of his leaving Pontefract has been the subject of some dispute. General Fairfax wrote to him on 28 November, summoning him to headquarters 'with all convenient speede possible'.[52] It has been argued that this must have reached Pontefract by 30 November – although in practice the distance of 175 miles, the short days, the weather and the state of the roads would have made this virtually impossible – and that Cromwell left on that day.

The distance could be covered in two days only in good conditions. Sixty or seventy miles a day was possible when there were more hours of daylight hours than at the end of November, and the roads were dry.[53] Three or four days is much more likely, and even five not unreasonable. Cromwell's letter of 5 November was not discussed at Derby House until the 10th, an indication that it had reached London on the 9th or 10th. Lambert's letter of 22 March 1649 announcing the agreement to surrender Pontefract was received in the Commons on the 27th.

Cromwell had told General Fairfax that he expected to leave on Tuesday [28th].[54] However, Sanderson's diary is very clear that it was Wednesday 29 November, well before the letter could have reached Pontefract, when he, in company with Lambert, 'Set Leeut: generall onwards towards wentbridge' some four miles south of Pontefract.[55] Wentbridge is so close that it cannot have been Cromwell's destination for the night and gives no indication of the route he took. A report from Mansfield, recording his intended arrival in Nottingham, may mean that he went through that town; if so, travel through Doncaster and Worksop is probable.[56] The distance is about sixty miles, which he covered in three days, arriving in Nottingham on 1 December.

He marched with a number of regiments that had been with him in Scotland; some of them, probably the foot, had left Pontefract for the south as early as 20 November.[57] He told General Fairfax[58] that the regiments coming from Pontefract were the Lord General's foot, Okey's dragoons, Cromwell's and Harrison's horse, and some others. Overton's also left at some point, as they were not among those around Pontefract for whom pay was assigned in early December.[59]

From Nottingham to London is about 130 miles, which Cromwell covered in five days. When close to London he left most of his troops: 'The three Regiments that guarded him up, he left behind (as was most proper) at Dunstable.'[60] The mention of three regiments suggests that he marched with his own and Harrison's horse, and Okey's dragoons, without any foot. If he rode the thirty-five miles from Dunstable with only a small escort on the fifth day, he had four days to march to there from Nottingham, a rate of almost twenty-four miles a day, which is quick for a large body of horse. Any criticism lies in the delay of his departure, and for his remaining with the regiments rather than riding ahead.

Cromwell had waited in Pontefract for nine days after the arrival of Lambert, who was perfectly competent to carry out any reorganisation of the siege in Cromwell's absence.

It is probably no coincidence that he began his move south the day after Lambert's three regiments of horse arrived in the vicinity of Pontefract with Colonel Lilburne on the 28th. There was an indication in a letter written over a week before he left that he was only waiting for these regiments, which were expected on the 23rd or 24th, and the march south would begin on the 27th or 28th.[61] Prior to that it may not have been wise to leave the castle less than fully besieged, and the need to take regiments to London meant that he could not have left earlier. He presumably felt it necessary to bring from Pontefract several regiments as the developing political crisis might call for the largest army presence near London.

Given all these factors, the date of his departure from Pontefract is wholly explicable and the speed of his journey was by no means unreasonable, although he does seem to have timed it all very carefully. If it were not planned it was a remarkable coincidence that he arrived a few hours after Colonel Pride had purged the Commons of Members unfriendly to the army. As a contemporary put it: 'and when all was done, in came Nol. Cromwell to Towne at night, as if he (poore man) had no hand in the Busines'.[62]

December 1648

On Cromwell's departure Lambert took over command of the sieges of Scarborough and Pontefract. The two towns had, as explained above, been taken in the middle of September and the middle of October respectively, but the castles still held out. During November there were false hopes that Scarborough was about to surrender, due to the number of men running from the castle – it was even suggested that it was now an empty castle being besieged – but, as with so many wars, there was a certainty that it would be over by Christmas.[63]

At Pontefract work was proceeding on the siege works, and by the first week of December the line had been drawn three parts around the castle. Batteries were being established and artillery pieces were ready to fire on the castle. The garrison, although down to about 300 with few horse, was also active, firing large and small shot, but could not be induced to make a sally. However, despite sickness, deaths, poor clothing and desertions, they were said to have sufficient provisions to maintain themselves for a year. One letter describes the desertion of a Lieutenant Cole on Monday [11 December], who was followed two days later by a Mr Hawkins, who accused Cole of intending to stab Lambert. One wonders whether Hawkins were a disinformation agent. Both men were imprisoned while the case was examined. The besiegers were also suffering, especially from shortage of quarters, for which they needed money.[64]

There was also another adverse report on Morris: 'The cruelties of Morris the governour of this castle to our prisoners are not to be paraleld, all of them that either have escaped, or been released, make lamentable comments of him.'[65] Morris complained to Colonel Fairfax that one of his men – who had left the castle only to get his horse – had been unjustly hanged, but Fairfax replied that the man had confessed to seeking intelligence. At the end of November Morris told Fairfax to 'save the labour of writing to him as this is the last answer to anie of your starved Apothogmes'.[66] Virtually all Morris' correspondence with the Parliamentary forces throughout the siege appears to have been addressed to Colonel Fairfax, rather than to Cholmley, Cromwell or Lambert, although this may reflect the chance survival of the letters.

The answer to Cromwell's request for money made at the beginning of November came to Lambert early in December, claiming to enclose warrants for a month's pay for two regiments of horse [Lambert's and Lilburne's], Bright's foot and five loose Companies of Foot.[67] The warrants were apparently not enclosed, and on 16 December there was a complaint made in strong terms:

> Our service is difficult, and our duty as hard, but for pay, are in greatest of
> want; the Committee of the Army promised us a monthes pay fourteen dayes
> since . . . but as yet we hear nothing of either. Wee cannot expect any thing
> from the poor Country, though (for want of pay) we are forced to desire
> Victuals of them, and I am perswaded, that many that give us it, stand in as
> great, if not greater need thereof than our selves. It pities us, that we must of
> necessity be so burthensome to them and we are the more troubled, that we
> should be so slighted.[68]

Not only does this give an impression of what life was like for civilians, but saying that the besieging army felt slighted seems designed as a threat to those responsible. However, the identities of sender and recipient are not known, and it may be no more than a private grumble.

Lambert's army was also occupied with political considerations, and on the 4th there was a meeting of officers in support of the army Remonstrance, although it was adjourned until Monday [11th] to allow 'divers officers being absent by reason of their imployments somewhat remote' to attend. They actually resumed on the 12th with thirty-six officers of all ranks present, from General Lambert to cornets and ensigns, and Thomas Margetts as secretary. Only two officers voted against a declaration supporting the Remonstrance – Colonel Bright and a Captain Westby.[69]

The declaration was taken to London by Captain Adam Baynes, who was to meet Captain Bradford there and present it to the Lord General and the General Council of the army. As the writer of the letter of the 16th[70] put it rather charmingly: 'Though we have not the honour to bring up the Van in the great undertaking, yet we know there is much honour to bring up the Rear. We are not good Leaders, but may be good followers, and I am confident will be in this engagement.' The army of the north was in no mood to compromise with the man they saw as responsible for the suffering of a renewed Civil War.

In Scarborough the siege was still thought to be drawing to a close, this time with more reason. On 28 November the besiegers under Colonel Bethell took the garrison's boat, causing the governor's ensign to speak of their alarm as it had been hoped to use it to get shoes and clothing, which were in short supply. Although they had corn and butter, they had only a month's fish and three weeks' firewood. The soldiers were all for making terms, and a Lieutenant Sallet came out and surrendered upon mercy.[71]

On 19 December the surrender of the castle was agreed by Bethell under reasonable terms. The garrison were allowed to march out with: 'Colours flying, Drums beating, Muskets laden, Bandaleers filled, Matches lighted and Bullet in Mouth' – a way of indicating that the end had come by negotiation rather than defeat. The governor, field officers and captains were to go to a place appointed, the rest were allowed to go home. It was said that the terms reflected the imminent arrival of ships from the Prince of Wales to relieve the castle with men and provisions.[72] One of Lambert's problems was now solved, leaving him with the siege of Pontefract and the disbanding of the surplus militia forces.

On 23 December Lambert found it necessary to write again about pay for his force. Each regular regiment had an establishment for a surgeon and two mates, and Lambert's three (Lambert's and Lilburne's horse, and Bright's foot) were short of pay and lacking their full complement of mates. There were still some of those wounded at Preston, as well as at the siege, who needed attention: 'Amongst the rest of our discouragements, that is not a little one: That when Souldiers are wounded, they cannot be provided for as is fit and necessary for them.'[73] Some pay was available, however, for on 21 December Major Sanderson of Lilburne's was able to pay his commissioned officers for fourteen days and non-commissioned officers and men for fifteen days.

Lambert also had to attend to the matter of the discharge of the militia, and on 25 December Sanderson was put in charge of an escort for Lambert, consisting of seven men out of each troop of both regiments of horse, a total of eighty-four. The composition of the escort may have been to spread the duties among all the troops, or it may have been a selection of the more reliable men, as the militia was often opposed to disbanding. From 25 to 30 December, the troops of Sir Edward Rhodes, Captain Byards. Captain Wentworth, Captain Cook and Major Pearson were disbanded at several locations from Barnsdale to Addingham (map 3).[74]

Events in London had been moving apace. On 16 December the army sent a party of horse to bring the king to Windsor, where he was expected on 23 December.[75] The Council of War of the Army was now managing all business in relation to the king, and on the 27th they ordered that all ceremonial should cease and the number of his attendants be reduced.[76] The king was now being regarded simply as a prisoner. On the 28th the Commons held the first reading of the formal charges against the king – that he had broken his trust and been the 'occasion of much Bloodshed and Misery to the People' – and on 1 January passed an ordinance accusing the king of treason and declaring that he be tried. The Lords threw this out, but on the 3rd and 4th the Commons resolved that they were the supreme power in the nation and could act without the Lords, and on the 8th passed the Act for trying the king with the endorsement: 'That it be enacted for Law; and have the Force of a Law.'[77] The dubious legality of the tribunal has been discussed by many writers; put simply, it was an expedient to solve a pressing problem.

JANUARY 1649

At the end of December, John Baynes recorded that: 'The Gunns are not yet come to Pontefract nor can we certainly know where they are . . .' On 6 January the siege guns were still awaited, although they were expected the next week and the batteries to contain them were being raised.[78] In April a Mr Streeter was paid £32 8s. 0d. for eighty-one days' work on the fortification at the rate of 8s. a day. If he were discharged from the work when the siege ended, this pay dates from 1 January; his service may well have begun before this date. At the same time, Edward Smith was paid £1 17s. 6d. 'for charges about the Ordinance'.[79]

By 2 January 1649 Lambert was in Easingwold, about fourteen miles north of York. From there he wrote to Colonels Fairfax, Bright, Mauleverer and Wastell, suggesting that they send officers to Leicestershire and Staffordshire both to spur them on to raise a promised levy and to enquire whether they might send a party of twenty horse to each place to assist with the collection. He records that he was busy with disbanding, had already dealt with the six troops of Bethell's and four companies of Lascelles', and that he had at least another ten days' work ahead of him.[80]

Several other letters record the task of disbanding in January. Cornet Baynes mentioned Lambert's absence on this work, and Margetts described the disbanding of Rhodes' and Cholmley's regiments of horse as: 'having proved very difficult and troublesome; yet by this time the business is well nigh over . . . our miserable hard duty in this extremely unseasonable weather'. Disbanding was clearly not an easy task, owing partly to lack of money and partly to the reluctance of the troops to depart.[81]

Lambert returned from dealing with Rhodes' and Cholmley's, but by 13 January had gone to York to discuss further disbanding, and from there to Scarborough to disband Bethell's horse and the foot regiments. The work detained him at Scarborough until the end of the month.[82]

Back in London there was nothing now to prevent the trial for high treason, with little doubt about the verdict. A fortnight before it began the Commons ordered a new Great Seal: 'on which the Sculpture of the House of Commons is engraven . . . [and] . . . In the First Year of Freedom by Gods' Blessing restored, 1648[9]', and three days before the trial read an ordinance for Inventorying and Preserving the goods in the king's houses.[83] The trial began on 20 January, in the absence of Lord Fairfax who had been named as one of the Commissioners, and on 30 January the king was executed.

Another Commissioner, Colonel Lilburne, had left Pontefract for London by the 13th, where he took part in the trial and signed the death warrant. Most of the other officers were absent from Pontefract although it is not clear whether their absence was for business or pleasure. The fact that 'Coll. Bright (who you know dissents . . .)' remained in Pontefract could be an indication that the others were in London.[84] Lambert, who had also been nominated as a Commissioner,[85] was not there either, perhaps because he did not want to have any part in the quasi-judicial proceedings, whatever his views might have been.

If he had been determined, attending the trial would not have been difficult, for his presence at Pontefract was no longer necessary – and in fact he was elsewhere for most of January. There were now sufficient troops to maintain a close siege and to prevent any supplies or reinforcements reaching the castle, although there were continuing exchanges of prisoners and some passes were issued to visitors. There was no point in trying an assault on such a strong castle, which was now the only centre of Royalist opposition and need only be contained to be ineffective. There seems no good reason why Lambert could not have insisted that Lilburne remain to command in the north as he had done in the previous June. Whether this was from motives of conscience or politics is not at all clear.

The Lancashire militia raised more problems in January, when there was another report[86] that the men under Colonel Ashton were discontented at the news that they were to be disbanded and there were suggestions that they should fight the army, or join with the Scots, rather than return to civilian work. Early in February Colonel Ashton asked for powder and bullet from Lancaster, but this was refused, and it was reported that Colonel Shuttleworth had lifted men and horses, apparently from the Kendal area. The countryside around Pontefract was also said to be discontented, but this may have had more to do with the large number of soldiers in the area than political affiliations.[87]

It will be convenient to note here that there were still problems with the militia early in March, when there was a report of: 'dissention and jangling; Col. Ashtons forces are extreamly *unsatisfied* with the proceedings at *Westminster*'.[88] Lambert went over to Lancaster in the week beginning 5 March,[89] and later in the month he was said to be ready to defeat them if needs be. Ashton and Shuttleworth were believed to be prepared to fall into line if the arrears were paid and past insolence forgiven.[90] Birch's company was disbanded on 29 March: 'Wee lodged our collours, laid down our armes and disbanded.'

By 4 April the disbanding of the Lancashire forces was complete, apart from the troop of a Captain Bamber from Fleming's regiment, who was refusing to disband. Throughout April and May there were reports of him recruiting men up to the figure of 210, taking free quarter and oppressing the countryside. Lambert was ordered by the Council of State (which had replaced the Committee of Both Houses) to disband them by force if necessary, and to restore their arms and horses to their rightful owners. Ashton and the other Deputy Lieutenants of Lancashire were also instructed to take measures against them.[91]

During January the siege works approached close to the castle and shots from the garrison with both stones and bullets were killing some of the besiegers. The approaching works would not have been the fortified circumvallation, which was fixed, but saps and parallels to allow the besiegers to close in with minimum risk of casualties. On 24 January the Royalists made a sally, killed three or four men and took fourteen prisoners before being forced in again.[92]

FEBRUARY 1649

The execution of the king spurred the garrison of Pontefract to greater efforts, declaring that they would have a king whatever it cost them. On 2 February they made another sally, hoping to beat the besiegers out of their trenches near the outlying Swillington tower on the north side of the castle and killed one man, but were beaten back. One suggestion was that they were also trying to send emissaries out to find out just what was happening and to look for orders.[93] There were reports of Royalists gathering in the woods to plot the relief of the castle, and Parliamentary patrols were sent out to apprehend them. It was thought that the garrison, while they hoped for relief, were ready to come to terms if given another summons. However, they continued to harass the besiegers as best they could, and although they no longer had shells for their mortar they were able to fire stones from it. One landed in Colonel Lilburne's quarters, next to Lambert's room, but both men were away and no one was hurt. Lambert had by this time (3 February) returned from disbanding but was now visiting his wife.[94]

The besiegers had their own problems. At the beginning of January there had been several Councils of War for trying offending soldiers with 'exemplary justice' for the satisfaction of the countryside and to restore and maintain discipline. There were also fears among local people of another Scottish invasion, although Margetts did not think this very likely.[95]

Late in January cipher letters had been intercepted between George Beaumont, the rector of South Kirkby seven or eight miles south of Pontefract, and the garrison. He was also accused of having had a principal hand in the capture of Pontefract in June, and was hanged in front of the castle 'that his old friends might see him' on 15 February 1649.[96]

Following this execution, the garrison made another sally with the loss to the besiegers of six or eight killed and twice as many taken prisoner. A significant loss was that of the Chief Gunner who had come from London to assist with the siege. A Royalist newsbook made the most of it, claiming that the 'couragious renowned Royalists' killed fifty, and took forty prisoners along with provisions and ammunition. It also claimed that the garrison was able to last for another year, during which time relief was certain.[97]

There were other considerations that Lambert had to attend to around this time. On 13 February the Commons voted money for paying off the Northern Forces, and gave Lambert instructions for those who were to be added to the army establishment.[98] In addition there was an alarm of Royalist ships operating on the west coast. This was said to be causing alarm to the West Riding and, although at its westernmost extent it is only thirteen miles from the coast at Morecambe, there must be some doubt about the accuracy of the report. But at the same time there was another report of some Lancashire men being sent home from Pontefract to secure castles there as 'that Country (as is all the North) being evill disposed', so perhaps there was some sort of threat in the west.[99]

The siege proceeded without any major actions reported on either side. In his Letter[100] Paulden dismissed the last four months of the siege, December to March, thus: 'Major-General Lambert came against us; and then we were close shut up.' However, in his Account[101] he describes how two Parliamentary batteries caused the garrison to remove guns from the top of the towers into chambers, from where they were able to silence the besiegers' guns, apart from their mortar, which caused a large explosion. After that, the only thing worth reporting was a fever that raged among the garrison and killed many, and other diseases such as scurvy, which Paulden put down to the salt diet.

The reference to the besiegers' mortar shows that this episode should be dated to late January or February, when the heavy siege guns and mortars were at last coming into use.[102] This had been slow progress, perhaps explained by the difficulty of moving heavy artillery at any time of year, and especially in the winter when snow, frost, rain and mud could make wheeled transport next to impossible. The weather was presumably unusually poor for the time of year, as it was described as unseasonable.[103] Letters from Pontefract were being delayed owing to the frost and snow in the area.[104]

The fever in the castle was known to the besiegers on 10 February, as was the death from it at this time of Captain William Paulden, the commander of the raid on Rainsborough. Even details of damage and injuries were known: a Captain Benson had his hand broken by a grenade (perhaps a mortar shell), which fell in the governor's chamber. The garrison's ability to fire back was said to be decaying, although they were still resolute.[105]

Much of this information no doubt came by messengers passing letters to and from the besiegers, as correspondence between Colonel Fairfax and the garrison had resumed and was frequent during January and February. Morris even asked to be supplied with a quire of paper, for which he was prepared to pay. This request also explained that the garrison was putting out bodies from the castle, and offered a pass for a surgeon to visit.[106] Many of the letters are concerned with passes and requests for medicines and the tone is more civil than formerly, perhaps due to deteriorating conditions in the castle and the inevitability of a final surrender.

News reports delighted in making fun of the opposition. A Royalist sheet announced that: 'The *King-Choppers* are as Active in mischief as such Thieves or murderers need to be . . .' On the other side, the garrison was referred to as being 'all notable Incendiaries though they want Fuell', and a newsbook editor took pleasure in recounting a fire in the castle, which: 'with great Industry was immediately quenched they complaine for the want of fire, and yet they sweate and labour by the excesse thereof'.[107]

On 14 February, Morris wrote to pass on a complaint from his prisoners that they were not receiving straw, strong waters and tobacco, and at about the same time was also suggesting a general exchange of prisoners. Lambert replied to the latter point on the 18th and named his commissioners to discuss terms. The following day he provided them with detailed instructions, principally to ensure that no Royalist prisoners were allowed into the castle, and that none of the garrison was to be allowed out before the conclusion of a treaty. No more than two hours were to be spent on the discussions. The soldiers and junior officers would be free to go home to live quietly, with no mention of the fate of their seniors.[108]

The talks came to nothing, largely because it was clear that six unnamed persons were to be excepted from the general pardon and would have to surrender on mercy. The garrison refused these terms and the siege went on. Margetts was not sanguine about the situation and feared that if the 'Jockeys' (Scots) were to rise again Parliament would be at a disadvantage owing to the recent disbanding. Although secretary to the moderate Lambert, Margetts seems to have been something of a hardliner who regretted the long demurs in justice being meted out to prominent Royalist prisoners. He wanted all malignants to be disarmed, and all disaffected priests to be punished.[109]

Meanwhile, some of the besiegers occupied themselves with horse racing, although at the beginning of March Lambert ordered a race at Clifford, south of Wetherby (map 3), to be postponed for a month.[110]

A Royalist report at the end of February explained that the valiant garrison was beating up the besiegers' guards daily and had declined another summons from Lambert, declaring that they would hang the messenger who brought any more summonses. Relief might be long delayed, but it was certain. [111]

MARCH 1649

The upbeat tone of the report seems to have been based on hope rather than reality, for by 3 March Margetts was able to report that the Royalists had asked for a treaty, difficult though it might be to persuade them to deliver some to mercy, while at the same time he was afraid that dissensions on the Parliamentary side 'at home' would lead to their own destruction. Another letter suggests that it was disease that had led to the request for a treaty, plus the greater effect of mutiny and disaffection among the rank and file.[112]

John Baynes, who had a similar outlook to Margetts, wrote on 10 March that the treaty between the two sets of Commissioners was to be held that day, with hopes of a satisfactory outcome as good terms were to be offered to all but the six excepted men. On the same day, Bright explained that letters, wrapped around stones and thrown over the castle wall in order to make it clear to the non-excepted that fair terms were being offered to them, had caused dissension among the garrison. He feared that, despite now having both mortars at work, only a few rooms in the castle were ruined. This was due to the strength of the timber used in castle roofs and floors, which mean: 'that if our grenadoes break through one storey it goes no further'. The only effect was to provide the garrison with more firewood.[113]

It seems that the letters had had some success, for on Thursday 8 March Morris sent Colonel Roger Portington and Captain Thomas Paulden as Commissioners to request another meeting. On Friday 16 March a surrender on the following Monday (19th) was agreed, and the only outstanding point was the excepted persons. On receiving intimation that the governor was to be one of these, Paulden asked to be relieved of his duty. Morris ordered the other Commissioners to conclude the treaty saying that: 'if he was excepted, he would take his Fortune, and would not have so many worthy Gentlemen perish for his sake'. The six men to surrender on mercy were: Colonel Morris, Lieutenant Austwick, Cornet Blackborne (the latter two for the murder of Rainsborough), and three who had been in the Parliamentary garrison and had assisted with its betrayal – Major Ashby, Ensign Smith and Sergeant Floyd.[114]

The garrison asked for a stay of the surrender for six days to allow the excepted men to escape if they could, a proposal to which Lambert agreed. The day after signing the treaty, the garrison sent a party out two or three times, but without attacking. On the following day a determined attack was made by the garrison, to cover the escape of the excepted persons. Morris and Blackburne got away, but the other four went back into the castle. On the fourth day another attempt was made, during which Ensign Smith was killed. The other three were hidden in the castle, walled up in a sally port, from which they escaped after the surrender. On 24 March, the garrison announced that all six had already escaped, and prepared to surrender. It appears that the garrison came out of the castle on the 25th, the first day of the new year in the old-style calendar.[115]

Lambert wrote to the Speaker on the 22nd, in a letter delivered by Margetts, announcing the terms, which he hoped were acceptable despite their leniency. One of his reasons for the terms was that the garrison still had two months' supplies, and the alternative of starving them out would mean more hardship for the 'poor distressed country'.[116]

Pontefract Castle was dismantled almost at once, but not simply at the behest of Parliament. Lambert included in his letter the: 'desires of the Mayor, Aldermen and well-affected of the Towne of Pontefract, who earnestly pray for the demolishing of the castle' – a petition that he supported. The articles of surrender were approved by Parliament on 27 March, when it was agreed that 'the said castle of Pontfract [sic] be forthwith totally demolished, and levelled to the Ground'.[117] Work began on 9 April, and by the 18th around 140 tons of lead from the castle had been sold.[118]

Also on 27 March, perhaps partly in response to a letter to the Speaker from General Fairfax, the Commons ordered an Act to be prepared giving Lambert and his heirs £300 a year out of the demesne lands of Pontefract, at full value as in 1641:

In respect of his many great and eminent Services, performed with much Care, Courage and Fidelity, by the said Major-General Lambert, in the Northern Parts, as well against the Scotts Army, the last Summer, as against the Forces of Sir Marmaduke Langdale, and otherwise, and in reducing the castle of Pontfract, being the last Garison in England held out against the Parliament; and in respect of his extraordinary Charges therein, he having not been allowed any Pay as a Major-General.[119]

Lambert's campaign in the second Civil War was finally over.

Appendices

Appendix 1

SOURCES

Newsbooks

The main source of information for this study is the contemporary collection of pamphlets and newsbooks made by George Thomason and known as the *Thomason Tracts* (*TT*). This is held in the British Library and accessible elsewhere on microfilm, and online as part of the Early English Books Online (EEBO) e-resource, which is less widely available to independent researchers. The tracts are referred to in the endnotes by the BL shelfmark thus: *TT* E475/6.

There are over 1,400 publications in the collection from 1648 listed by G. K. Fortescue in his catalogue, of which more than a quarter are sermons, ballads, satires in prose and verse, or reprints of earlier items, which are less relevant here. The collection contains some 700 issues of sixty-two 'periodical' or newsbook titles. Many of these appeared only in late 1647 or in 1648, fourteen of them in one issue only, particularly in the middle of that year in response to the unrest across the country. Several of these addressed a single news item (e.g. three issues of *Colchester Spie* in August, or the single issue of *Treaty Traverst or, Newes From Newport in the Isle of Wight* in September), others attacked another title (e.g. *Mercurius Impartialis or an Answer to That Treasonable Pamphlet, Mercurius Militaris; Together with the Moderate*, published in December).

Newsbooks developed from the manuscript newsletters sent between the gentry in the late sixteenth and early seventeenth centuries, particularly from London out to the rest of the country. The earliest printed newsbooks or 'corantos' came from the continent with news of the foreign wars, to be translated into English for the home market. Manuscript newsletters continued to be written by correspondents working for particular families even after the huge increase in printed material during the Civil Wars, and on occasion there were close links between the two means of distributing information. John Dillingham, who was employed as a newsletter writer by the Montagu family, was one of the earliest newsbook editors, and responsible for *The Moderate Intelligencer* in the second Civil War. Gilbert Mabbott, appointed assistant to John Rushworth, Clerk Assistant to the House of Commons, in 1643, and later his deputy licenser of printing, corresponded regularly with individuals such as Ferdinando, Lord Fairfax. As agent for the army during the Civil War and Interregnum, he kept commanders in England and Scotland up-to-date with foreign and domestic affairs by means of newsletters; he was also said to have been involved in editing two newsbooks, the *Perfect Diurnall* and *The Moderate*.[1]

The letter format was seen as a reliable means of distributing news, and was adopted by many of the writers and editors of the most informative of the later journals. These were rarely signed, and even if initials are given at the end, it is often difficult to identify the writer. On occasion the text could be based on a genuine letter with additions to clarify the text for the reader who might not be familiar with the background. A good example of this is the letter written by Margetts from Aberforth on 11 August 1648, which forms the basis for the unsigned letter in *Packets of Letters*.[2] Such was the value of the format as seen by the editor of the newsbook and his reader that on many occasions initials would be added to give a report an air of authenticity, when in fact there may not have been an original letter.

References throughout the text to 'a letter' indicate only that the newsbook presents what purports to be a genuine letter. Where the news is given in straightforward journalistic style, the reference is to 'a report' even although this was probably based on a letter.

The majority of the newsbooks were printed and published in London, the notable exception being *Mercurius Aulicus*, the leading Royalist paper started in Oxford in 1643. The news would be gathered from reports, official or otherwise, sent to the capital, and the printed versions could then be sent to friends in the provinces. Evidence of this traffic can be found in letters sent by Francis Thorpe, Recorder of Hull, from London to the townspeople, when he writes 'the prints will tell you the news' and assumes that others will have sent the 'diurnalls and occur[en]ces'. Following the defeat of the Scots army at Preston, Thorpe recommends *The Diurnall*: 'being the p[er]fect relacon of the passages touching the treaty for peace . . .'[3]

Dating

In his article on Thomason in *ODNB*, David Stoker notes that his 'practice of adding the dates of publication or acquisition on the works' title pages has proved invaluable in establishing the chronology of events during this turbulent period [the Civil War]'. However, as indicated at various points in the foregoing text, dating reports and the events described in the pamphlets in Thomason's collection can reveal discrepancies. The dates may be illegible because of worn type[4] or the printer may have picked up the wrong piece of type, as in the letter from Pontefract, Upper town, which is dated 'July 39. 1648' (*TT* E456/18). It may help if the date of publication of the pamphlet can be established, but much has been written on the difficulties inherent in this. Spencer notes that Thomason started to date the publications in his collection more consistently in 1642, with a manuscript note, giving day and month, on title pages. But doubt has been expressed, particularly by Greenberg, and by Mendle in his article published in 1990, as to whether this is a date of publication or acquisition. In his catalogue, which is arranged chronologically with a separate listing of the newsbooks, Fortescue used the title page ms dates only occasionally, arranging the pamphlets by the date of the first or only dated item or, in the case of those describing particular events, by the date given for the event, which is not always helpful.

A study of the newsbooks and pamphlets for 1648 shows that Thomason's manuscript dates normally occur when there is no day and month printed on the title page, either in the imprint or as the date of receipt by, or reading in, Parliament. *Packets of Letters*, published weekly from mid-March to the beginning of November 1648 as a supplement to *Perfect Occurrences of Every Daies iournall in Parliament*, contain reports written in letter form 'brought by the post' on Monday with the date following: no. 12, brought on 5 June, was licensed by Mabbott on the 6th; nos 13 and 14, brought on 12 and 19 June respectively, were similarly licensed the following day; no. 15, brought on the 26th, has no *imprimatur* but is dated 27 June in manuscript on the title page.[5] (For further examples of the importance of the manuscript dates see Chapter 7, where reports of the battle of Preston are discussed.) Thomason himself states in the introduction to the manuscript list of his collection that: 'The Method that hath been Observed throughout is Tyme, and Such Exact Care hath been taken that the very day is written upon most of them that they came out.'[6] Mendle's comment that Thomason writes this 'with a little inaccuracy' may not be strictly correct.[7]

There must have been many sources for the reports contained in the newsbooks. Peacey outlines the links between intelligence gathering, propaganda and journalism in the Civil War and Commonwealth, and gives evidence of the leaks of official documents to the press.[8] Many of the letters found in the news reports were first sent to Parliament, or to one or other of its committees, and must have been available for view by newsbook editors. Diethe suggests that there was a news distribution system in London, with agents receiving letters and selling them to editors.[9] This may have led to letters being copied with different origins given, as in those purportedly from Newcastle 13 July and Penrith on 16 July.[10] A letter written from Lambert's quarters at Bowes on 19 July 1648 reached London by the 24th, and was reported briefly in *Packets of Letters Numb. 19 brought by the Post Monday July 24 1648* (*TT* E454/19). The full text of the letter appeared in a separate pamphlet (*TT* E454/14). The day and month of printing are not given but the manuscript date on the title page is 27 July.

A very similar text, although lacking details of the forces that met Lambert's army at Bowes after their withdrawal from Appleby, is printed in *Perfect Diurnall of some Passages in Parliament Numb. 261, 24–31 July* (*TT* E525/10). A badly printed version is to be found in *Perfect Occurrences of Every Daies iournall in Parliament Num. 82, 21–28 July* (*TT* E525/9), which has several errors of transcription, including 'runles' for 'two miles' and 'Kirlep-Stephen' for Kirkby Stephen. It may be that the news gatherer in this case had difficulty in, or little time for, reading the report, but was anxious to publish it before his rivals. There are no names, or initials, appended to the letter in any of these publications, but it appears genuine, and was probably a report sent to the Army Committee, the papers of which are no longer extant. This letter was apparently not reported to the House of Commons or to the Committee of Both Houses. Letters from the major-general himself, however, are reported: from Wetheral dated 3 July, two from Penrith on the 10th and 14th, and one from Barnard Castle on the 20th.[11] The reason, no doubt, was because action was required on the part of the Commons or Derby House.

The post and messengers

The letters quoted above were read in London four or five days after the date of writing. But how did they reach the capital? A system of posts, for carrying royal and government documents, had existed since Tudor times, and there were gradual developments in the late sixteenth and early seventeenth centuries, with monopolies and regulations introduced. These included rules for the number of horses kept at any one post, the need for stout leather bags for carrying the packets, and a horn to blow at intervals en route. Following a suggested reorganisation to cover thirty-two counties and 512 market towns in England, with a new central office in London and fixed days for delivery and collection, in July 1635 Thomas Withrington was given the job of setting up a new system.

Charges were set at 2*d.* for a single letter sent up to eighty miles, 4*d.* for 80–140 miles, 6*d.* above 140 miles and 8*d.* to the border with Scotland and beyond. Turn-around time at any stage was to be no more than a quarter of an hour, and the expected speed of travel was, as in the past, 7 m.p.h. in summer and 5 m.p.h. in winter. Ledgers were to be kept to record the movement of packets, and labels with similar details to be attached to them. 'OHMS' communications had to take precedence but private post was also carried until royal orders introduced further limitations in July 1637. In the same year Witherington was demoted to deputy when the Secretaries of State became joint Inland Postmasters.

Three years later he was replaced by Charles I's appointee, a London merchant, Philip Burlamachi. As relations between king and Parliament deteriorated, Burlamachi in turn was dismissed when Parliament seized control of the London office, and thereafter the Lords and Commons supported separate claimants for the office. The successful contender was the Commons nominee, Sir Edmond

Prideaux (1601–1659), a lawyer and MP for Lyme Regis in the Long Parliament, who was involved with the service from 1644 to 1653.

The route from London to Berwick had been established by 1509, and a century later there were five other principal routes for the post, to Kent, Chester, the West, Bristol and Yarmouth. By this time there were twenty stages on the Great North Road, and a further two between Berwick and Edinburgh, at Haddington and Cocksburnpath. It was calculated that footpost carrying letters to Scotland would average 16–18 miles per day, and therefore it would take two months before a reply could be received back in London. The projected new service would average 120 miles in twenty-four hours, and a reply could be had from Scotland in six days. This was in fact wildly optimistic as the shortest route between London and Berwick is 340 miles, and, to achieve the desired turnaround, the messenger would have had to ride twenty-four hours a day.[12] There is evidence in the Duke of Northumberland's papers that post from London to Alnwick took twelve days in 1648: the letter written from London by Hugh Potter, Secretary to the Earl of Northumberland, on 20 February was received by the Earl's agent in the north, Robert Watson, on 4 March, and another written by him on 5 December was delivered in Alnwick on the 17th of that month.[13]

Although travel, and the organisation of the official post, was disrupted during the war, the service still existed (e.g. Prideaux was asked to alter the stages between Conway and Holyhead in July 1648[14]), but at the suggested speed it cannot have been used for urgent military reports and instructions. Although the government, whether royal or Parliamentary, was always keen to have a monopoly on collection and delivery of post, in order to control it, individuals were still able to send letters by private messenger or carrier, and the stages could be used by them.

Many of the reports of action in the north would be carried by the ordinary post; newsbooks and 'separates' record this: 'by Post came letters from the north'. They also mention when there had been an interruption to the post: *Packets of Letters*, no. 16 contained letters only from Manchester and Stamford as those from Edinburgh, Berwick, Newcastle and York had been intercepted by 'the Cavaliers that took Lincoln', and later that month: 'the Northern letters sent from London were intercepted near Stamford in Lincolnshire, by a scouting party of Royalists'. The weather could also be a problem: at the beginning of February 1649: 'Letters from the North (by reason of the Frost and Snow) were somewhat longer coming than usual.'[15]

Urgent messages, such as reports of major military manoeuvres and the accompanying need for reinforcements, would be carried by special messenger, and there are records of payment to them by way of rewarding good news. The first report of Rossiter's action at Willoughby Fields on 5 July, brought by a Mr Weaver, reached Derby House on 8 July, but Captain Charles Norwood appears to have delivered an official 'narrative' which he was asked to put in writing, and to arrange for it to be printed. For this he was paid £100.[16] The official account was ordered to be printed the same day and dated 11th in the imprint.[17]

Although it took place further from London, the victory at Preston was of far greater significance than the nearer fight at Willoughby Fields, so that efforts were made to take the news to Parliament as quickly as possible. One of the first reports of the defeat of the Scots, a short letter dated 17 August written by Cromwell to the Lancashire Committee and enclosed in a letter dated the 19th from W. L. (probably William Langton, MP for Preston), was published by order of Parliament on the 22nd (*TT* E460/16). According to the pamphlet published by Robert Ibbitson, the Commons had received this letter on the 21st, and Thomason had a copy the following day (*TT* E460/17). Cromwell wrote a much fuller account on the 20th to William Lenthall, the Speaker of the Commons. This was seen by the Committee of both Houses two days later, and published by order of the Commons assembled in Parliament,[18] with the imprint of 23 August 1648. There is no manuscript date. The

Lords ordered that the letter be printed and published on the 23rd; no day or month is given in the imprint but 24 August is noted in manuscript on the title page.[19] Major James Berry (later major-general) received £200, and Edward Sexby (the agitator and conspirator) £100 for taking the letter to London. Cromwell refers to sending up 'this gentleman' with the letter, but the importance of the despatch would require two riders to ensure safe delivery, and Sexby, who was said to have left the army by this time, must have been available and asked, or volunteered, to accompany Berry.[20]

The distance from Warrington to London is 190 miles. The 20th was a day of rest after the fighting, and it might reasonably be assumed that the letter would have been ready for the courier by midday. It is recorded as having been seen at Derby House on the 22nd, as the last item in the day's business, perhaps arriving at the end of the day, in which case its transmission would have taken two and a half days, with an average of 75–80 miles a day. But a letter from Maidstone written on 2 June 1648 was received by Derby House the following day.[21] The speed of military despatches is not relevant to the speed of the post.

Parliament and its various committees had a team of messengers, although it is not clear whether these took letters all the way to their destination or were responsible only for sending them out of London. The letter concerning the taking of Pembroke and Cromwell's march north was 'sent' to Lambert by Mr Bulmer. But 'what other occurrences are here you will be informed of by Capt Lister', who had delivered to Derby House a paper concerning the needs of the Northern Army.[22] The Committee of both Houses wrote to Hesilrige with an enclosure 'formerly sent to you by an express to be forwarded to Col. Lambert' and the instruction to send the enclosed, 'being a matter of great consequence', if he is 'in doubt whether the former Bulmer has come to him safe'.[23]

Other letters were 'sent by the post', as when Derby House wrote to Rossiter and the County Committees of Northampton, Leicester, Rutland, Nottinghamshire and Derby with information on the enemy's taking of Lincoln. All were sent to Grantham, those to the County Committees specifically to Mr Bury there.[24] In *Some Civil War Accounts, 1647–1650* there are several entries in 1648 detailing money paid out for messengers, individuals riding post, and the carrying of letters, ranging from 1s. 6d. paid to a post boy on 21 March to £8 disbursed to Mr Rich. Winsmore for 'letters out of Wales' on 26 July.[25] Robert Watson notes in a postscript to his letter dated 7 March 1648 to Hugh Potter that previous letters from London were 'a weeke retarded, and lay at New castle at the poast house there who alledgeth because they were not payed above'.[26]

Provision was made for sending less urgent official government messages by the ordinary post free of charge. In this case the sender was required to put his name on the outside of the letter, and we have evidence of this in the correspondence sent in early 1649 from Pontefract by John Baynes to his cousin Adam. In each case, below John's name on the verso of the folio is written '*nihil*' (no charge), although not all the content would seem to be official.[27]

Rushworth

Another source of information for the period is the final volume of *Historical Collections* compiled by John Rushworth. As secretary to Thomas Fairfax since 1645, he would have had access to the proceedings and correspondence of Parliament and the army, but like Thomason he collected newsbooks and pamphlets and it is principally upon these that his 'collections' are based, with connecting text and comment. The relevant volume for 1648, no. 7, was published in 1701, eleven years after Rushworth's death. Although the title page states that it had been 'fitted for the Press in his Life-time', the volume lacks the personal preface of earlier volumes, and it is not clear whether the editorial comments are by Rushworth or some later, unknown editor.[28] In the case of the letter from Bowes dated 19 July and quoted above, we cannot be sure whether he had sight of the original letter or took the text from the newsbook or pamphlet. His account of the action at Preston is the text, with minor differences such as the use of figures rather than words for numbers, to be found in *The Perfect Diurnall of some Passages in Parliament*, no. 265, 21–28 August (*TT* E525/21), presumably the newsbook recommended by Francis Thorpe, above. This is a shortened version of Cromwell's letter of 20 August, yet another précis of which is found in *Perfect Occurrences of Every Daies iournall in Parliament*, no. 86, 18–25 August (*TT* E525/20).

One might expect Rushworth to have relied on his own knowledge when writing his *Collections*. He had been involved in the delivery of messages from before the first Civil War; in August 1641 he made a complaint against the postmaster at Ware for not supplying him with horses when he was carrying a letter from the House of Lords to York with instructions for 'the speedy disbandment of the army', and he was 'forced to go some distance on foot carrying his saddle'.[29] In June and July 1648 he was in Colchester with Fairfax, and is recorded as sending information to Derby House. It may be that the letter from 'a Person of Credit' in Maidstone on 2 June, the text of which is given in full in the *Collections*, and described as 'not before Published', was written by him, but only a short précis is given of one from Colchester written on 6 July and another to Speaker Lenthall on the 15th describing action in the town.[30] Gualter Frost, co-secretary to the Committee of both Houses at Derby House, had been instructed on 3 June 1648 to 'communicate any intelligence he receives from time to time to Mr Rushworth'. As with other contemporary accounts, Rushworth's description of the events of the second Civil War may offer additional detail but much of it may simply be copied or edited from other sources.

Diaries and personal accounts

The only known surviving diary of an officer is that of Major John Sanderson, which is generally very accurate although there are occasional slips as to days and dates. Sanderson's detailed 'relation' of the battle of Preston, written on 20 August, is also informative, but he says that Langdale himself fled north with his cavalry whereas he is known to have rejoined Hamilton.[31] This letter, the only known copy being with the Clarke Papers in Worcester College, Oxford, was addressed to his father and printed, presumably in the north of England, where William Clarke may have acquired his copy. It appears not to have found its way into any of the newsbooks or pamphlets printed and published in London. Sanderson's letter describing the events of 1 July was, however, reported in the London press as the first letter in the newsbook, dated 3 July, with his full name given.[32]

Captain John Hodgson's *Memoir* has some very useful information, but it was written long after the events and contains a number of errors. The fighting at Appleby is described as Hamilton catching Lambert's rearguard while the latter was retreating, whereas Lambert had actually been at Appleby for three days. He gives the opening of the battle of Preston on 17 August as 'about 20 August'. Carlyle rightly described the publication as 'left full of blunders, of darkness natural and adscititious'.[33]

Captain Samuel Birch left what is usually, but incorrectly, referred to as a 'diary'. It is in fact a record of his service in the Lancashire Militia regiment of Colonel Ashton, written by Birch in April 1650 on his leaving the army, as a justification of either his expenditure or his service. A partial transcript was published in 1894,[34] and that part dealing with his marches on active service, which has been checked against the original manuscript, appears in appendix 4. A peculiarity is that the marginal dates do not always tie in directly to the text of the journal. In a number of places words are inserted above the line: for example, 4 November: 'they receive a months pay ^from Cap. West^ out of ye 4700ˡⁱ'.[35] The insertion may have been omitted in error while copying from a diary, or may have been added from memory after writing the sentence. If from memory, was this correct, and have other additions been made during the writing as part of the text?

A major source for the siege of Pontefract are the records of Captain Thomas Paulden, a Royalist who was in the castle garrison for almost all of the siege. He probably left two versions, one written in the form of a letter in March 1702, the other account, almost certainly by him, of unknown date. They are referred to in the text as Letter and Account. Both have errors of date, and differ in significant details, as will be seen in the chronological text, Chapters 3 and 9. Richard Holmes, the nineteenth-century Pontefract historian who published both texts, excuses errors and variations of time and place between the two versions, partly because of his very strong bias in favour of the Royalist cause and partly on the grounds that Paulden had a 'disregard of accuracy in matters not dealing with military details'. The real reason is probably simpler: Paulden wrote the Letter at the age of seventy-eight, looking back more than fifty years. However, most of the events Paulden describes are also covered by contemporary reports and it is unlikely that he will have deliberately falsified events although hindsight may have added a rosier glow than was always justified.

Reliability of sources
All sources of information on the second Civil War need to be treated with some caution. As indicated in 'Intelligence' (see p. xxvi), poor communication in an age without modern technology was one of the chief causes of lack of, or incorrect, information, whether local or national. Two conflicting reports of the negotiations for a treaty at Pontefract are given in *The Moderate*, no. 36, 13–20 March 1649 (*TT* E548/2), but the editor of the newsbook 'knowing my first Intelligence true' was prepared to believe that the treaty would be broken off if there was no agreement before night, rather than the second report that the castle had surrendered to mercy. *The Perfect Weekly Account* [no. 53], 14–21 March 1949 (*TT* E548/10) has only the first report, written in the third person. Uncertainty is evident in no. 14 of the same title, which mentions a letter 'produced from a private hand in the North' with news of a fight between Langdale and Lambert, the victory going to Lambert's forces, with Langdale wounded and Lambert slain: 'the grounds of this relation are but slender (no packet coming this week) therefore I shall leave the certainty hereof till we receive the next packet'.[36]

There were also the deliberate attempts to misinform, either for positive or negative reasons. *Three Letters out of the North to Friends here in London* (*TT* E452/13, printed 12 July) has a letter from York declaring: 'We are full of good news, Langdale shattered to pieces, Pontefract routed . . .' Later in July, it was falsely rumoured that: 'Major Gen. Lambert is totally routed, and that he hath lost 17. Foot Cullers, and 9. of Horse.' Another letter in the same pamphlet gave Colonel Lilburne as the victim, suggesting that he had lost '27. prisoners, 50. horse and two Cullers'.[37] There is no truth in either account. Much more blatant and scurrilous is the anti-Parliament propaganda in the Royalist 'mercuries', of which a large number were published in 1648. Several of these are quoted in the text (e.g. chapter 4, n. 10; chapter 5, n. 7). Typical of the Royalist press is the false report in the issue of *Mercurius Psiticus* quoted above: '. . . goodman Lambert is cleare routed by Sir Marmaduke Langdale, bag and baggage, Luke Poison beard will needs have Sir Marmaduke Langdale to have lost all. Sirrah, know Lambert is a certainly routed and slain, as ever thou preached out of the pillory.' Further examples can be found in two reports on Cromwell's victory at Preston – a letter from Manchester reports: 'a glorious mock-Victorie gain'd upon the Scottish Army, by Nol magnificent, the contents you have already in print, the truth thereof remains invisible . . .'[38] The writer of *Mercurius Fidelicus*, no. 1, 17–24 August 1648 (*TT* E660/32) claims that the 'Relation of a great fight in Lancashire between the Scots and Cromwell' is false, because, as he was writing the book, he received a letter from a friend in Lancashire dated 20 August who assured him that there had been no such fight as

Appendix 1

Cromwell dared not engage with Callander, Hamilton and Langdale who were now 30,000 strong. The report ends typically, with a poem:

> And Cromwell flyes and dare not stand the shot
> Of loyall Langdale and the bonny Scot
> For if he doe, they'll make his Saints to feele
> The power of Blew caps, with the rod of steele.

Interesting though these anti-Parliament publications are, they contain little genuine news, as these extracts show, and less use has been made of them as sources for the text of this book. More reliable, if dull in comparison, are the pro-Parliament pamphlets and periodicals.

Appendix 2

THE CASTLES CAPTURED, OCCUPIED OR OTHERWISE MENTIONED IN THE TEXT

Alnwick
The second largest inhabited castle in England, it was begun in the eleventh century and has been much modified and added to since. As the principal seat of the Percy family, it was never allowed to decay as were many other castles. Colonel Bright, Major Sanderson and others were based there intermittently during the early part of 1648, but it does not seem to have been held by a permanent garrison at that time.

Appleby
Dating from the eleventh to fifteenth centuries, Appleby Castle was one of the largest in the northwest. It was held by the Scots for forty years in the twelfth century, and in the fifteenth century was deliberately damaged to prevent further occupation. It seems to have been in a dilapidated state by the start of the Civil War, but was sufficiently strong to withstand several sieges.

Barnard Castle
This was a very large, strong castle dating from the twelfth century. In the thirteenth century two of its four baileys were abandoned, but it was still in a condition to withstand a siege in the sixteenth century. In the early seventeenth century it was at least partly unroofed to provide materials for work on Raby Castle, but it was able to provide some shelter and accommodation during the Civil War. Lambert probably used the castle rather than the town as his headquarters in June and July 1648.

Bowes
The castle was built in the mid-1130s in the northwest corner of the Roman fort of *Lavatris*, 300 yards north of the river Greta, and stands alongside the Roman road from Scotch Corner to Carlisle (A66). It was strengthened and rebuilt by Henry II in the 1170s against raids from Scotland; his keep is the only major part now visible, and there may never have been a curtain wall. In the early fourteenth century the castle had outlived its usefulness, and had become very ruinous. In the mid-seventeenth century the keep may have provided shelter. It was briefly used as a guard post as part of the watch on Stainmore in late July 1648.

Brough
The castle was begun in the late eleventh century and occupied the northern part of the Roman fort of *Verteris*, which lies just to the south of the Swindale Beck. The castle is nearly half a mile south of the Roman road (now A66) and stands in Church Brough. This planned village did not prosper and in the late twelfth century the centre of population moved north to the Roman road where the present

(Market) Brough was established. Major rebuilding and modernising of the castle were carried out in the early fourteenth century, but a serious fire in 1521 made it uninhabitable. By the mid-seventeenth century it was not defensible and was not occupied by either side.

Brougham

The northwest part of the Roman fort of *Brocavum*, on the Roman road to Carlisle (A66), was used as the site for the castle in the early thirteenth century. It was greatly extended and improved in the late thirteenth century, and again in the 1380s, but was almost immediately sacked by the Scots. By the time of the Civil War the castle was in poor condition and probably in no state to withstand a siege. It was surrendered to Lambert as soon as summoned in June 1648.

Cartington

This was begun in the fourteenth century as a defended enclosure, and by the mid-fifteenth century it had a large tower in the northeast corner, with a hall and solar alongside. It was by no means a strong, or even a true, castle, but was held by the Royalists at the beginning of May and the end of July 1648; after the former occupation, the 'house', perhaps the hall, was dismantled by the Parliamentary forces.

Cockermouth

The castle was rebuilt in stone in the thirteenth century at the confluence of rivers Derwent and Cocker, and extended in the fourteenth century. In September 1645 the then owner, the earl of Northumberland, twice described it as 'neither strong nor useful' but this was said in opposition to a proposal to put a Scottish garrison into it. After the siege it was probably partially slighted, and by 1688 only the gatehouse and the courthouse were habitable. There was some rebuilding in the nineteenth century.

Greystoke

A fourteenth-century fortified house and earlier pele tower. Lambert's forces occupied it in June 1648 without a fight, but it was almost all demolished by Parliament after the war. Most of the present house dates from the eighteenth and nineteenth centuries.

Harbottle

The building of this once strategically important castle began in the twelfth century, and in the thirteenth century it had a stone keep and two baileys. In the sixteenth century there was some refurbishment, with a small garrison placed in it in 1564, but by 1604 it was described as 'an old castle much decayed'. Its brief occupation by Sir Gilbert Errington in 1648 was probably more of a token than a serious effort.

Morpeth

The castle was first built in the late eleventh century, and totally rebuilt in the thirteenth; it was never a large one. In 1644 it was garrisoned for Parliament by 500 Scots, who withstood a twenty-day siege from Royalist Scots. In the same year it was described as 'a ruinous hole, not tenable by nature far less by art'. It does not seem to have been held during the second Civil War, but may have offered shelter to passing troops. The only part of the building to survive is the fourteenth-century gatehouse, much altered in the nineteenth century.

Penrith

Major work on the castle began in the late fourteenth century, and more buildings were added during the fifteenth principally by Richard Duke of Gloucester. In the sixteenth century the gatehouses and gates were in ruins, although two of the towers and some domestic buildings were in good repair. It was not seriously defensible during the Civil War and was not garrisoned, although Major-General Lambert probably used it as his headquarters in June and July.

Pontefract

This was one of the strongest and most important castles in the north, founded on a rocky hill, which stands over thirty feet above the valleys at either side. It had two baileys: the sloped outer one on the southeast side rising in two parts, Upper and Lower, from the Pontefract–Knottingley road; and the more or less level inner bailey, the walls of which had six towers plus the keep known as the Round Tower, which was some sixty feet in diameter. In addition there was an outlying tower to the north, the Swillington Tower, connected to the castle by a stone wall. Following the first siege, which began at the end of 1644 and with a brief interlude ended in July 1645, some repairs were carried out to the castle. As soon as the final siege, which lasted from June 1648 to March 1649, was over, the castle was totally demolished at the request of the local population.

Raby

This was a heavily fortified house with several towers and walls up to ten foot thick, surrounded by a moat. It was probably in a very good state, as Sir Henry Vane had been improving it at the expense of Barnard Castle. The exterior mostly dates to the fourteenth century. It appears to have been besieged in 1648, although there is no record in the newsbooks. The Parish Register (Staindrop) says that on 27 August a soldier killed in the siege was buried in the church, and many others were buried in the park. This event may have involved those retreating after Preston, similar to the siege of Cockermouth.

Rose

Rose Castle, the principal residence of the bishops of Carlisle from the thirteenth century (to 2009), was besieged by the Scots on several occasions. At the time of the Civil War it formed a quadrangle with five towers surrounded by a curtain wall and moat, but much of it was destroyed when Major Cholmley fired it on 7 July 1648. Considerable remodelling has been done since then.

Scaleby

A small castle in a double circular moat, which was probably begun in the late thirteenth century and much rebuilt in the fifteenth century with sixteenth-century additions. It was besieged by Parliament in 1644, and again in 1645 when it was taken and seems to have been badly damaged and burnt. It was held again for the king in 1648, but surrendered after firing one shot, probably because it was in poor state.

Skipton

A strong castle dating in its present form from the fourteenth century, it was held for the king and withstood a three-year siege, which ended in 1645. Slighting was ordered, but it was briefly held again in May 1648 before being recaptured by Lambert at the beginning of June.

Appendix 2

Warkworth

A very large and strong castle, rebuilt in stone in the thirteenth century, it began to decline in the sixteenth century, accelerated by the removal of timber and other material under Elizabeth. The castle was garrisoned on Sir Arthur Hesilrige's orders at the beginning of May 1648, more to prevent a Royalist occupation than for any offensive purpose, and is said to have been further damaged in this period.

Appendix 3

BRIEF BIOGRAPHIES OF SOME SIGNIFICANT PEOPLE MENTIONED IN THE TEXT

Ralph Ashton (Assheton) (1606–1651)

Of Middleton, Lancashire, he was colonel of a foot regiment that his son Ralph took over in summer 1645. He fought in most of the first Civil War engagements, and was thanked for his services by the House of Commons in January 1645, and again after the battle of Preston. But in February 1644, as one of the Receivers of the King's Revenues, he was sent to the Tower for withholding £1,500. In 1648 he was appointed major-general/commander-in-chief of all the militia Lancashire forces, but two years later a warrant was issued for him to be brought before the Council of State on a charge of High Treason.

Robert Batten

Sometimes confused with Admiral William Batten, Robert may be the lieutenant recorded in the garrison of Portsmouth in January 1643. He was nominated as captain of Holy Island in June 1646, having been sent there with forces to guard the area from Royalist incursions by land and sea. In 1648 Langdale made unsuccessful efforts to subvert him. Nothing more is known of him.

Bethell

Colonel Hugh Bethell (1615–1679), captain of horse in the Parliamentary army by 1643, commanded a regiment in the Northern Association army at Marston Moor and Rowton Heath the following year, and was badly wounded but received £200 for his service. He was again in command of a regiment of Yorkshire horse in 1648, when he took part in the siege of Scarborough, and thereafter became governor of Scarborough Castle (c.1649–1651), and an MP in the 1650s. He also continued his military service, and assisted General Monck in bringing about the Restoration.

His cousin **Walter** served as a major in Colonel Horton's regiment in the New Model, and was present at the Army council meetings in November 1647 and December 1648. He was given £150 for his service in bringing to London the news of the victory in South Wales in May 1648.

Major Jno Bethell [name uncertain, probably John] was named as a captain of Yorkshire horse in the commissions granted by the Council of State to Officers of the Militia in August 1650. This may be another of Hugh's brothers, known as John of Skyrlaw, who died in 1652, and is perhaps the Captain Bethell, who was active in the north of England in 1648.

The summons to the governor of Scarborough in 1648 was signed by **Tho. Bethell**, according to the report in a contemporary newsbook. He has not been identified, and the name may be an editorial error.

Appendix 3

Samuel Birch (1620/21–1680)
The younger brother of Colonel John Birch, Samuel came from Manchester, matriculated at Brasenose College Oxford in 1637, and was commissioned as a captain in the Parliamentary army. In 1648 he served in the regiment of Ralph Ashton junior, which was disbanded at the end of March 1650, after which he composed his record of service. He left 'when he found things were run to extremity' and returned to Oxford. He subsequently entered the ministry but was ejected in 1662, and three years later had opened a school for the sons of dissenter parents, where several future government ministers seem to have been educated. He continued teaching until just before his death.

Colonel Boynton (d. 1651)
Matthew Boynton, second son of Parliamentarian Sir Matthew Boynton of Burton Agnes, Yorkshire, fought for Parliament until he changed sides when governor of Scarborough Castle in 1648. The following year he was banished from England as an enemy and traitor, and excluded from the royal court in Scotland in 1650. He died in action at Wigan Lane in 1651.

Colonel Bright (bap. 1619; d. 1688)
Of humble Yorkshire origins, John Bright soon emerged as a leading Parliamentarian in the West Riding. Early in 1645 he became a colonel under Ferdinando, Lord Fairfax, and fought in several major engagements. In 1648 he was a colonel in the Northern Army under his brother-in-law John Lambert. He opposed the execution of the king, and resigned his commission in 1650 under some small pretext but probably because he was against the invasion of Scotland. The following year he served as a colonel of militia to repel the Scottish advance in to England. He supported Lambert in the late 1650s but at the Restoration devoted himself to his private affairs.

Cholmley
Sir Henry Cholmley (1608–1666) was a member of the cadet branch of the Cheshire family of Cholmondeley. He was commissioned a colonel in a Yorkshire-trained band that fought at Edgehill in September 1642. Elected MP for Malton in 1641, he was a JP in the West Riding 1642–1648 and on a number of local committees. In 1642–1644 and 1648 he was colonel of a Parliamentary foot regiment, and had charge of the third siege of Pontefract until October. He died in Tangier after going to deputise for his nephew as superintendent of the harbour works there.

His elder brother **Sir Hugh (1600–1657)** initially supported Parliament, and defended Scarborough against the Royalists, but sickened by the effect of the Civil War he changed sides in 1643 and held the town for the king for five months in 1645. Thereafter he fled to France, returning to his home in Whitby only in 1649.

There is no apparent connection between this family and that of **Major Cholmley** of Lilburne's, who came from Carlisle.

Fairfax
Ferdinando, 2nd Lord Fairfax of Cameron **(1584–1648)**, MP for Boroughbridge in the 1620s and for Yorkshire in the Long Parliament, commanded the Parliamentary forces in Yorkshire, and was governor of Hull 1643–1644 and of York 1644–1645. He commanded the infantry at Marston Moor, where his younger son Charles was killed.

His elder son **Thomas (1612–1671)** was knighted in 1640 and inherited his father's title in 1648. In 1645 he was appointed commander-in-chief of the New Model army. He supported the army in its demands for pay and punishment of the king, but was opposed to the execution, and resigned from the army because of his antipathy to the invasion of Scotland in 1650.

Colonel Charles Fairfax (1597–1673), younger brother of Ferdinando, was taken prisoner by the Royalists in the first Civil War but was rescued. He was commissioned as a colonel in 1648 and took a major part in the siege of Pontefract. The regiment is often quite wrongly said to have taken part in the battle of Preston; it was the Lord General's regiment of foot which was there. He later served in Scotland under Monck.

Lady Fairfax of Gilling was probably Alethea, granddaughter of William Howard of Naworth, and wife of Thomas, 2nd Viscount Fairfax of Emly (d. 1641), a member of the senior branch of the family, descended from Richard Fairfax of Walton who died in 1432. This branch on the whole remained Catholic, whereas the branch to which Ferdinando and his family belonged became Protestant.

Colonel George Fenwick (c.1603–1657)

Originally from Brinkburn in Northumberland, he went to New England in 1636 and set up Saybrook Fort where he served as *de facto* governor till 1644. He then returned to England and was elected MP for Morpeth the following year. In 1648 he commanded a regiment of northern militia, took part in the defeat of Sir Richard Tempest, relieved Holy Island and recaptured Fenham Castle. On the surrender of Berwick he became governor, apparently as Heselrige's deputy whose daughter Catherine he married as his second wife. Appointed a commissioner for the trial of the king he refused to act. In 1650 he took part in Cromwell's invasion of Scotland and was made governor of Leith and Edinburgh Castle in December. He served as MP for Berwick 1654 and 1656.

Sir Thomas Glemham (1595–1649)

Born in Suffolk, where he became a JP and deputy lieutenant, he at first pursued a military career abroad. As a Royalist army officer in the first Civil War, noted for his ability to defend besieged towns, he was governor of York in 1642 and 1644, defended Carlisle against the Scots in 1644/1645, and became governor of Oxford in October 1645. He was seen in Edinburgh at the beginning of April 1648 and assisted Musgrave in capturing Carlisle for the king at the end of the month, but appears to have taken no further part in the war, and went into exile in France where he died the following year.

Colonel Harrison (bap. 1616; d. 1660)

Thomas Harrison first enlisted in the Parliamentary army in 1642, and joined the New Model when it was founded in 1645. He sided with the army in 1647 and opposed further negotiation with the king. A Puritan, he became a leader of the Fifth Monarchists in the 1650s, and continued his military command. Having initially had Cromwell's friendship and support, they fell out when Harrison was suspected of involvement in plots against him and the state. He was executed as a regicide in October 1660.

Sir Arthur Hesilrige (1601–1661)

MP for Leicestershire, he was one of the five members whom Charles I tried to arrest in 1642. Having raised a troop of horse in October of that year, he played a full part in military and political developments during the Civil Wars. In December 1647 he was appointed governor of Newcastle with overall charge of the forces in northeast England, where he amassed a personal fortune through the purchase of sequestered estates. He did not support the trial of the king, but returned to Parliament thereafter, and then became a bitter opponent of Cromwell when the Rump was dissolved in 1653.

John Hodgson (1617/18–1684)

A native of Yorkshire and Parliamentary army office, he is best known for his autobiography. In 1642 he was an ensign, and two years later was in Bright's regiment and served at the siege of Pontefract in 1645. He took a prominent part in the merger of the Northern Association army into the New Model in 1647, and as a lieutenant was in the forlorn of foot with Major Pownall at Preston the following year. He continued in the army until 1659 when, as a supporter of Lambert, he refused to join Monck in Scotland. His memoirs may have been written in response to the persecution he suffered after the Restoration.

Sir Marmaduke Langdale (1598–1661)

A Royalist army officer in the Civil Wars, after attending St John's College Cambridge, he fought in the service of the Queen of Bohemia. Knighted in February 1628, High Sheriff of Yorkshire in 1639 and appointed Commissioner of Array in June 1642, he was commissioned colonel and defeated the Covenanter cavalry at Corbridge in February 1644. He then formed the Northern Horse from the remnants of the Earl of Newcastle's army, and relieved Pontefract in March 1645. Following defeats he went to France but returned to Britain in 1648 to lead English forces in support of the invading Scots. He was captured after Preston but escaped, fled abroad again and was in the Venetian service by 1652. In 1660 he returned to England, and died a year later.

Francis Lascelles (Lassels) (1612–1667)

Born at Stank, Northallerton, he was admitted to Gray's Inn in 1628, and paid a £10 fine for refusing a knighthood. Appointed a JP in 1642, he was MP for Thirsk (1645), Yorkshire (1653) and the North Riding (1654 and 1656), and served on the Assessment Committees for Yorkshire and the North Riding, but devoted most of his time to military duties, serving first as a captain of foot (late 1642), and eventually as colonel, at Selby, Guisborough, Skipton, Helmsley, Bolton Castle and both sieges of Scarborough. He was with Lambert at Preston in 1648. Although a Parliamentary radical, he refused to sign the king's death warrant.

Lilburne

Robert (bap. 1614; d. 1665) was the elder brother of **John**, the noted Leveller. He served first with the Earl of Essex's army in 1642, then having raised a regiment of horse in his home county, Durham, he was in the Northern Association army the following year. In 1646 he was put in command of the Kentish New Model regiment, which refused to follow him north when he was appointed governor of Newcastle in August 1647. That year he was involved in the petitions of the army against serving in Ireland. Following his service in the north in 1648, as colonel of a regiment of horse, he was one of the signatories of the king's death warrant, and became commander-in-chief of the English forces in Scotland until May 1654, when he was made governor of York. He was a deputy to Lambert during the rule of the major-generals. At the Restoration he surrendered as a regicide, was imprisoned in October 1660 and died in prison.

The youngest brother **Henry (1618–1648)** was a cavalry colonel, who served under his brother at the second siege of Skipton in late 1645, when he saw many defections from his troop. On 9 August

1648, when governor of Tynemouth Castle, he defected to the king, and was killed in the recapture of the castle by Hesilrige two days later.

Captain Thomas (bap. 1621/2; bur. 1665) of Lilburne's, was their cousin. He was one of the many attorneys for the purchase of Crown lands on behalf of various regiments after the end of the second Civil War.

Thomas Margetts (c.1620–1691)
The son of Thomas and Dinah Margetts of Bedford, Thomas, according to his own testimony in 1659, was clerk to the Irish Committee from 1642 until 1645, then to Judge Advocate Dr John Mills, until in 1647 he was appointed Judge Advocate to the Northern Army, and became Lambert's secretary. As such he was the source of many valuable letters and news reports. He was given £50 for taking to London the news of the surrender of Pontefract, but his correspondence with Adam Baynes usually contained requests for money, and in March 1658 Margetts 'being now eight months in arrear' petitioned the Council of State for three months' pay, which was approved the following month. When his duties allowed, he returned to Bedford where he had property in St Peter's parish. He served on local committees and represented the town in Richard Cromwell's Parliament. In June 1659 he was nominated as Judge Advocate for Scotland, but refused on the grounds of ill-health. However his petition failed and ten days later his appointment was confirmed. His will, written in 1688, names his wife Elizabeth, son Thomas and four daughters.

Colonel John Mauleverer (c.1610–1650)
Of Letwall, Yorkshire, at the start of the Civil War he sided with Fairfax, who commissioned him as a colonel. In July 1643 he was captured by Royalists at Bradford, but escaped or was exchanged, and was put in charge of the Hull garrison the following year. After service at Pontefract in 1648, he went to Scotland with Cromwell's army in 1650 and died in Edinburgh in December of that year.

Sir Philip Monckton (1622–1679)
Captain in a trained band regiment and Commissioner for Array in Yorkshire in 1642, he had joined the cavalry by June 1643, and fought at Marston Moor. Knighted for his gallantry at Corbridge in February 1644, the following June he was with Langdale's Northern Horse at Naseby, and commanded it at Rowton Heath in September that year. In May 1646 he compounded but was in arms again in 1648. With 600 men from Pontefract he took the bishop's palace at Lincoln but was captured at Willoughby Field by Colonel Edward Rossiter (q.v.), who wrote to Fairfax recommending mercy. Monckton was thus able to go overseas where he remained until December 1651.

Sir George Monro (d. 1694)
Having joined the Scottish regiment of the Swedish army, he returned to Scotland in August 1640 and was appointed lieutenant-colonel in the Scottish army commanded by his uncle Robert, which was sent to Ireland in 1642. He was commissioned as major-general of the forces to be sent back to Scotland to support the Engagers in 1648. After the defeat at Preston he wanted to return to Ireland but was forced to disband, and fled abroad, returning to Ireland the following January. His allegiance was suspect as his second wife was an Irish Presbyterian, but he continued to be called for military service, and became MP for Ross-shire just before his death.

Appendix 3

Lieutenant-Colonel John Morris (c.1615–1649)

Born near Pontefract, he was brought up in the household of the future Earl of Strafford, and was an ensign in his foot regiment. By January 1642 he was serving as a major in Ireland. He returned to England to join the Royalist army, but changed sides in November 1644 after the Parliamentary army captured Liverpool. Refused a command in the New Model, he changed sides again and took Pontefract Castle for the Royalists in 1648. When the castle finally surrendered in 1649, he was one of the 'excepted' who escaped, but was captured, imprisoned in Lancaster Castle and executed in August that year.

Sir Philip Musgrave (1607–1678)

Committed Royalist and strict Anglican, he was a JP and deputy lieutenant of Cumberland and Westmorland, captain of Trained Bands, and MP for Westmorland in the Long and Short Parliaments. At the outbreak of the Civil War he became commander-in-chief of the Royalist force in Cumberland and Westmorland, but had difficulty in persuading the forces to fight outwith the county boundaries. They did, however, capture Carlisle at the end of April 1648, and he went to Edinburgh to negotiate with the Scots. He did not serve at Preston, but after the defeat he and his forces went to Appleby, where they capitulated on 9 October. He left England after the king's death, then went to the Isle of Man, where he was governor for a short time. He returned to England at the Restoration, and became governor of Carlisle.

Paulden

Timothy (1622–?1651), Thomas (1625–1702/10) and **William (1628–1649)** were from Wakefield, and came to prominence in the Royalist garrison at Pontefract in 1648. On hearing of the Scots' plans to invade England in 1648, they enlisted 300 foot and fifty horse from among their disbanded colleagues and, with Colonel Morris, hatched the plot to seize Pontefract for the king. **Thomas,** captain of foot, who may have been the Captain Paulden captured at Naseby, served throughout the siege, which he survived. After the surrender in 1649, he went into exile with Prince Charles, but secretly visited England several times in the 1650s. He finally returned in 1660, and died in poverty sometime between 1702 and 1710, leaving two accounts of the siege of Pontefract.

William, captain of horse, died of fever in Pontefract Castle in February 1649. **Timothy**, also captain of horse, left his brothers after the failed attempt on the castle in May and went off to join Langdale. Thomas says that he was killed at Wigan fighting under the Earl of Derby, which *ODNB* places in 1648. However, there is no record of the earl taking part in the second Civil War, and Timothy's death is more likely to have taken place in 1651, when Colonel Robert Lilburne defeated the earl at Wigan on 25 August.

Colonel Thomas Rainsborough (Rainborow, Rainsborowe) (d. 1648)

The son of William Rainsborough, an officer in the king's navy, Thomas also went to sea, but after serving in the navy guarding the Irish Sea to prevent Irish volunteers joining the Royalist army in the north of England he transferred to the army during the fighting at Hull in October 1643. He was appointed colonel in the New Model army and fought at Naseby, and the several sieges including Bristol, Sherborne, Oxford and Worcester. In 1646 he was elected MP for Droitwich but continued to play a major role in the army, siding with the radicals the following year, and with his regiment when it mutinied. Appointed vice-admiral in September 1647, but initially refused permission to go to sea by the House of Commons, he finally began a disastrous five-month command on 1 January

1648. He then returned to the army and saw the end of the siege of Colchester before being sent to take command at the siege of Pontefract in October. When the incumbent there, Sir Henry Cholmley (q.v.), refused to leave, Rainsborough retired to Doncaster, and was killed on 29th by a Royalist group who had hopes of exchanging him for Sir Marmaduke Langdale (q.v.).

Thomas Reade

Nothing is known about him other than the detail given in his narrative concerning the Scots invasion of England in 1648. He is not to be confused with the Royalist army officer and civil lawyer, nor with the Parliamentary colonel of the same name. A Mr Read was added to the Commission of Assessors in November 1643, which might confirm his assertion that he was involved in army disbanding. In early 1648 he was forced to flee from London, took ship to Scotland, and became secretary to the English Commissioners in Edinburgh, while apparently being in communication also with the Scottish Royalists and Callander.

Edward Rossiter (Rosseter) (1618–1669)

A Parliamentarian and staunch Presbyterian, he was distantly related to Cromwell. Major in 1644, he was appointed colonel of a regiment of horse in the New Model army. The regiment, being local to Lincolnshire, was very active there and in the neighbouring counties during the first Civil War, and was present at Naseby. Rossiter lost his command in 1647, being succeeded by his major, Philip Twistleton, but he saw service again in 1648, when he was ordered, on 3 June, to secure the ferry boat at Chelsea and to provide a troop of 120 horse 'for the guard of Parliament'. Two days later he was put in command of the forces at Stamford, and ordered down to Lincolnshire. When the forces from Pontefract under Sir Philip Monckton (q.v.) were routed at Willoughby field on 5 July, Rossiter was 'shott in the buttocks'. MP for Great Grimsby in 1646, he abstained after Pride's Purge, but represented Lincolnshire in 1654, 1656, 1659 and 1660. That year he interrupted the night of his second wedding to take part in the operations against Lambert.

Major John Sanderson (1616?–1650)

John may have served in the Parliamentary army as early as 1642. By 1647 he was active as a major of horse on his home ground in the north of England, and wrote a diary of his duties the following year and a 'relation' of the battle of Preston when serving as a captain in Lilburne's. In 1649 he worked as a regimental attorney for the purchase of crown lands. Full details of his life and transcripts of all his known writings are given in Hill and Watkinson.

Major George Smithson (b. c.1620; d. after August 1665)

Of Moulton, Yorkshire, he married in 1653 Eleanor, daughter of Sir Charles Fairfax. As a major in the Parliamentary army he served under Sir Thomas Fairfax (q.v.) in Lincolnshire in 1643, and probably fought in the campaign in the west when Fairfax was ordered to march to the relief of Taunton. He was at Preston in Lilburne's in 1648 and Parliament him awarded £100 for his good service there. Returned as MP for the North Riding in 1654, he appears not to have been involved in the work of local committees, but played a significant part in the Restoration.

Major Archibald Strachan (d. 1652)

Born in Scotland, Archibald joined Waller's army in 1642 but was excluded by the Self-Denying Ordinance and returned north to join the army of the Solemn League and Covenant. In 1648 he liaised with Cromwell on Argyll's behalf. He professed to be against the English invasion of Scotland in 1650 while secretly corresponding with Cromwell. He and Gilbert Kerr, whose regiment of horse he joined early in 1649, became the leaders of the Covenanters in southwest Scotland.

Major Thimbleby

The Thimblebys were a prominent Catholic family in Lincolnshire in the seventeenth century. John of Irnham's son **John** (bap. 20 February 1567/8) married Mary, daughter of Charles Jackson of Snydale in Yorkshire, and had eight sons, the eldest being **Charles** (aged twenty-three in 1612) who begged to compound in 1653 and was fined £2,053. The younger John petitioned to compound in June 1646. It is likely that he and his son John are the Thimblebys listed as volunteers for the defence of Pontefract in the first siege. In November 1648 Major Thimbleby of Snidale (probably the younger John or one of his brothers) was included in the list of those ineligible to receive a share of the £3,000 paid to Yorkshire soldiers as he was reported to have been a delinquent in the 'late insurrection', probably because he served in the garrison at Pontefract.

John Wastell (c.1593–1659)

Born at Scorton in Yorkshire, he was admitted to Sidney Sussex College Cambridge in 1611 and Gray's Inn two years later. He followed a legal career in his native county, being elected Recorder of Ripon in 1626, and of Richmond in 1631, and was MP for Northallerton in the Long and Rump Parliaments. During the Civil War he accepted a commission as colonel, and in the first Civil War served under Lord Leven and Lord Fairfax (q.v.) in the north of England. In the second Civil War he commanded a regiment of foot, which was disbanded in May 1649.

Edward Wogan (d. 1654)

Having been born in Ireland to an English Protestant family, Edward may have been sent to live with relatives in Wales when the Ulster rebellion broke out in 1641. He was commissioned as a captain in Okey's Dragoons in 1645 and, following the king's flight to the Isle of Wight in 1647, he was sent to Wales to await disbanding. He preferred to continue as a soldier, and in March 1648 took his men to Edinburgh to join the Engager army. He does not appear to have fought at Preston, but fled to Ireland after the defeat, then to France in 1650. He was back in Scotland the following year, a colonel of horse in 1653, and died of a sword wound in a minor skirmish near Loch Earn.

Colonel Francis Wren (d. 1684)

Francis was the son of the Parliamentary supporter Francis Wren of Henknoll, County Durham, and nephew of Sir Charles Wren of Binchester, a noted Royalist. He was colonel of a horse regiment under the command of Ferdinando, Lord Fairfax (q.v.), by April 1646. James Fawcett of Goswick, four miles from Berwick, claimed in 1651 that he was unable to pay the fine imposed on him six years earlier as his estate had been wasted by the coming and going of the cavaliers, the Scots army and Cromwell's forces, and Colonel Wren's regiment, which had plundered him of all he had – which was £300. A member of the Committee for Compounding in Durham, Francis was appointed its treasurer in May 1650, and in this capacity received the £150 fine of his cousin, Lindley Wren of Binchester, in January 1651. Later that year, he commented on the wide area that he and his fellow committee member had to cover, and the difficulty of transferring the rents collected, amounting to £3,000, to London 'as we live so far remote'.

Appendix 4

CAPTAIN BIRCH'S ACCOUNT
OF HIS SERVICE AND HIS DIARY

Introduction to the transcript

This is a corrected version of the transcript in the *Portland Papers*,[39] and is included for comparison with the diary of Major John Sanderson of Lilburne's regiment of horse.[40] It is treated in the same way, with the places identified by National Grid reference and the mileage marched totalled for each day.

The distances are derived from both computerised route planners and large-scale maps, with care taken to use all minor roads when appropriate; modern roads that deviate from more ancient routes have been avoided. Complete accuracy of mileage is impossible but distances probably average out to a good approximation. There is also the point, discussed in appendix 1, that Birch's record was a summary of his service written eighteen months after the event rather than a diary written up every day or two, although it may well have been based on a diary.

Mileage in the Subtotal column is entered in fractions of a mile but displayed to the nearest whole mile, and may appear to disagree with the Total column, which adds the fractions.

Birch's period of active service was from 15 May to 9 October 1648, exactly twenty-one weeks. In this time he and his company of foot marched 573 miles at an average of 11.7 miles per marching day. At the same rate of activity he would have marched 1,420 miles in a full year. This compares with 4,360 miles covered by Sanderson, a cavalryman, in the fifty weeks of his diary, which was at the rate of 20.6 miles per marching day.

Birch's account goes on to March 1649 when his company was disbanded, but his movements from 9 October 1648, when he was made governor of Appleby, are not included. The subsequent marches relate to only part of the company and seem to be more concerned with moving from quarter to quarter than with any military purpose. His later comments are given, however, as they have a bearing on the disbanding of the Lancashire militia.

Note: In the seventeenth century a superscript symbol was used to represent letter 'r' preceded by one or two vowels (er, or, our etc.), and is shown in the transcript as ᵉʳ. A letter 'p' with a line across the tail was used to represent 'per', and is shown here thus: p̶

The 'diary' of Samuel Birch

Mileage in the Subtotal column is entered in fractions of a mile, but displayed to the nearest whole mile, and may appear to disagree with the Total column which adds the fractions

Date	Day	Transcript	From	To	Miles		Grid	Notes
					Sub Tot	Daily Tot	(for To col)	
1648								
		1648, May 15, to 1650, April 2. A true and perfect account of the receipts and disbursements of Captaine Samuel Birch in relation to himselfe and Company with their Charge upon ye Countrey, marchings, freequarter, etc. since their last raysings. May 15, 1648. As followeth:						
	15	After much moneys spent and paines taken in raysing men, preparing Armes, engaging officers, etc. haveing received the second orders from ye Committee of our Countrey to march, I delivered out Armes						
	18	and march't my men from Manchester to Worsley.	Manchester	Worsley	7		SD744006	
	19	From thence to Houghton where wee quarter'd (all upon free Quarter from ye first day) till Monday, which	Worsley	Houghton	9		SD651060	if this is Westhoughton
	22	day wee march't to Wigan by ye Committee's order; And	Houghton	Wigan	3		SD580055	
June	2	there wee quarterd till wee march't away p[er]d[er] [per order], June 2d. to Euxton Burgh where wee stayd till Lord's day in the	Wigan	Euxton	9		SD555185	
	4	afternoone, at which time wee remov'd to Leyland; wee	Euxton	Leyland	4		SD540220	
	5	stayd but one night, ye next day wee marcht to Preston.	Leyland	Preston	6		SD540300	

Day	Description	From	To	Miles	Total	Grid ref	Notes
7	We march't by Quartermaster Pigotts order to Wood Plumpton, where wee stayd and passd our muster upon Haworth Moore and return'd into our Quarters untill Wednesday Thursday, which	Preston	Wood Plumpton	4		SD500345	
		Wood Plumpton	Haworth Moor	1		SD550366	probably Hollowforth, 1m north of Wood Plumpton
		Haworth Moor	Wood Plumpton	1		SD500345	
					6		
15	day wee advanc't by order to Garstang & from thence to Lancaster in extreame foul weather. Free quarter all.	Wood Plumpton	Garstang	9		SD490455	
		Garstang	Lancaster	10		SD485615	
					19		

Day		From	To			Grid ref	Note
		Lancaster	Halton Moore	4		SD515660	?between Halton Green and Moorgate?
16	I received money, according to my muster on Haworth moore, viz.: a Three weekes pay for: £ s. d. £ s. d. Capt 7ˢ 6ᵈ ꝓ diem 07 17 06} Lieut 4ˢ ꝓ diem 04 04 00} Ensigne, 3ˢ ꝓ diem 03 03 00} 2 Serg.ᵗˢ 3ˢ ꝓ diem 03 03 00} 119 03 06 2. Drums, 2ˢ ꝓ diem 02 02 00} 4. Corp.ˡᵇ 4ˢ ꝓ diem 04 04 00} 135 private souldiers 8d. ꝓ diem 94 10 00} This same day wee march't away from Lancaster to Kirkby Lansdale after the Randesvouz upon Halton Moore. Wee stayd at Kirkby Lansdale till Munday, & then	Halton Moore	Kirkby Lonsdale	11	15	SD611788	
19	Marched towards Beetham house which was surrendred	Kirkby Lonsdale	Beetham House		9	SD499791	
20	to us ye 2.d day After wee had Quarter'd in ye field all night. This day wee marched from thence (all but 5. men wᶜʰ came to us ye next day) to Kendall! Still wee receive free quart.ᵉʳ	Beetham House	Kendal		9	SD515925	
23	This day wee advanc't from ~~Shapp~~ Kendall to Shapp and send in to ye Countrey for provisions to meete us.	Kendal	Shap		17	NY656155	
24	From Shapp wee advanc't to Penrith and ye next day	Shap	Penrith		10	NY515300	

Date		From	To			Grid ref	Notes
25	being Lord's day wee march't towards Carlisle to Heskett moore, where wee met with Major Gen^ll Lamberts forces; And then march't to Warwicke bridge in extreamity of wet and foul wether and want of provisions etc. Wee quart^red in a Barne on ye further side Warwicke bridge after the enemy was beaten off from ye Bridge & divers p^rson^rs taken. a miserable time for the souldiers as I have seene at any time.	Penrith	Hesket Moor	10		NY475455	Between High Hesket and Low Hesket
		Hesket Moor	Warwick Bridge	9	19	NY469568	
26	Wee advanc't towards the Borders of Scotland, Randesvouzd in Guillsland, sent out a party out of every Company as forlorne, with my Lieut. wch advanc't to Stanwick banke on ye otherside Carlisle, beate the enemy out of their Entrenchments, out of ye Towne and church into ye City: wee kept their hould and kept guard at ye wood bridge foote. Wee quarter'd in Bramstocke (a small village [last word overwritten, ??p—pe] this night. the souldiers are in great want of victualls, noe drinke at all but water either for officer or souldier, wee sent out for pvisio	Warwick Bridge	Guillsland	4		NY471605	??Gill House 4m from Warwick Bridge by roads, 3m by cross country
		Guillsland	Stanwix	6		NY565401	Measured to bridge
		Stanwix	Brunstock	3	13	NY416595	
27	We march't backe to warwicke bridge where wee kept guard.	Brunstock	Warwick Bridge	6		NY469568	
July 4	Wee advanc't from our guards to Warwicke Bridge, four miles on the other side Carlisle. Quarter'd in ye field, noe provisions.	Warwick Bridge	Dalston	10		NY369505	or thereabouts. Perhaps Orton Grange. Both are about 4m from Carlisle

5	Next day wee march't to Bolton; I Quarter'd wᵗʰ my Company in Sandall and sent for provisions out of ye Countrey, all free.	Dalston	Bolton Low Houses	10		NY 238444	
		Bolton Low Houses	Sandale	3	13	NY 249401	
7	Wee marcht, betweene Cauldbecke & sowerby, Quarter'd in ye field.	Sandale	between Caldbeck and Sowerby		3	NY365375	Taken as Millhouse. Distance about same whether Sowerby Hall or Sowerby Row
8	Wee marcht from ye same place to Penrith, much rayne hath beene: such a wet time, this time of ye yeare hath not	between Caldbeck and Sowerby	Penrith		12	NY515300	
9	beene seene in ye memory of man: the souldiers in great want of provisions. Wee are every day at exercise in ordinary. Wee Quarter free in ye towne & send for provisions into ye Countrey, but						
13	at 3ᵈ or 4ᵗʰ part of 4ᵈ a day for a souldier hath not come in.						
14	At night the whole body of both Scotts and English marching against us wee drew out of Penrith and march't all night & ye next morning (extreamly wet as it was) wee came about eleven a clocke to Appleby; wee guarded ye Magazine wᶜʰ was extreamly troublesome. wee had some provisions out of	Penrith	Appleby		14	NY685200	
16	Ye Countrey whilst wee stay'd here.						

Date							
17	The Scotts fell upon us before wee were aware; our horse being (ye greatest part) absent: drave up our horse guards within our Centryes and Quarters of foote. drew out partyes which kept them off from us till night and made divers works, but by day breake in ye morning we march't away. I had the Rereguard of ye foote with Major Greenlishe.	Appleby	Kirkby Stephen	10		NY774085	
		Kirkby Stephen	Bowes	17		NY995135	
					27		
18	In ye skirmish some '4 or 5' of our Kild, some wounded. Wee came safe in oer Retreit to Kirkby Steeven, from thence to Bowes, wee quarterd upon ye bare walls of a Cottage after long fasting.						
19	Wee marcht to Barnard Castle. and quarterd in Wharleton. Wee recd provisions from Langleydale, Hunwicke &c. to assist our Quarters. Kept a small guard in Barnard Castle.	Bowes	Barnard Castle	4		NZ050160	
		Barnard Castle	Whorlton	4		NZ105150	
					8		
24	Wee Randesvouzd upon Girlington Moore, returned to Wharleton.	Whorlton	Girlington Moore	1		NZ129138	Girlington Hall
		Girlington Moore	Whorlton	1		NZ105150	
					3		
August 2	Upon this day wee left Wharleton, where wee lay upon free quartrers 12. dayes. And march't to Gatterley moore and from thence to Richmond; Quarter'd in Towne.	Whorlton	Gatherley Moor		8	NZ 190070	
3	Wee march't to Ripon, quarter'd there, had assistant Quarters.	Gatherley Moore	Ripon	26		SE 310710	

	Narrative	From	To			Grid ref.	Notes
7	Wee advanc't from Rippon to Knaresbrough had assistant Quarters from Langthorpe, & Hunburton *cum* Milbie &c. All this while wee have beene without money or any other	Ripon	Langthorpe	7		SE390673	Langthorpe is just north of Boroughbridge. Humburton SE 423685 2.7m east of Boroughbridge. Milby 1m northeast of B'bridge. Looks as though 2 day trip via Boroughbridge, could be 6th and 7th or 7th and 8th
		Langthorpe	Knaresborough	8	14	SE355575	
9	Accomodation saving Quarter, which sometimes was good, sometimes exceeding bad; Only part of the provisions came in In money, which serv'd the souldiers to supply some extraordinaryes of small valew.						
13	Lord's day wee quarter still in Knaresbrough, ye valews of provision was set downe by some officers appointed for yt purpose betweene ye souldier & ye Countrey. The souldier ordered to receive 6ᵈ valew in provision every day: but could not but seldome obteine so much.						
~~14~~ 13	Wee advanc't from Knaresborough 'to Oaxly & thence,' (where wee had lien	Knaresborough	Otley	13		SE205465	
		Otley	Carleton	18	31	SD972498	Near Skipton
14	upon free quarter & had assistant Quarters 7 dayes), to Carleton neere Skipton, quarter'd (upon bare walls) one night,						This is doubtful as a daily total

15	wee advanc't to Downham where wee quarter'd (of such as the enemy had left us) in towne. And from thence wee	Carleton	Downham	14	SD785443	
16	March't to Stanyhurst finding still ye quarters so bare as an enemy could leave them y^t had quarterd still every night before us till wee came to Preston. this night wee quarter'd in a field close by Stanihurst hall:	Downham	Stoneyhurst	8	SD 691391	
17	This day wee march't to Preston, had ye great dispute with ye Scotts and English Armie, see ye Acc^t on ye file. I had ye charge of o^r Lancashire Brigades forlorne, my Lieut. had ye charge of my division of musquettiers, my Ensigne, by Command of G. C. Ashton, lead ye pykes & Collo^{ers} up agt ye Defend.^{ts} on Rible Bridge & beat them off: allmost all my officers mark't, none kill'd. divers souldiers shott & hurt, some very dangerously, most performed very well: Bless'd bee God for his great deliverance.	Stoneyhurst	Preston	12	SD530290	
18	After my Company had quarter'd y^t night in ye field, the next morning by L. G. Cromwells order wee drew into ye Towne to Guarde ye 3,000. prison^{ers}, all ye Magazine & a great Store of provisions which wee tooke from the Enemy, our Lancashire forces being only left for y^t, whilst L. G. Cromwell pursued ye Enemy: And notwithstanding Monroes and S^{ir} Tho. Tildisleys Threatenings who with 9 or 10000 men lay at Lancaster, God assisted us to secure all, wee lay there upon free quarter					
23	Till this day, at which time wee removed into ye field countrey, not fare from ye sea side for 5. dayes, and then	Preston	'field countrey'	16	SD345395	The Fylde (Poulton-le-Fylde, 3m from the sea, for mileage)

			'field country'				
	29	wee return'd to Preston where wee stayd this night.		Preston	Preston	16	SD530290
	30	Wee marched to Blackburne, quarter'd there one night, the		Preston	Blackburn	12	SD680280
	31	Next day wee went to quarter in Pleasington and Witton: I quarter'd some small time at Blackburne at Jno Sharples, & in Preston I either was at home or pd my quarters. In		Blackburn	Pleasington	5	SD643262
Sept-ember	18	This posture wee stayd till this day; all ffree quarter: which day we advanc't my Company by order to Waddington. Recd 3 weekes pay 15. instant & pd it my Company 5. dayes after, I thanke God my company stayd and went with mee upon ye service when most of ye rest runne away after they had recd their money: I say a three weekes pay just according to ye last muster recd & payd ye officers and souldiers Capt. 7ˢ 6ᵈ ꝑ diem — 007 17 06} Lieut. 4ˢ ꝑ diem — 004 04 00} Ensigne 3ˢ — 003 03 00} 2 Serg.ᵗˢ 3ˢ — 003 03 00} — 119 03 06 2. Drums 2ˢ — 002 02 00} 4. Corpˡˢ 4ˢ — 004 04 00} 135. private souldiers — 094 10 00}		Pleasington	Waddington	16	SD789438
	19	ffrom Waddington wee march't to Long Preston where wee stayd 2. nights still upon ffreequarter, after which wee		Waddington	Long Preston	13	SD835583
	21	Advanc't from thence to Gigleswicke, stayd one night, and		Long Preston	Giggleswick	4	SD810640
	22	ffrom thence to Thornton and Wastus, stayd one night,		Giggleswick	Westhouse	11	SD672740	Thornton Hall about 1m due east

23	ffrom thence wee advanc't this morning to Kirkby Lunsdale, where wee stayd in miserable quarters two nights; the enemy haveing left noe provision behind him.	Westhouse	Kirkby Lonsdale	5	SD611788
25	Wee marcht this day to Kendall, where wee stayd only two nights, wee all passe upon every 3.^{d} nights duty.	Kirkby Lonsdale	Kendal	12	SD515925
27	Wee advanc't this day to Shapp, my company still continueing above 120. men notwithstanding ye mutiny and running away of so many. ffreequarter still.	Kendal	Shap	17	NY656155
28	Wee march't this morning to Penrith, the enemy not appearing but in Scouts only.	Shap	Penrith	10	NY515300
29	Wee continued our advance towards ye Enemy this day as farr as Cauldbecke, where wee quarter'd in a barne, quite without victualls or any reliefe after a	Penrith	Caldbeck	15	NY323398
30	hard march; Before day or breakfast wee marcht this morning away towards Cockermouth, which ye enemy had close besieg'd, but hearing of our comeing, went hastily away, leaving their great gunne and some victualls behind, which the garison seised, wee had our quarters in towne, this night wee had the unhappy losse of 3. horse collo^{ers}, and divers horses and men, out of o^{ur} Lancashire regim^{t}; by ye enemyes falling into our horse and foote quarters at Talantyre.	Caldbeck	Cockermouth	15	NY120305

Oct-ober	1	Wee quarter still free and bare in Cockermouth towne. Wee have had at divers times assistant or provisionall quarters assigned us, where wee have quarter'd so narrow, yt noe possibility of provisions was to bee had from ye quarters wee possess't, and where meate nor any kind of provision was to bee had or not to ye valew assigned us, wee recd ye residue in money wᶜʰ				
	3	The souldier either found himselfe victualls withall or at least drinke; where meat was not to bee had: All which is but to bee accounted as part of our freequarter, ye receipts and disbursmᵗˢ with ye valews are as followeth, since the beginning of our march, till this present day. [The rest of this folio and half of the verso is accounts, not included in this transcription] This is the account of the receipts and disbursements of what in money hath beene recd from oᵘʳ pᵛisionall quarters; the remainder was recd in provisions, was at the same times distributed for the sustenance of ye Souldiers in their too narrow quarters, only very many times wee recd not halfe, nor scarce any sometimes for ye warrants yt were sent out. This is before this day.				
	4	Wee quarter still in Cockermouth upon free quarter.				
	5	wee marcht from Cockermouth to Tarpenney where wee quarter'd (miserably for want of victualls) 2 nights & one day, whilst the Enemy came to Treaty with us:	Cockermouth	Torpenhow	9	SD202397
	7	wee marcht from Turpenny to Cauldbecke our ould and greivous quarters still miserably distrest for want of meat.	Torpenhow	Caldbeck	8	NY323398

8	And from thence to Penrith, where wee pass't upon duty.	Caldbeck	Penrith	15	NY515300	
9	wee all advanc't for Appleby, had the castle surrendred to Us, of which I was made Governor, and my whole company kept it. Hitherto wee have paid nothing in ye Countrey for meate or drinke, and now for theese few dayes wee make a	Penrith	Appleby	14	NY685200	
13	Shifte to live upon ye ill condicone victualls in the Castle					
				573	Total mileage	In 21 weeks = 1,420m in 12 months
				11.69	Average miles per travelling day	

This completes the active service part of Birch's account.

Remainder of the 'Diary'

Date	Day	Transcript
1648		
October	15	for about 6. or 7. dayes. And then had six^d p^{er} diem allowed them out of severall partes in Westmorland by order from L. C. Jackson, adjutant. Gen.^{ell} according to ye appointm^t of Major Gen^{ell} Asshton, as may appeare in punctuall particulars in ye lists and in ye booke of ye garison of Appleby pag. 1, 2, 3, 4 &c.
November	4	Untill saturday November 4. At which time after ye whole company had punctually paid their Quarters in towne and pass't upon constant and hard duty in the Castle. they rec'd a months pay from ^Cap. West^ out of ye 4,700li. I say out of the 4,700li raysed or yt should have beene raysed out of ye sequestracons in ye county of Westmorland. Viz. li s d Capt. 7^s 6^d p diem 050 10 00} Lieut. 4^s 004 04 00} Ensigne 5^s 004 04 00} 2. Serg.^{ts} 3^s 004 04 00} 193 06 00 2. Drums 2^s 002 16 00} 4. Corp^{lls} 4^s 005 12 00} 129. private souldiers 120 08 00} p diem
	5	At this time also I disposed into quarters the one halfe of my company (of which as many as were willing had licence to goe home which
	6	was ye greatest part of them, ye rest went to Quarters) to Egremont. The other halfe of Officers and souldiers were by Major Gen^{ell} Ashtons command appoint^{ed} to stay in ye Castle of Appleby till further order & to receive 6^d per diem and proportionable still, wch is very meane allowance all things being so extreame deare. and in this posture they continued, sometimes passing upon every 4.^{t} nights duty, sometimes upon every 3.^{d} dayes duty and sometimes oftner, they payd their Quarters punctually and had their six pence per diem punctually allowed, whilst the other 1/2 of ye Company were part in Quarters and part at home,
December	10	untill the 10th day of December 1648, at which time, by order, I left the castle to be demolished. I had also some other officers whilst I had the Castle, and my whole company in it, viz. a surgeon, a marshall and his two men, a brewer, a cooke or farrier, and a quartermaster, which did not properly belong to a foote company. When I sent away the half of my company, I reserved only a surgeon and a quartermaster, besides ensigne, one sergeant and four corporalls and one drum. The accounts of my receipts and disbursements in relation to the said castle, are punctually and at large in the booke and lists thereunto belonging. That part of my company with me marcht very speedily towards Lancashire, and had in many places, free quarter: the rest went to St. Bees, to Burrowdale, and Irton, into quarter.

Month	Day	
	11	I staid all Lords day at Appleby, and this day went towards Kirkby Lansdale and so to Lancaster. From the 9th day of October till the 6th day of January next, I had not had free quarter at all for myselfe or horse. We disposed of some armes in Lancaster and so marched to Manchester.
1649		
January	5	I returned towards my company lying in Cumberland
	6	and this night came to Mr. Irton's of Irton, my quarters, where now I beginne of free quarter, but my company, as many as have beene in quarters, have lien in part of StBees parish, and in Burrow-dale, and in Irton, about fifty men apeece. or evenly if not so many.
	29	I marcht those two parts of my company that lay in St Bees and Irton to Mockergen, and the next
	30	day to Cockermouth. Quarterd in Pap Castle and Bridekirke.
	31	This day wee march't backe towards Westmorland as
February	1	farr as Keswicke, and this 1st of February to
	2	Ambleside. Then wee advanc't this day and
.	3	quartered in Under Barrow, and this day wee came into Lancashire and quartered in the
	4	Yealands where wee spent this Lords day and lay
	5	still. The next morning marcht my company to Halton.
	6	I marcht this day, the regiment through Lancaster, quartered my company in and about Ellell, but I lay at charges two dayes in Lancaster about our meeting and money.
	8	I march't my company and quarterd this night in Barton.
	9	March't this day and quartered in Blackburne, and
	10	the next day quartered in our settled quarters in Rossendale. Wee received our 4,000*l.* out of Cumberland being a month's pay.
		Notwithstanding my orders otherwise my officers agreed with the grave and heads of the Forest at his and their earnest importunityes – in my absence – for a weekely allowance and to pay for our quarters. I went home. See the agreement and the reason of it under the grave's hand, with divers others. I received in six weekes and odd dayes the sum of twelve pounds for my selfe and man and two horses, and a horse and a man of the adjutant's, Lieutenant-General Jackson's, so long as hee stayd. And notwithstanding I was there but about five or six dayes I spent with my men and horses there about 9*l.* of it. None of my company demanded anything of his landlord for his absence from quarters unlesse they did joyntly agree and condition to doe it. Thus wee con-
		tinued upon free quarter till the 28th day of March,
March	28	on which day I marched them out of Rossendale in Blackburn hundred unto Bury cind the parts adjacent where I quartered that one night. And

	29	Thursday, betimes, I marched them to Manchester where wee lodged our collours, laid down our armes and disbanded. And there I received and payd eighteen dayes pay to my officers and souldiers, being their part of 2,400l. graunted us by the parliament.
		Sum total 'received by mee and my souldiers in way of pay since the second raising of my company, viz.: May 15, 1648, till our late disbanding, March 29, 1649,' was £768 8s.
December	21	'This day haveing received from Mr. Norres – viz. : by his order and assignation of bonds, Richard Twiford's 22l. and Richard Hoghton's 30l. and the rest in money – I payd my souldiers – their last – twenty dayes pay.' [Summary of payments omitted]
		But because of the distraction of the times and for that the late Lancashire brigade is looked on as not well affected to the present powers and proceedings, wee looke upon the other 800 and odd pounds yet remaining in arreare, together with the rest of our arreares – if things continue as they are – in a soart desperate. So that wee may account that which thus farr wee have received to bee the full account of what wee – as yet – can expect for our last yeares service, 1648.
1650		
March	20	So that at this present day – March 27 1650 – wee may make up our full receipts to bee: [Summary of payments omitted]
		f.156-162 These pages of accounts and muster rolls omitted

NOTES

Introduction

1 Braye, *The manuscripts of . . . Lord Braye . . . &c*, Historical Manuscripts Commission 10th report, appendix, part VI, London: HMSO, 1887, p. 172, Thomas Margetts to John Browne, Seaton, 3 October 1648.

2 Stephen Bull and Mike Seed, *Bloody Preston: The Battle of Preston, 1648*, Lancaster: Carnegie, 1998.

3 Ian Gentles, 'The Civil Wars in England', in Kenyon, J. and Ohlmeyer, Jane (eds), *The Civil Wars: A Military History of England, Scotland, and Ireland, 1638–1660*, Oxford: Oxford University Press, 1998, p. 152.

4 J. Binns, 'Scarborough and the Civil Wars 1642–1651', *Northern History*, vol. xxii (1986), p. 97.

5 See Chapter 1, n. 19.

6 Richard Pococke, *Tours in Scotland 1747, 1750, 1760*, ed. by D. W. Kemp, Scottish History Society, vol. I (1887), p. 19; Letter IV from Orton [Westmorland] 10 May 1760.

7 Wilbur Cortez Abbott, *The Writings and Speeches of Oliver Cromwell*, 4 vols, Cambridge, Mass.: Harvard University Press, 1937–1947, vol. 1, p. 633; Cromwell to the Honourable Committee of Lancashire, 17 August 1648.

8 *LJ, Journal of the House of Lords*, vols 9–10 (1802), vol. 10, p. 66; 19 February 1648.

9 See p. 76 and Chapter 6, n. 3.

10 See Chapter 3, nn. 19 and 57, and Chapter 6, n. 24.

11 *CSPD 1648–1649, Calendar of State Papers Domestic . . . 1648–1649*, ed. by W. D. Hamilton, London: HMSO, 1893, p. 202; 20 July 1648.

12 P. R. Hill and J. M. Watkinson, *Major Sanderson's War: The Diary of a Parliamentary Cavalry Officer in the English Civil War*, Stroud: Spellmount, 2008, pp. 62, 142.

13 *TT* E454/16 *The Moderate Intelligencer*, no. 175, 20–27 July 1648, report from Newcastle 21 July.

14 Abbott, vol. 1, p. 637; Cromwell to Speaker Lenthall.

15 Malcolm Wanklyn, *The Warrior Generals: Winning the British Civil Wars 1642–1652*, New Haven, Conn., and London: Yale University Press, 2010, p. 213.

Chapter 1: Lambert and His Army

1 *TT* E13/19 *The Kingdomes Weekly Intelligencer*, no. 77, Tuesday 15–23 October 1644; *TT* E14/2 *Mercurius Civicus*, no. 74, Thursday 17–24 October 1644; *TT* E256/28 *Perfect Occurrences of Parliament*, no. 11, 18–25 October 1644, letter from Fairfax 8 October; *TT* E256/26 *Perfect Passages of Each Dayes Proceedings in Parliament*, no. 1, 16–23 October 1644, letter from quarters at Otley 11 October 1644; *TT* E14/5 *The Scotish Dove*, no. 53, 18–25 October 1644. The raid was in answer to a Royalist raid which seized 100 horses at Ripon, and 'Plumpton' may be Plumpton Hall near Ripon (SE 290697) rather than Plompton Hall near Harrogate (SE 355540).

2 *TT* E258/17 *A Perfect Diurnall of some Passages in Parliament*, no. 78, 20–27 January 1644[5], report on 21 January.

3 Bulstrode Whitelocke, *Memorials of the English Affairs . . . From the Beginning of the Reign of Charles the First, to King Charles the Second His Happy Restoration . . .* new edn, London: J. Tonson, 1732, p. 132, 17 February

1644[5]; *TT* E258/34 *Perfect Passages of Each Dayes Proceedings in Parliament*, no. 20, 5–11 March 1644[5], report on 7 March; *TT* E273/2 *The Kingdomes Weekly Intelligencer*, no. 90, 4–11 March 1645; *TT* E273/5 *Mercurius Civicus*, no. 94, 6–13 March 1644[5]; *TT* E258/33 *A Perfect Diurnall of some Passages in Parliament*, no. 84, 3–10 March 1644[5] report dated 7 March; *TT* E273/10 *The Scotish Dove*, no. 73, 7–14 March 1644[5]

4   H. M. Reece, 'The Military Presence in England, 1649–1660': a thesis submitted for the degree of Doctor of Philosophy at the University of Oxford, 1981 (unpublished), pp. 60–1.

5   Lucy Hutchinson, *Memoirs of the Life of Colonel Hutchinson*, ed. with introduction by J. Sutherland, Oxford: Oxford University Press, 1973, p. 209.

6   Clements R. Markham, *A Life of the Great Lord Fairfax*, London: Macmillan, 1870, p. iv.

7   Braye, p. 168; letter from Thomas Margetts to John Browne, 14 September 1648.

8   See Chapter 1, n. 6.

9   Reece, pp. 60–1.

10 Whitelocke, pp. 271–2, 275; 27 September; 25 October 1648.

11 Braye, pp. 171–2; letter from Thomas Margetts to John Browne, 3 October 1648.

12 David Farr, *John Lambert, Parliamentary Soldier and Cromwellian Major-General, 1619–1684*, Woodbridge: Boydell, 2003, p. 37; *CSPD 1644–1645, Calendar of State Papers, Domestic . . . 1644–1645*, ed. by W. D. Hamilton, London: HMSO, 1890, p. 128, 14 November 1644 records his imminent arrival in London; letter to General Fairfax, 21 January 1644[5], quoted without attribution by W. H. Dawson, *Cromwell's Understudy: The Life and Times of General John Lambert and the Rise and Fall of the Protectorate*, London: Hodge, 1938, pp. 37–8. The authors appreciate correspondence with Dr David Farr on this point. *TT* E448/16 *Packets of Letters*, no. 14, letter from Penrith 14 June 1648.

13 Whitelocke, p. 254.

14 *CJ, Journal of the House of Commons*, vol. 5, London: n.p., pp. 459–60, 9 February 1647[8] It is not clear whether the foot companies within a regiment were of differing strength, as previously, and here they are assumed to be each of eighty men.

15 Hill and Watkinson, pp. 25, 95. Unit strength of the horse is discussed there, pp. 23–6.

16 *TT* E472/5 *The Kingdomes Weekly Intelligencer*, no. 285, 7–14 November 1648, letter from the four Northern Counties to the Commons, Barnard Castle 25 October 1648.

17 *CJ*, p. 268, 17 July 1647; C. H. Firth and Godfrey Davies, *The Regimental History of Cromwell's Army*, 2 vols, Oxford: Clarendon Press, 1940, p. xx; *TT* E522/10 *Perfect Occurrences of Every Daie iournall in Parliament*, no. 65, 24–31 March 1648. Ian Gentles, *The New Model Army in England, Ireland, and Scotland, 1645–1653*, Oxford: Blackwell, 1992, p. 232, n. 242 gives also Mauleverer's and Fairfax's foot. But Fairfax's was raised in May 1648 as the West Riding regiment of foot, (*TT* E446/29 *The Declaration of Sir Thomas Glenham . . . With a List of the chief Commanders belonging to the Parliaments Forces*) and added to the New Model in February 1649 (Firth and Davies, p. 501). Mauleverer's was already in existence in 1648 but remained outside the New Model.

18 *LJ*, vol. 10, p. 267, 19 May 1648, letter from General Fairfax; C. H. Firth (ed.), *The Clarke Papers*, vols i, ii, Camden Society new series, vols 49 and 54 (1891, 1894), vol. ii, pp. 20–2, Newsletter from Thomas Margetts, York, 27 May 1648. Fairfax notes that forty of Twistleton's had been diverted to secure Belvoir Castle, making it clear that this was very much a temporary detachment; they may be the part of the troop which came north long after the rest of the regiment in late July.

19 *CSPD 1648–1649*, p. 101, 5 June 1648. The letter itself has not survived. Col. Ewer had commanded the siege of Chepstow. Gentles, 1992, p. 258, says the move was to assist Lambert, but Coventry is over 100 miles from Pontefract and 180 from Barnard Castle.

20 *CSPD 1648–1649*, p. 56, 1 May 1648.

21 *CSPD 1648–1649*, p. 112, 8 June 1648.

22 B. P. Lyndon, 'The Parliament's Army in Essex, 1648', *Journal of the Society for Army Historical Research*, vol. 54 (1981), p. 145, lists the units with General Fairfax but makes no mention of Thornhaugh's.

23 Gen. Fairfax actually says '. . . *Cromwell*, out of his own regiment and Colonel *Thornhaugh's*, hath sent Five Troops of Horse with some dragoons . . .' But four of Cromwell's were with Lambert by early June, so it is probable that only one of Thornhaugh's was sent to north Wales.

24 All six troops of Harrison's were certainly with Lambert at the end of June when he sent them to support Lilburne in Northumberland (see Chapter 3).

25 Abbott, vol. 1, pp. 615–6, Cromwell to Major Thomas Saunders, 17 June 1648. John Roland Phillips, *Memoirs of the Civil War in Wales and the Marches 1642–1649*, London: Longman, 1874, vol. i, p. 413, gives his rank incorrectly as Colonel Saunders. He discusses Thornhaugh's in Wales, but assumes that the whole regiment marched north with Cromwell.

26 *TT E457/24 The Perfect Weekly Account*, no. 21, 2–9 August 1647 [*sic*], undated letter from Nottingham, reported 7 August.

27 John Rushworth, *Historical Collections Fourth and Last Part.*, 2 vols, London: R. Chiswell & T. Cockerill, 1701, pp. 1113–4; 15 May 1648, letter from Newcastle dated 11 May.

28 Hill and Watkinson, 11–18 May 1648; *TT E525/9 Perfect Occurrences of Every Daies iournall in Parliament*, no. 82, 21–28 July 1648.

29 Rushworth, p. 1132, 29 May 1648, letter from Newcastle dated 25 May; Whitelocke, p. 308, 27 May 1648; *TT E442/9 Packets of Letters*, no. 9, letter from York 12 May 1648; *TT E522/33 Perfect Occurrences of Every Daies iournall in Parliament*, no. 74, 26 May–2 June 1648.

30 Hill and Watkinson, p. 106, Sanderson's Diary entries for 16 and 18 May 1648.

31 Hill and Watkinson, pp. 106, 108, Sanderson's Diary, 18 May, 3 June.

32 Firth, *The Clarke Papers*, vol. ii, pp. 20–2, Newsletter from Thomas Margetts, York, 27 May 1648. One troop of Twistleton's joined towards the end of June (*TT E525/9 Perfect Occurrences of Every Daies iournall in Parliament*, no. 82, 21–28 July 1648, letters from York reported 20 July).

33 Two companies of Gen. Fairfax's were left in York and marched towards Lambert on 15 July; *TT E453/21 Packets of Letters*, no. 18, letter from Helmsley Castle 15 July 1648.

34 *TT E446/12 A True Relation of the Proceedings of the Northern Forces Under the Command of Col. Lambert, Col. Blakemore, and Col. Harrison*, letter from Manchester 1 June 1648. Lt-Col. Blakemore was appointed major of Cromwell's regiment on 14 June 1648 in place of Huntingdon and was presumably commanding the detachment of four troops from that regiment. *TT E448/7 The Severall Fights Neere Colchester in Essex . . . Also Major-Generall Lamberts Victories in the North*, letter from Kendal 12 June 1648.

35 *TT E448/16 Packets of Letters*, no. 14, letter from Newcastle 15 June 1648.

36 *TT E449/23 The Declaration of the Citizens of Edenborough*; *TT E447/4 Packets of Letters*, no. 13, letter from Wigan, 9 June 1648; Arthur Hesilrige, Leicester Record Office, The Hazlerigg Collection, DG21/275/d Letters to Sir Arthur Hesilrige, 2nd Bart *c.*1648–1650, Lambert to Hesilrige, Penrith 11 June 1648; Rushworth, p. 1165, Monday 26 June.

37 Rushworth, p. 1165, 26 June 1648, gives 8,000; *TT E449/23 The Declaration of the Citizens of Edenborough*, letter from T. S. at Penrith 17 June 1648 says 8,000–9,000.

38 *TT E454/19 Packets of Letters*, no. 19, letter from York 21 July 1648.

39 *Portland Papers, The Manuscripts of His Grace the Duke of Portland preserved at Welbeck Abbey*, 10 vols, London: HMSO, 1891–1931, vol I, p. 471, Lambert to unknown correspondent, Brampton, 2 July 1648; Hill and Watkinson, pp. 53, 58, 139–40.

40 *Portland Papers*, vol I, pp. 474–5, Lambert to Sir William Lister, Weatheral [*sic*], 4 July 1648. It is not clear to what regiments the four troops in Yorkshire belonged. The only possibilities seem to be one from Lambert's, perhaps one from Twistleton's, perhaps Harley's (unidentified and here assumed to be militia), and possibly one of General Fairfax's.

41 Abbott, vol. 1, p. 618, Cromwell to Lord Halifax, 28 June 1648. Pennyfeather (or Pennyfather) was in Horton's regiment at Pembroke (Firth and Davies, p. 86). The other three of Scroope's had previously been sent to join General Fairfax's command.

42 *TT E525/9 Perfect Occurrences of Every Daies iournall in Parliament*, no. 82, 21–28 July 1648, letters from York reported 20 July. The name printed as Losseth is clearly meant for Lascelles. See also *TT E453/29 The*

Notes – Chapter 1: Lambert and His Army

Moderate Intelligencer, no. 174, 13–20 July 1648, letter from Newcastle 13 July 1648; *TT* E453/34 *Bloody Nevves rom* [*sic*] the *Scottish Army*, letter from Penrith 16 August 1648; *TT* E454/16 *The Moderate Intelligencer*, no. 175, 20–27 July 1648, letter from the Army of Major Gen. Lambert, 17 July. All these references give a total of 600 men for the troops coming from Wales, perhaps an indication that they were all now at their war strength of a hundred.

43 *TT* E454/16 *The Moderate Intelligencer*, no. 175, 20–27 July 1648, letter from the Army of Major Gen. Lambert, 17 July 1648.

44 See Chapter 1, n. 42.

45 *TT* E456/1 *Another Fight between the Two Armies of Scotch and English*, letter from Barnard Castle 25 July 1648: 'we have lately some Troopes of Horse, and some Companies of Foot come to us out of Yorkshire.' *TT* E525/13 *A Perfect Diurnall of some Passages in Parliament*, no. 262, 31 July–7 August 1648; Rushworth, p. 1211, Monday July 30 [*sic, recte* 31], both quoting a letter of 28 July from Barnard Castle giving a date of 27th for some of the reinforcements.

46 *TT* E453/21 *Packets of Letters*, no. 18, letter from Helmsley Castle 15 July 1648.

47 *TT* E454/14 *A True Relation of the Fight Between Maior Gen. Lambert, and the Scots Army neer Appleby, July 24 1648*, the letter itself is undated, title dated in ms 27th July.

48 *TT* E525/13 *A Perfect Diurnall of some Passages in Parliament*, no. 262, 31 July–7 August 1648; Rushworth, p. 1211, Monday July 30 [*sic, recte* 31], both quoting a letter of 28 July from Barnard Castle.

49 *TT* E525/10 *A Perfect Diurnall of some Passages in Parliament*, no. 261, 24–31 July 1648, report of letters from Lambert's quarters 19 July; Whitelocke, p. 323, report for 26 July. Their wording, 'the Yorkshire Horse and a thousand of Lieutenant-General Cromwell's Foot are joined with him', is virtually identical and both say that the letter was from Lambert himself.

50 Cromwell, marching with infantry, took twenty-six days to reach Pontefract at the end of July.

51 Abbott, vol. 1, pp. 618–9, Cromwell to Lord Fairfax, Pembroke 28 June 1648.

52 *TT* E456/26 *Another Bloudy Fight at Colchester upon Tuesday night last*, letter from Skipton Castle 1 August 1648.

53 Rushworth, p. 1211, Monday July 30 [*sic, recte* 31]; Whitelocke, p. 325, 31 July 1648; both refer to a letter from Lambert's quarters 28 July. This may be the letter in *TT* E456/18 *The Resolution of The Kings Majesties Subjects . . . And a Defeat given to Lieutenant Generall Cromwells Forces neare Pontefract in Yorkshire*, letter from Tho: Derton 39 [*sic*] July 1648. Listed in G. K. Fortescue (ed.), *Catalogue of the Pamphlets, Books, Newspapers, and Manuscripts relating to the Civil War, the Commonwealth, and Restoration, collected by George Thomason, 1640–1661*, 2 vols, London: British Museum, 1908, under 28 July; Thomason has a manuscript date of 2 August.

54 *TT* E457/24 *The Perfect Weekly Account*, no. 21, 2–9 August 1647 [*sic*]; *TT* E456/20 *The Perfect Weekly Account*, no. 20, 20 July–1 August 1647 [*sic*] gives 'his own Regiment, Col. Prides Regiment, and Col. Deanes Regiment.' But Cromwell did not have a foot regiment of his own at this time, and his horse had already joined Lambert.

55 *CSPD 1648–1649*, p. 210, 24 July 1648.

56 Rushworth, pp. 1133–4 (i.e. pp. 1141–2), 6 June 1648, letter from Pembroke dated 1 June.

57 Firth and Davies, p. 387. Stuart Reid, *All the King's Armies: A Military History of the English Civil War 1642–1651*, Stroud: Spellmount, 2007, p. 223 and n. 1.

58 Rushworth, p. 1036, 24 March 1648.

59 Rushworth, p. 1206, 28 July 1648; *CSPD 1648–1649*, pp. 219, 227, 230; 27 July, 1 and 2 August.

60 *CSPD 1648–1649*, p. 219, 27 July 1648. Dolphin's appears to have been a loose troop, and Dolphin himself was apparently taken into Thornhaugh's old regiment (now Saunders') in January 1649 (Firth and Davies, p. 283). However, elsewhere Firth says that he is in a list of officers proposed for Col. Marten's regiment, 1 February 1649, which was to be made up of loose troops (Firth, *The Clarke Papers*, vol. ii, p. 213).

61 Firth and Davies, 108; Firth, *The Clarke Papers*, vol. ii, p. 27; *CSPD 1648–1649*, p. 186, 12 July 1648.

62 Abbott, vol. 1, p. 637, Cromwell to Speaker Lenthall, Warrington 20 August 1648.

63 *CSPD 1648–1649*, p. 208, 21 July 1648. On the same day two troops of Ireton's were sent from London to partly offset this move.
64 Firth and Davies, p. 108, say that Scroope was sent to Yarmouth in July, but this is far from confirmed. He was asked to monitor the road to Yarmouth to prevent movement of those in sympathy with the revolted ships who arrived there with the Prince of Wales on 22nd, but it was Captain Brewster's company and one from Norwich which were ordered to occupy the town, although the order was cancelled on 25th, the ships having sailed off on 24th (*LJ*, vol. 10, p. 399, *CSPD 1648–1649*, pp. 201, 202, 208–9, 214–5; 19, 20, 24, 25 July 1648; Bernard Capp, *Cromwell's Navy: The Fleet and the English Revolution 1648–1660*, Oxford: Clarendon Press, 1989, p. 32). The only mention of Scroope as being any further connected with the town is Rushworth, p. 1205, 26 July 1648, according to whom he was ordered by Gen. Fairfax to march towards Yarmouth with eight troops of horse and dragoons. Rushworth appears to be referring to something a week or more old. Similarly Rushworth reports (p. 1216, 4 August 1648) that two days earlier information had been received that Scroope was now satisfied that Yarmouth was no longer in danger. This is again probably an old report. Scroope could have had orders to march north by around 27 July, allowing about fourteen days to join Cromwell, perhaps at Pontefract, on 10 August. Assuming that he was somewhere near Yarmouth, this would allow fourteen days to cover the 170 miles. Marching fifty-six miles in four days, followed by a rest day, would have been a steady rate of fourteen miles a day. Cromwell's 3,000 foot marched at no less than this rate over twenty-one days from Pembroke to Nottingham (see p. 96, fn.).
65 *TT* E460/35 *The Moderate Intelligencer*, no. 179, 17–24 August 1648, report from Warrington 20 August.
66 Abbott, vol. 1, pp. 632–3, Cromwell to the Lancashire Committee, 17 August 1648; Hill and Watkinson, p. 143, Sanderson's Relation.
67 Abbott, vol. 1, p. 707, Cromwell to Lord Fairfax, [29?] November 1648; *TT* E473/1 *The Moderate*, no. 19; 14–21 November 1648, report from Pontefract 18 November 1648.
68 *CSPD 1648–1649*, p. 210; 24 July 1648.
69 E.g. Abbott, vol. 1, p. 628; Gentles, 1992, p. 260. An exception is Maurice Ashley, *The English Civil War*, rev. edn, Gloucester: Alan Sutton, 1990, p. 158, who has Cromwell reinforcing the besiegers before marching on.
70 Richard Holmes (ed.), *The Sieges of Pontefract Castle 1644–1648*, Pontefract: Holmes, 1887, pp. 308, 320, Paulden's Account.
71 *CSPD 1648–1649*, p. 192, 15 July. Reminders were issued on 25 July, *CSPD 1648–1649*, p. 204.
72 See Chapter 1, n. 54.
73 See Chapter 1, n. 42.
74 *TT* E453/21 *Packets of Letters*, no. 18, letter from Helmsley Castle 15 July 1648, describing these regiments as marching towards Ferrybridge.
75 *CJ*, vol. 6, p. 46, 25 July 1648; *CSPD 1648–1649*, pp. 217, 222, 227, 228, 246; 27 and 28 July, 1 and 18 August 1648.
76 See Chapter 1, n. 55.
77 Abbott, vol. 1, p. 638, Cromwell to Speaker Lenthall from Warrington 20 August 1648.
78 Ian Gentles, *The English Revolution and the Wars in the Three Kingdoms 1638–1652*, Harlow: Longman, 2007, p. 344 n. 43. Gentles, 1992, p. 261 gives a similar figure, but p. 514 n. 103 suggests 'well over 11,000'.
79 Hutchinson, p. 181; Ashley, p. 158.
80 Sir James Turner, *Memoirs of His Own Life and Times 1632–1670*, Edinburgh: Bannatyne Club, 1829, p. 78.
81 The size of Hamilton's army is discussed by, among many others, Ashley, p. 158; Gentles, 1992, p. 259; Reid, p. 226; Malcolm Wanklyn, *Decisive Battles of the English Civil War: Myth and Reality*, Barnsley: Pen & Sword, 2006, p. 191; Peter Young and Richard Holmes, *The English Civil War: A Military History of the Three Civil Wars 1642–1651*, Ware: Wordsworth, 2000, pp. 280–2.

Chapter 2: The Condition of England
1 Trevor Royle, *Civil War: The Wars of the Three Kingdoms 1638–1660*, London: Abacus, 2005, p. 338.
2 *CJ*, vol. 5, pp. 106–8, 124, 126; 5, 8, 25 and 26 March 1647.

Notes – Chapter 2: The Condition of England

3   *CJ*, vol. 5, p. 128; 29 March 1647.
4   *LJ*, vol. 9, p. 115; 30 March 1647.
5   *CJ*, vol. 5, p. 158; 30 April 1647.
6   *CJ*, vol. 5, pp. 166, 173; 7 and 14 May 1647.
7   Charles Hoover, 'Cromwell's status and pay in 1646–47', *Historical Journal*, vol. 23 (1980), pp. 708, 715.
8   *CJ*, vol. 5, p. 183; 25 May 1647.
9   *LJ*, vol. 9, p. 226; 1 June 1647.
10   *LJ*, vol. 9, p. 232, 3 June 1647; *CJ*, vol. 5, p. 197, 3 June 1647.
11   Gentles, 2007, pp. 308, 312.
12   *PCHE, The Parliamentary or Constitutional History of England; From the Earliest Times, to the Restoration of Charles II . . . By Several Hands*, 2nd edn, 24 vols, London: J. & R. Tonson, A. Millar & W. Sanby, 1761–1763, vol. XV, pp. 401ff.
13   *CJ*, vol. 5, pp. 206–8, 11 June 1647; *LJ*, vol. 9, pp. 256, 257, 261, 11 and 12 June 1647; the Order for Indemnity was passed on 19 June (C. H. Firth and R. S. Rait (eds), *Acts and Ordinances of the Interregnum 1642–1660*, 3 vols, London: HMSO, 1911, vol. 1, pp. 957–8).
14   Royle, p. 401.
15   Gentles, 2007, pp. 313–4. Fairfax later denied that the army intended to treat separately with the king (*LJ*, vol. 9, p. 323, 9 July 1647), but the evidence is against him.
16   *LJ*, vol. 9, p. 267, 15 June 1647; J. G. Fotheringham (ed.), *The Diplomatic Correspondence of Jean de Montereul and the brothers Bellievre . . .*, 2 vols, Scottish History Society, vols XXIX, XXX (1898–1899), vol. I, pp. 176–7.
17   *CJ*, vol. 5, p. 214; 16 June 1647.
18   *CJ*, vol. 5, p. 225, 26 June 1647; *LJ*, vol. 9, pp. 295–6, 26 and 28 June 1647.
19   *CJ*, vol. 5, p. 226, 28 June 1647; *LJ*, vol. 9, p. 306, 30 June 1647.
20   Firth, *The Clarke Papers*, vol. i, pp. 146–7.
21   *CJ*, vol. 5, p. 245, 15 July 1647; Rushworth, pp. 626, 777–8, 17 July, 16 August 1647; Whitelocke, pp. 259, 265, 15 and 17 July, 16 August 1647. An accounting entry for 27 July 1647 shows 'To Coll. Lambert for charges into the North, £150 0s. 0d.' (Ethel Kitson and E. K. Clark, 'Some Civil War Accounts 1647–1650', *Thoresby Society Publication XI: Miscellanea,* 1904, p. 141) which presumably relates to his journey there on or around that date.
22   *CJ*, vol. 5, pp. 236, 251–2; 6 and 20 July 1647.
23   *LJ*, vol. 9, pp. 340–1, 20 July 1647; *CJ*, vol. 5, pp. 110–11, 254, 4 May, 22 July 1647; Whitelocke, pp. 260–1, 26 July 1647. Fairfax's letter justifying the actions of the army gives a good summary of these events at the end of July (*LJ*, vol. 9, pp. 357–8, 6 August 1647).
24   *LJ*, vol. 9, pp. 358–65; 30 and 31 July 1647.
25   Rushworth, p. 646, 30 July 1647; *LJ*, vol. 9, p. 366, 1 August 1647; Whitelocke, p. 261, 29 July 1647.
26   *LJ*, vol. 9, p. 363, 30 and 31 July 1647. A hogshead is equal to 52.5 gallons. Cashor is properly Cashio, a large Hundred which included St Albans, Watford and Rickmansworth.
27   *LJ*, vol. 9, pp. 372–3; 3 August 1647.
28   Rushworth, pp. 750, 756, 4 and 6 August 1647; Whitelocke, pp. 263–4, 3, 4, 6 August 1647.
29   *LJ*, vol. 9, pp. 375, 379; 6 August 1647.
30   *CJ*, vol. 5, p. 280; 20 August 1647.
31   Rushworth, p. 790; 26 August 1647. The foregoing paragraphs owe much to Gentles, 2007, Chapter 10, where is to be found a most useful summary of the political situation.
32   *CJ*, vol. 5, pp. 307–8, 17 and 18 September 1647.
33   C. H. Firth (ed.), 'Narratives illustrating the Duke of Hamilton's expedition to England in 1648 II: Sir Philip Musgrave's Relation', *Miscellany of The Scottish History Society,* vol. 2 (1904), p. 304 n.1; Gentles, 2007, pp. 320–1.
34   *CJ*, vol. 5, p. 415, 3 January 1647[8].

Chapter 3: Escalation to War

1   David Stevenson, *Revolution and Counter-Revolution in Scotland. 1644–1651*, rev. edn, Edinburgh: John Donald, 2003, p. 82; Firth, 1904, p. 304.

2   *CJ*, vol. 5, p. 416, 3 January 1647[8]; *CSPD 1648–1649*, p. 6, 20 January 1648. Derby House stood between Canon Row and the Thames, just north of Westminster Bridge. Cromwell's daughter Bridget was given lodging there in 1655, and in 1674 it became the Admiralty Office under Samuel Pepys.

3   Whitelocke, p. 291, 9 February 1648.

4   Rushworth, p. 995, 14 February 1648.

5   Austin Woolrych, *Britain in Revolution 1625–1660*, Oxford: Oxford University Press, 2002, p. 404.

6   Hill and Watkinson, pp. 27–8; Rushworth, p. 1047, 3 April 1648; *TT* E433/12 *The Kingdomes Weekly Account of Heads of Chief Passages in Parliament*, no. 11, 15–22 March 1647[8], letter from York 18 March.

7   *CSPD 1648–1649*, May, June, July 1648.

8   Gentles, 1992, p.250.

9   *CJ*, vol. 5, p. 442; 24 January 1648.

10   Rushworth, pp. 982, 1020; 31 January, 6 March 1648.

11   *CSPD 1648–1649*, pp. 29–30, 14 March 1648; *TT* E431/16 *The Kingdomes Weekly Post*, no. 9, 2–9 March 1648; *TT* E431/18 *The Moderate Intelligencer*, no. 155, 2–9 March 1648; Rushworth, pp. 1023, 1024, 1031.

12   Rushworth, pp. 1040–1, 27 March 1648, letters from the English Commissioners in Scotland.

13   Rushworth, p. 1031, 20 March 1648; *TT* E433/9 *A Plot Discovered*, letter from George Stuart, Berwick, 15 March 1647[8].

14   *TT* E522/10 *Perfect Occurrences of Every Daie iournall in Parliament*, no. 65, 24–31 March 1648.

15   Rushworth, pp. 1040–1, 27 March 1648, letters from the English Commissioners in Scotland; Rushworth, p. 1047, 3 April 1648, letters from York 31 March 1648.

16   *CSPD 1648–1649*, pp. 41–3; 7 April 1648.

17   *TT* E435/13 *Packets of Letters*, no. 4, letter from Edinburgh, 4 April 1648.

18   Firth, *The Clarke Papers*, vol. ii, pp. 1–2, Thomas Margetts to William Clarke, York 8 April 1648.

19   See Chapter 3, n. 57, and Chapter 6, n. 24.

20   Rushworth, pp. 1064, 1071, 19 and 25 April 1648; Henry Guthry, *The Memoirs of Henry Guthry . . . Containing an Impartial Relation of the Affairs of Scotland, Civil and Ecclesiastical, from the Year 1637, to the Death of King Charles I*, 2nd edn, Glasgow: A. Stalker, 1748, p. 268.

21   Fairfax, Transcripts of the Collection of Letters known as The Fairfax Correspondence 1645–1648, British Library, Add Mss 36,996 (late nineteenth/early twentieth century manuscript copy), f. 12, letter from Edward Rhodes and others, dated 25 April 1648, York.

22   *TT* E438/8 *The Perfect Weekly Account*, no. 8, 26 April–3 May 1647 [*sic*]; Rushworth, p. 1098, 1 May 1648.

23   Rushworth, pp. 1099, 1105; 2 and 8 May 1648.

24   Whitelocke, p. 303; 1 May 1648.

25   Rushworth, pp. 1121, 20 May 1648 (Carmarthen), 1130, 29 May 1648 (Chepstow), 1133 (i.e. 1141), 6 June 1648 (Tenby).

26   *LJ*, vol. 10, p. 267, 19 May 1648. Lambert's letter of 2 July confirms that he had four troops of Cromwell's with him (*Portland Papers*, vol. I, p. 471).

27   *TT* E442/11 *The Declaration and Propositions of Maj. Gen. Langhorne and Col. Rice Powel* 'The Copy of a Letter from the North . . .' Newcastle 8 May 1648; Rushworth, p. 1105, 8 May; *Portland Papers*, vol. I, p. 505, Examination of George Clavering, 29 December 1648; p. 508. Statement by Major John Mayer, 28 January 1648[9]; *CJ*, vol. 5, p. 54, 9 May 1648; *CSPD 1648–1649*, p. 57, 2 May 1648; *TT* E444/9 *The Moderate Intelligencer*, no. 166, 18–25 May 1648, report from Newcastle 18 May.

28   *TT* E441/19 *The Kingdomes VVeekly Intelligencer*, no. 259, 2–9 May 1648; *CSPD 1648–1649*, p. 158, 9 May 1648; *CJ*, vol. 5, p. 554, 9 May 1648.

29   *TT* E441/4 *A Great Fight in Wales*, undated letter from Northumberland by S. J., published 8 May 1648.

30   *TT* E467/1 *The Moderate*, no. 13, 3–10 October 1648.

31 Hill and Watkinson, pp. 45–6, 103–4; Rushworth, p. 1106, 8 May 1648; *TT* E444/9 *The Moderate Intelligencer*, no. 166, 18–25 May 1648, report from Newcastle 18 May. Walton Hall was the house of the Waterton family, on an island in a small lake three miles southeast of Wakefield, SE 363162, eight miles from Pontefract. The present house dates from 1767. The garrison seems to have been a small one, as on 26 June they wrote to Col. Fairfax asking for ten or twelve musketeers and for a party of horse to get supplies in for them as they had only four horse, and also for pay (Fairfax, f. 22, letter from William Pell to Col. Charles Fairfax).

32 *HMC Third Report of the Royal Commission on Historical Manuscripts*, London: HMSO, 1872, pp. 86–7 (and original in Alnwick Castle Archives, DNP Ms 16) letter from Wressell 30 May 1648.

33 Fairfax, f. 13, letter from Lambert to Col. Fairfax, dated 4 May [no year, but clearly 1648].

34 *TT* E442/9 *Packets of Letters*, no. 9, letter from York 12 May 1648.

35 Rushworth, p. 1106; 8 May 1648.

36 *TT* E442/9 *Packets of Letters*, no. 9, letter from Newcastle 11 May 1648; *TT* E443/14 *A Great Fight at Chepstow Castle*, undated but other reports in the pamphlet dated 13 and 16 May 1648, with ms date 18th May; Hill and Watkinson, p. 47.

37 *CJ*, vol. 5, p. 555, 10 May 1648; *CSPD 1648–1649*, p. 62, 9 May 1648. The instruction was issued by the Commons on 11 May, but Derby House was instructing the Commissioners two days earlier.

38 Rushworth, p. 1113, 15 May 1648.

39 *TT* E442/11 *The Declaration and Propositions of Maj. Gen. Langhorne and Col. Rice Powel* 'The Copy of a Letter from the North . . .' Newcastle 8 May 1648. A similar false rumour was repeated late in June, *TT* E450/12 *Tvvo Letters, One from Penrith Another From Northumberland*, Gisford [Gosforth] 22 June 1648.

40 *TT* E444/9 *The Moderate Intelligencer*, no. 166, 18–25 May 1648, report from Newcastle 18 May.

41 National Library of Scotland, Add. Mss 35.5.11, ff. 32–3, letter from Thomas Margetts to William Clarke, York, 12 May 1648, printed in part in Firth, *The Clarke Papers*, vol. ii, p. 25.

42 *TT* E442/9 *Packets of Letters*, no. 9, letter from York 12 May 1648. Cholmley was probably the captain in Lilburne's (Hill and Watkinson, pp. 166–7).

43 Rushworth, p. 1114, 15 May 1648, quoting letter of the 11th. Hartley Castle, a fortified manor half a mile east of Kirkby Stephen, was the Musgrave family seat until 1677 when they moved to Edenhall, Penrith.

44 Hesilrige, DG21/275/j, Bright and Smithson to Hesilrige, Alnwick 15 May 1648.

45 see previous note.

46 Rushworth, p. 1113, 13 May 1648; Hesilrige, DG21/275/k, Ireton to Hesilrige, Windsor 16 May 1648; *LJ*, vol. 10, pp. 267–8, 19 May 1648.

47 Hesilrige, DG21/275/k, Ireton to Hesilrige, Windsor 16 May 1648.

48 Rushworth, pp. 1122–3, 22 May 1648; Guthry, pp. 268, 269.

49 Guthry, pp. 271, 278.

50 Turner, p. 246.

51 *TT* E522/10 *Perfect Occurrences of Every Daie iournall in Parliament*, no. 65, 24–31 March 1648; Hill and Watkinson, pp. 54, 106.

52 Hill and Watkinson, p. 54.

53 *TT* E445/5 *Packets of Letters*, no. 11, letter from Newcastle 26 May 1648.

54 *LJ*, vol. 10, p. 267, 19 May 1648.

55 Rushworth, pp. 1121, 1123, 1127, 20, 22 and 24 May 1648; Whitelocke, pp. 306, 307, 20 and 22 May.

56 Rushworth, p. 1132, 29 May 1648, letter from Newcastle 25 May 1700 [*sic*]; Whitelocke, p. 308, 27 May 1648; *TT* E522/33 *Perfect Occurrences of Every Daies iournall in Parliament*, no. 74, 26 May–2 June 1648; *TT* E444/9 *The Moderate Intelligencer*, no. 166, 18–25 May 1648, report from Newcastle 18 May.

57 Firth, *The Clarke Papers*, vol. ii, pp. 20–2, Newsletter from Thomas Margetts, York 27 May 1648.

58 *TT* E522/33 *Perfect Occurrences of Every Daies iournall in Parliament*, no. 74, 26 May–2 June 1648, letter from York 26 May.

59 See Chapter 6, n. 81.

60 See Chapter 3, n. 33.

61 W. H. Dawson, *History of Skipton,* London: Simpkin, Marshall, 1882, p. 136, quoting from the Parish Registers.

62 National Library of Scotland, Add. Mss 35.5.11, ff. 28–9, letter from Thomas Margetts to William Clarke, York, 9 June 1648, printed in part in Firth, *The Clarke Papers,* vol. ii, p. 25.

63 *TT* E446/31 *The Scots resolution,* letter from York signed H. W., 1 June 1648; *TT* E446/27 *Exceeding Good Newes From South Wales,* undated but other reports dated 5, 6, 7 June 1648, and ms date 8 June.

64 *CSPD 1648–1649,* p. 87, 30 May 1648; *TT* E447/4 *Packets of Letters,* no. 13, letter from Wigan 9 June 1648; Rushworth, p. 1148, 12 June 1648.

65 See Chapter 3, n. 57.

66 Rushworth, p. 1132 (i.e. 1140), 5 June 1648, letter from Newcastle 1 June; *TT* E447/2 *A Bloody Fight In Essex* 'A declaration of the Parliament's Forces in the North'.

67 *TT* E446/12 *A True Relation of the Proceedings of the Northern Forces,* letter from Manchester 1 June 1648; *TT* E522/33 *Perfect Occurrences of Every Daies iournall in Parliament,* no. 74, 26 May–2 June 1648, report from Newcastle 25 May.

68 *CSPD 1648–1649,* p. 58, 5 May 1648; *TT* E444/9 *The Moderate Intelligencer,* no. 166, 18–25 May 1648, report from Newcastle 18 May (where the name is given as S. Forbrits Island).

69 *TT* E446/12 *A True Relation of the Proceedings of the Northern Forces,* letter from Manchester 1 June 1648; *TT* E522/33 *Perfect Occurrences of Every Daies iournall in Parliament,* no. 74, 26 May–2 June 1648, report from Newcastle 25 May.

70 *CSPD 1648–1649,* pp. 85, 87, 28 and 29 May 1648; Capp, 1989, pp. 182–8; Bernard Capp, 'Naval Operations', in J. Kenyon. and Jane Ohlmeyer (eds), *The Civil Wars: A Military History of England, Scotland, and Ireland, 1638–1660,* Oxford: Oxford University Press, 1998, pp. 182–3.

71 Gardiner gives 1 June, and is followed by some modern commentaries, but it is clear that it was the 3rd: see *TT* E446/16 *Mercurius Elencticus,* no. 28, 31 May–7 June 1648; Nathan Drake, 'A Journal of the First and Second Sieges of Pontefract Castle, 1644–1645, with an appendix of evidences relating to the Third Siege', edited by W. H. D. Longstaffe, *Miscellanea,* Surtees Society, vol. 37 (1860), p. 89; Holmes, 1887, p. 259, quoting the statement of the governor, Col. Cotterell.

72 The ladder was reported to be of forty-two rungs, hinged in the middle on an iron bolt (*HMC Various, Report on Manuscripts in Various Collections, vol. viii: The Manuscripts of the Hon. Frederick Lindley Wood; M.L. S. Clements Esq,; and S. Philip Unwin Esq.,* London: HMSO, 1913, p. 61, letter from Thomas Carter to Mr West, 23 May 1648).

73 George Fox, *The Three Sieges of Pontefract Castle,* Burton Salmon: Old Hall Press, 1987, pp. 120–4, and Holmes, 1887, pp. 149–54, both quote the letter.

74 There are several versions of the methods used to take the castle, e.g.: Cotterell's Deposition in Holmes, 1887, pp. 259–60; *CJ,* vol. 5, p. 587, 6 June 1648; Rushworth, p. 1133 (i.e. 1141); *TT* E446/27 *Exceeding Good Newes From South Wales,* undated but other reports dated 5, 6, 7 June 1648, and ms date 8 June; Drake, pp. 88–90. Clarendon says that the successful attempt was made using ladders.

75 *CJ,* vol. 5, p. 60, 21 January 1647[8], announcing his discharge from the investigation.

76 S. R. Gardiner (ed.), *The Hamilton Papers . . . relating to the years 1638–1650,* Camden Society, new series 27 (1880), pp. 209–10, no. 135, J. Thomson to W. Black, Carlisle 9 June 1648.

77 Fox, p. 104. Fox published a history of Pontefract in 1827, and continued to add to his notes and illustrations thereafter. The complete manuscript was transcribed and published in 1987.

78 *Portland Papers,* vol. I, p. 455, Col. Thomas Stockdale to Francis Thorp MP, 3 June 1648.

79 Holmes, 1887, p. 302.

80 Fairfax, f. 14. The companies were those of Capt Skyer, Capt Spencer and Capt Siddall.

81 Fairfax, f. 17, letter from Tho: Dickinson to Charles Fairfax at Leeds 5 June 1648.

82 *CJ,* vol. 5, p. 589, 7 June 1648, recording the receipt of a letter from Lambert sent from Ferrybridge.

83 National Library of Scotland, Add. Mss 35.5.11, ff. 28–9, letter from Thomas Margetts to William Clarke, York, 9 June 1648, printed in part in Firth, *The Clarke Papers,* vol. ii, p. 25.

84 Rushworth, p. 1148, 12 June 1648. Helmsley Castle had been partially slighted in 1644 but was clearly still defensible.

85 Le Fleming, *The Manuscripts of S .H. Le Fleming Esq. of Rydal Hall*, Historical Manuscripts Commission 12th report, appendix part VII, London: HMSO, 1890, p. 19 (document 200), letter from Sir Marmaduke Langdale at Houghill Castle to Sir Thomas Sandford *et al.*, 2 June 1648.

Chapter 4: Gatherley Moor to Carlisle and Penrith

1   Rushworth, p. 1132 (i.e 1140), 5 June 1648.

2   Gardiner, p. 208, no. 134, J. Thomson to W. Black, Carlisle, 7 June 1648.

3   Rushworth, p. 1148, 12 June 1648; *TT* E447/24 *The Moderate Intelligencer*, no. 169, 8–15 June 1648; *TT* E449/23 *The Declaration of the Citizens of Edenborough*, gives a date of 15 June, clearly wrong as the letter is dated the 17th; this is discussed further on p. 51. David Underdown, *Revel, Riot and Rebellion: Popular Politics and Culture in England 1603–1660*, Oxford: Oxford University Press, 1987, pp. 4–5, defines 'champion country'.

4   Firth, 1904, pp. 306–7.

5   Hill and Watkinson, pp. 94–5, 101, 102.

6   See p. 42.

7   It was known in York on the 5th that Harrison's and Twistleton's regiments were on the way to Bainy [Barnard] Castle (*TT* E446/29 *The Declaration of Sir Thomas Glenham*, report from York 5 May [*recte* June] 1648).

8   *TT* E447/24 *The Moderate Intelligencer*, no. 169, 8–15 June 1648, report from Durham 8 June.

9   Hesilrige, DG21/275/f, Lambert to Hesilrige, Brough 10 June 1648.

10 *TT* E447/28 *The Parliament-Kite*, no. 5, 9–16 June 1648.

11 National Library of Scotland, Add. Mss 35.5.11, ff. 32–3, letter from Thomas Margetts to William Clarke, York, 12 May 1648, printed in part in Firth, *The Clarke Papers*, vol. ii, p. 25.

12 *TT* E449/23 *The Declaration of the Citizens of Edenborough*, letter from T. S. at Penrith 17 June 1648.

13 See Chapter 4, n. 14.

14 Hesilrige, DG21/275/f, Lambert to Hesilrige, Brough 10 June 1648.

15 William Whellan, *The History and Topography of the Counties of Cumberland and Westmorland*, Pontefract: Whellan, 1860, p. 735; William Page (ed.), *The Victoria County History of York, North Riding*, 3 vols, London: Constable, 1914–1925, vol. I, p. 43. The business of the inn was transferred one mile eastwards in the nineteenth century to become the New Spital, now, after a period as a farm, the Bowes Moor Hotel.

16 De La Veile was presumably one of the Delavals, a noted Northumberland family, but this individual has not been identified. Blackston may be Sir William Blakistone.

17 This paragraph is based on Humphrey Welfare, 'Maiden Castle Fortlet', in Blaise Vyner, *Stainmore: The Archaeology of a North Pennine Pass*, Tees Archaeology Monograph, no. 1 (2002), pp. 96–8.

18 NY 880124. CBA Defence of Britain Database, Site No. S001 3284, Black Riggs, Type FW3/24 (http://ads.ahds.ac.uk/catalogue; accessed April 2011)

19 Hill and Watkinson, p. 49; *TT* E522/40 *Perfect Occurrences of Every Daies iournall in Parliament*, no. 76, 9–16 June 1648, undated report from Newcastle under news for Monday 12 June.

20 Hill and Watkinson, p. 50.

21 *TT* E522/40 *Perfect Occurrences of Every Daies iournall in Parliament*, no. 76, 9–16 June 1648, undated report from Newcastle under news for Monday 12 June.

22 *CSPD 1648–1649*, June 1648, *passim*.

23 *CSPD 1648–1649*, p. 103, 6 June 1648.

24 E.g. *TT* E446/27 *Exceeding Good Newes From South Wales*, undated but other reports dated 5, 6, 7 June 1648, and ms date 8 June.

25 *TT* E447/4 *Packets of Letters*, no. 13, letter from Wigan 9 June 1648; Hesilrige, DG21/275/d, Lambert to Hesilrige, Penrith 11 June 1648. Ashton's command, under Lambert, was approved by the Commons on 20 June (*CJ*, vol. 5, p. 608). For numbers, see also Bull and Seed, pp. 111–12.

26 *CSPD 1648–1649*, p. 116, 9 June 1648.

27 Hesilrige, DG21/275/d, Lambert to Hesilrige, Penrith 11 June 1648.

28   See Chapter 6, n. 12.

29   See Chapter 4, n. 27.

30   *TT* E449/12 *The Perfect Weekly Account*, no. 14, 14–21 June 1647 [*sic*], letter from R. S. at Penrith 16 June.

31   Rushworth, p. 1165, 26 June 1648. Mr Neville Howard of Greystoke has kindly informed the authors that the castle was not defended but was abandoned to Lambert's troops, and was largely demolished after the Civil War as an act of spite.

32   *TT* E448/16 *Packets of Letters*, no. 14, letter from Penrith 14 June 1648. Part of the same letter in Rushworth, p. 1157, 19 June, letter from Penrith (dated 15 June), omits the first sentence which mentions Lambert's illness.

33   *TT* E448/7 *The Severall Fights neere Colchester in Essex*, letter from Kendal 12 June 1648.

34   See Chapter 4, n. 27.

35   E.g. *TT* E448/7 *The Severall Fights neere Colchester in Essex*, letter from Kendal 12 June 1648. 'The Enemy are at least 5,000 with fire Armes, and nigh as many more, some of which are armed'; *TT* E448/16 *Packets of Letters*, no. 14, letter from Newcastle 15 June 1648. 'Lambert is reported to be about 6,000 men, and Langdale as many and more armed, and as many more unarmed.'

36   See Chapter 4, n. 12.

37   TT E450/12 *Tvvo Letters, One from Penrith Another From Northumberland*, letter from Penrith 22 June 1648.

38   Hesilrige, DG21/275/e, Lambert to Hesilrige, Penrith 17 June 1648; *TT* E449/23 *The Declaration of the Citizens of Edenborough*, letter from T. S. at Penrith 17 June 1648.

39   www.fourmilab.ch/cgi-bin/uncgi/Yoursky; accessed April 2011. This gives uncorrected dates, to which ten days have to be added to allow for the correction of the calendar in September 1752.

40   Gardiner, p. 213, no. 139, Sir Philip Musgrave to the Earl of Lanerick, Carlisle 14 June 1648.

41   See Chapter 4, n. 12.

42   *The Declaration of the Citizens of Edenborough*, letter from T. S. at Penrith 17 June 1648.

43   *TT* E449/29 *Another Fight at Colchester* 'Two Fights, one in the North of England near Carlisle . . .', letter from Kendal 21 June 1648.

44   *TT* E449/12 *The Perfect Weekly Account*, no. 14, 14–21 June 1647 [*sic*], letter from R. S. at Penrith 16 June.

45   *TT* E449/23 *The Declaration of the Citizens of Edenborough*, letter from T. S. at Penrith 17 June 1648.

46   See previous note.

47   Firth, 1904, p. 308 and note.

48   Hesilrige, DG21/275/e, Lambert to Hesilrige, Penrith 17 June 1648, appears to give a figure of 1,000 weight. This presumably indicate 10 hundred weight (10 cwt). Rushworth, p. 1165, 26 June 1648, says '1,500 Weight' (15 cwt).

49   *CSPD 1648–1649*, p. 124, 13 June 1648, Derby House to the Lord Admiral [Warwick].

50   See appendix 1, especially n. 36.

51   See Chapter 4, n. 40.

52   Peter Edwards, 'Logistics and supply', in J. Kenyon and Jane Ohlmeyer (eds), *The Civil Wars: A Military History of England, Scotland, and Ireland, 1638–1660*, Oxford: Oxford University Press, 1998, p. 256. A peck is a measure of volume equal to 2 gallons.

53   The authors are grateful to Mr Mark Corby for pointing this out.

54   Turner, p. 58.

55   *TT* E450/12 *Tvvo Letters, One from Penrith Another From Northumberland*, letter from Gisford [Gosforth] 22 June 1648; Rushworth, p. 1165, 26 June 1648; Firth, 1904, p. 308. *TT* E451/22 *A true and perfect Relation of a Great Victory obtained by the Parliament's Forces in Northumberland*. Carre may be Francis who served under Edward Grey in 1648, and Driveal one of the Delaval family, but neither has been positively identified.

56   *TT* E522/40 *Perfect Occurrences of Every Daies iournall in Parliament*, no. 76, 9–16 June, undated report from Newcastle under news for Monday 12 June.

57   *TT* E450/12 *Tvvo Letters, One from Penrith Another From Northumberland*, letter from Gisford [Gosforth] 22 June 1648.

58   Hesilrige, DG21/275/g, Lambert to Hesilrige, Penrith 22 June 1648.

59 *Portland Papers*, vol. I, p. 465, Col. Ralph Assheton to William Lenthall, Kendal 23 June 1648.

60 See Chapter 1, especially n. 36.

61 Rushworth, p. 1165, 26 June 1648.

62 Gardiner, pp. 217–8, no. 142, Sir Marmaduke Langdale and Sir Philip Musgrave to the Earl of Lanerick, Carlisle 24 June 1648.

63 Whitelocke, p. 319.

64 Rushworth, p. 1184, 10 July, quoting an undated letter from Lambert's quarters. From internal evidence it was written between 26 and 30 June. Langdale (n. 62, above) believed that the castle had been captured without loss.

65 *TT* E453/21 *Packets of Letters*, no. 18, letter from Helmsley Castle 15 July 1648.

66 See Chapter 3, n. 51.

67 Hesilrige, DG21/275/g, Lambert to Hesilrige, Penrith 22 June 1648.

68 *TT* E452/31 *A New Declaration Set forth by the Lord Gen. Hamilton*. This letter says that the action took place on Friday night [23 June]. Whitelocke, p. 319, mentions the action but the date is missing.

69 See Chapter 4, n. 64.

70 See Chapter 4, nn. 64 and 68.

71 See Chapter 4, n. 64.

72 *TT* E451/7 *Packets of Letters*, no. 16, letter from Manchester 1 July 1648.

73 *Skirmish, A Skirmish in Northumberland. Being a Reprint of a Very Rare Tract in Quarto Entitled 'Packets of Letters . . . 1648'* (Sunderland, 1842). Letter from Major Sanderson, printed in Sunderland, 1842, reprinted in Hill and Watkinson, pp. 139–41. Sanderson presumably got this information from Lilburne or his officers when they came over to reinforce Northumberland a few days later.

74 William Mannix and William Whellan, *History, Gazetteer and Directory of Cumberland*, Beverley: Johnson, 1847. Carlisle Archives, Q/11/1/234/49, records in 1649 that the Priestbeck bridge was shot through the battlements by a cannon ball, which sounds very much like a stone bridge.

75 M. A. E. Green (ed.), *Calendar of the Proceedings of the Committee for Compounding*, 5 vols., London: HMSO, 1889–1892, p. 812, 19 September 1649.

76 See Chapter 4, n. 64.

77 See Chapter 4, n. 67.

78 *TT* E450/12 *Tvvo Letters, One from Penrith Another From Northumberland*, letter from Gisford [Gosforth] 22 June 1648.

79 See Chapter 4, n. 78.

80 *Skirmish*, p. 2.

81 Cadwallader J. Bates, 'The Border Holds of Northumberland 1' *Archaeologia Aeliana*, 2nd series, vol. xiv (1891), pp. 400–1, letter from Hesilrige to the Speaker, 2 July 1648. *CSPD 1648–1649*, p. 168, 6 July gives the total for Lilburne's forces as 500, an apparent error. The numbers are discussed in Hill and Watkinson, pp. 52–3.

82 Hill and Watkinson, pp. 52–8, 113–14. The strength of Fenwick's regiment given there is almost certainly too low, as Cholmley's troop was incorrectly included in the total Parliamentary figure.

83 *CJ*, vol. 10, pp. 624–5, 5 July 1648.

84 G. E. Aylmer (ed.), *Clarke Trials, Clarke Papers microfilm*, Reel 9 2/10 (LXX), f. 145v.

85 See Chapter 4, n. 81.

86 *TT* E525/4 *A Perfect Diurnall of some Passages in Parliament*, no. 258, 3–10 July 1648, report read on 5 July, letter from Newcastle 2 July 1648; Bates, pp. 400–1; *TT* E452/13 *Three Letters out of the North*, letter dated 2 July 1648.

87 *Portland Papers*, vol. I, p. 471, Lambert to unknown correspondent, Brampton, 2 July 1648; *Skirmish*, p. 5.

88 See previous note.

89 *CSPD 1648–1649*, p. 195, 17 July 1648; *Portland Papers*, vol. I, p. 471, Lambert to unknown correspondent, Brampton, 2 July; 474, Lambert to unknown correspondent, Wetheral, 4 July 1648.

90 *CSPD 1648–1649*, p. 160, 4 July 1648.

91 *Portland Papers*, vol. I, pp. 474–5, Lambert to Sir William Lister, Wetheral, 4 July 1648.
92 Abbott, vol. 1, p. 618, Cromwell to Lord Fairfax, 28 June 1648.
93 Rushworth, p. 1188, 12 June 1648.
94 *TT* E452/13 *Three Letters out of the North*, undated letter preceding letter dated 2 July 1648.
95 *TT* E454/14 *A True Relation of the Fight between Maior Gen. Lambert and the Scots Army neer Appleby July 24 1648*, undated pamphlet with ms date on title page 27th July.
96 *TT* E462/18 *The Moderate Intelligencer*, no. 181, 31 August–7 September, report from Newcastle 1 September.
97 See George Jobey, 'A military redoubt on Burnswark Hill, Dumfriesshire', *Transactions of the Dumfriesshire and Galloway Natural History and Antiquarian Society* 3rd series, vol. i (1973), pp. 72–81, for a discussion of this feature and its possible dating.
98 John Ogilby, *Britannia, Volume the First, or an Illustration of the Kingdom of England and Dominion of Wales*, London: printed by the author, 1675 (facsimile reprint, n. p., 1939), plate 96; Emanuel Bowen, *Britannia Depicta or Ogilby Improved*, 1720, facsimile reprint Newcastle: Frank Graham, 1970, p. 261.
99 *Letter from Holland*, Rotterdam, 23 September 1648, *TT* E467/21.
100 C. H. Firth (ed.), 'Narratives illustrating the Duke of Hamilton's expedition to England in 1648 I: Mr Thomas Reade's Relation', *Miscellany of The Scottish History Society*, vol. 2 (1904), pp. 299, 300.
101 *TT* E453/5 *A Declaration from Scotland Concerning the Advance of the Scots Army*, letter from Penrith 10 July 1648.
102 Gilbert Burnet, *The Memoires of the Lives and Actions of James and William Dukes of Hamilton and Castleherald . . .*, London: R. Royston, 1677, p. 355.
103 *Letter from Holland*, *TT* E467/21; *TT* E453/5 *A Declaration from Scotland Concerning the Advance of the Scots Army*, letter from Penrith 10 July 1648; Burnet, p. 355.
104 The date is given in *Ane Information of the Publicke Proceedings of the Kingdom of Scotland and Their Armies*, Edinburgh?: Evan Tyler, 16 August 1648. Other details are from: *TT* E453/29 *The Moderate Intelligencer*, no. 174, 13–20 July 1648; *TT* E453/34 *Bloody Nevves rom* [sic] *the Scottish Army*, undated but ms date 21 July 1648.
105 Rushworth, p. 1195, 18 July 1648; *TT* E453/29 *The Moderate Intelligencer*, no. 174, 13–20 July 1648; *TT* E453/34 *Bloody Nevves rom* [sic] *the Scottish Army*, undated but ms date 21st July 1648.

Chapter 5: Actions around Pontefract
1 *TT* E450/12 *Tvvo Letters, One from Penrith Another From Northumberland*, letter from Penrith 22 June 1648.
2 Holmes, 1887, pp. 308, 320, Paulden's Account.
3 Rushworth, pp. 1169, 1174, 28 June and 3 July 1648; *CJ*, vol. 5, p. 629, 8 July 1648; Fairfax, f. 22, letter from the Walton garrison to Col. Fairfax, dated 26 June; Clive Holmes, *Seventeenth-Century Lincolnshire* (*History of Lincolnshire*, vol. vii), Lincoln: Society for Lincolnshire History & Archaeology, 1980, pp. 200–1. *TT* E451/41 *An Impartiall and true Relation of the Great Victory* begins with their entry into Lincolnshire and does not mention Axholme.
4 Holmes, 1887, pp. 305–6.
5 Fairfax, f. 22, Walton garrison to Colonel Fairfax, 26 June 1648.
6 *TT* E451/41 *An Impartiall and true Relation of the Great Victory*; Whitelocke, p. 317, 3 July 1648. There may be confusion over the names: there was a woollen draper Peart in Lincoln at this time, and a Capt Pie was serving in the north.
7 *TT* E452/43 *Mercurius Psitacus*, no. 6, 10–17 July 1648.
8 Holmes, 1887, pp. 307–8, 320.
9 *TT* E452/31 *A New Declaration Set forth by the Lord Gen. Hamilton*. There is a brief reference in *TT* E453/28 *The Parliament-Kite*, no. 9, 13–20 July 1648; *TT* E452/13 *Three Letters Out of the North*, letter from George Horner, York 8 July 1648; *TT* E449/21 *A Dangerovs Fight at Pembrooke Castle*, letter from Ferribridge [sic] 19 June 1648; Fairfax, f. 18–19, Col. Fairfax to his wife dated 5 June 1648 (*recte* 15th). Fox, p. 104, quotes

part of the Fairfax letter and says that Thimbleby was 'not sent' to York but the copy of the letter in the BL clearly reads 'now sent to York'.

10 Holmes, 1887, pp. 291–322.

11 *CSPD 1648–1649*, pp. 99, 102, 158, 5 June, 4 July 1648.

12 The following is based on the report in *TT* E451/41 *An Impartiall and true Relation of the Great Victory*, published by order of the Commons.

13 Hutchinson, p. 177, where the event is said to have been on the day before the battle.

14 Rushworth, p. 1182, 8 July 1648; *TT* E451/41 *An Impartiall and true Relation of the Great Victory*.

15 *TT* E525/5 *Perfect Occurrences of Every Daies iournall in Parliament*, no. 80, 7–14 July 1648; *CJ*, vol. 5, p. 628, 8 July 1648.

16 See Chapter 5, n. 14.

17 Holmes, 1887, pp. 307–8.

18 Fairfax, f. 27–9, letter from Charles Fairfax to unknown recipient, dated Ferrybridge 13 July 1648. The superscription is 'My lord and Gent.' and was probably written to Derby House, *vide* Cromwell's letter to Derby House, 23 August 1648 (Abbott, vol. 1, pp. 641–2). The event was clearly on or before 13 July, and Paulden indicates that it took place after the Ferrybridge raid. A date of 10–12 July would fit well with the date of Col. Fairfax's letter. When Lambert arrived at Pontefract just after its seizure he mentioned 'my Lord Generall own Troop of Horse' (Fairfax, f. 14, letter from Lambert to Col. Fairfax, 4 June 1648, from Ferrybridge).

19 Perhaps the Capt John Browne who was a captain in Fairfax's, in which case he survived his wounds and went on to become major of the regiment (Firth and Davies, pp. 58, 67).

20 A horse ferry was in operation on the Thames at Lambeth in 1513 (Sir Howard Roberts and Walter H. Godfrey (eds), *Survey of London*, vol. 23, London: London County Council, 1951, p. 118). There is still a Boat Lane on both sides of the river at Allerton giving access to the ferry, which was in operation by 1592 and closed in 1959. In the nineteenth and twentieth centuries there was also a horse ferry there.

21 Fairfax, f. 23–5, letter to Sir Tho Widdiston (?Widdrington), presumably from Charles Fairfax, 'of July last 1648', contained an urgent request for powder, match and bullet: 'Let us know when it is at Leeds and we will send an escort.' Powder was also requested from York.

22 Fairfax, f. 23–5, letter to Sir Tho Widdiston (?Widdrington), presumably from Charles Fairfax, 'of July last 1648'.

23 *TT* E453/28 *The Parliament-Kite*, no. 9, 13–20 July 1648.

24 In the grounds 300 yards east of the church. Not to be confused with the present Thornhill Hall, or Lees Hall also in Thornhill.

25 Fairfax, f. 23–5, letter to Sir Tho Widdiston (?Widdrington), presumably from Charles Fairfax, 'of July last 1648'.

26 *TT* E454/16 *The Moderate Intelligencer*, no. 175, 20–27 July 1648, report of 29 July.

27 Fairfax, f. 23–5, letter to Sir Tho Widdiston (?Widdrington), presumably from Charles Fairfax, 'of July last 1648'; *TT* E453/21 *Packets of Letters*, no. 18, letter from Helmsley Castle 15 July 1648; *TT* E454/16 *The Moderate Intelligencer*, no. 175, 20–27 July 1648, letter dated 26 July; *TT* E456/5 *Another great and bloody Fight in the North*, letters between Col. Fairfax and the rebel governor 16–18 July 1648; *Portland Papers*, vol. I, pp. 488–9; *TT* E525/9 *Perfect Occurrences of Every Daies iournall in Parliament*, no. 82, 21–28 July 1648, letter from York 20 July.

Chapter 6: Appleby, Stainmore and Bowes

1 *TT* E453/34 *Bloody Nevves rom* [*sic*] *the Scottish Army*, letter from Penrith 16 July 1648; *TT* E453/29 *The Moderate Intelligencer*, no. 174, 13–20 Thursday 1648, report from Newcastle 13 July.

2 Ogilby, plate 38 Garstang to Carlisle road. Plumpton is not marked, but at the same crossroads is Sancoldyate [Salkeldgate?], given as four miles from Penrith. One of the roads leads to Salkeld.

3 Wanklyn, 2010, p. 199 n. 46, places this when Lambert was in Barnard Castle, but Hodgson, *Original Memoirs, Written During the Great Civil War; Being the Life of Sir Henry Slingsby and Memoirs of Capt Hodgson etc.*, Edinburgh: Archibald Constable, 1806, p. 112, ties it firmly to when Lambert and his army were in Penrith.

4 E.g. Bull and Seed, p. 56; Reid, p. 226; Austin Woolrych, *Battles of the English Civil War*, London: Batsford, 1961, p. 161; Young and Holmes, p. 281.

5 Burnet, pp. 355–6.

6 *TT* E525/9 *Perfect Occurrences of Every Daies iournall in Parliament*, no. 82, 21–28 July 1648.

7 Firth, 1904, p. 299.

8 *Letter from Holland.*

9 www.fourmilab.ch/cgi-bin/uncgi/Yoursky; accessed April 2011; see Chapter 4, n. 39.

10 Braye, p. 168, from/to unknown, HMC editor suggests a date of 18 or 19 July 1648.

11 Burnet, p. 356. The newsbook *Ane Information* gives some details of Hamilton's entry into England and the fighting at Appleby on 17 July, but ignores Penrith entirely.

12 *TT* E454/14 *A True Relation of the Fight between Maior Gen. Lambert and the Scots Army neer Appleby July 24 1648*, undated pamphlet, with ms 'July 27th' on title page. Around Eamont Bridge one and a half miles south of Penrith there are bridges over Eamont and Lowther about 650 yards apart.

13 Abbott, vol. 1, p. 621, Cromwell to Speaker Lenthall, 11 July 1648; *CSPD 1648–1649*, p. 199, 18 July 1648. See also p. 96 for the date of Cromwell's departure.

14 *CSPD 1648–1649*, pp. 192, 214, 235, 15, 25 July and 8 August 1648.

15 E.g. *CSPD 1648–1649*, pp. 217, 219, 27 July, 28 July 1648.

16 *TT* E454/16 *The Moderate Intelligencer*, no. 175, 20–27 July 1648, report from Lambert's Army 17 July.

17 Braye, p. 168, from/to unknown, HMC editor suggests 18 or 19 July 1648; *TT* E454/14 *A True Relation of the Fight between Maior Gen. Lambert and the Scots Army neer Appleby July 24 1648*, undated pamphlet with ms 'July 27th' on title page; Rushworth, pp. 1200–1, 24 July 1648.

18 *TT* E454/10 *A Bloody Fight in the North on Munday last, July 17 1648*, letter from Manchester 21 July; *TT* E454/14 *A True Relation of the Fight between Maior Gen. Lambert and the Scots Army neer Appleby July 24 1648*, Undated pamphlet, with ms 'July 27th' on title page; *TT* E454/19 *Packets of Letters*, no. 19, letter from Manchester 21 July 1648; Rushworth, pp. 1200–1, 24 July 1648.

19 There are a number of large, Listed farmhouses in the Hoff–Drybeck area dating from the sixteenth century. Burrells is a hamlet, about one mile south of Appleby.

20 *TT* E454/2 *The Moderate*, no. 2, 18–25 July 1648, report from Appleby 21 July.

21 Braye, p. 168, from/to unknown, HMC editor suggests 18 or 19 July 1648. The Scottish newsbook *Ane Information* gives the guards as being 400 of Cromwell's and Harrison's.

22 *TT* E454/14 *A True Relation of the Fight between Major Gen. Lambert and the Scots Army neer Appleby July 24 1648*, undated pamphlet, with ms 'July 27th' on title page; *TT* E454/19 *Packets of Letters*, no. 19, letter from Bowes 19 July 1648; Rushworth, p. 1201, 24 July 1648.

23 *TT* E454/16 *The Moderate Intelligencer*, no. 175, 20–27 July 1648, letter from Newcastle 21 July.

24 *TT* E454/19 *Packets of Letters*, no. 19, letter from Bowes 19 July 1648.

25 The principal reports are: *TT* E525/9 *Perfect Occurrences of Every Daies iournall in Parliament*, no. 82, 21–28 July 1648; *TT* E525/10 *A Perfect Diurnall of some Passages in Parliament*, no. 261, 24–31 July 1648, letter from Bowes 19 July. The first one gives 11 a.m., the other 9 a.m. They are all printed variations of the same letter, from one of Lambert's officers. *TT* E454/14 *A True Relation of the Fight between Maior Gen. Lambert and the Scots Army neer Appleby July 24 1648*, undated pamphlet, with ms 'July 27th' on title page is a somewhat longer version of the same, but gives no time. There are around a dozen printed reports, all with slightly different wording. Another report, from Kendal (*TT* E454/21 *A Message Sent From His Highness the Prince of Wales to the Maior of Yarmouth*, letter from Robert Green, Kendal 13 [*recte* 23rd see Chapter 6, n. 57] July 1648) is by no means as detailed, but is an independent account. It gives noon as the time the Scots' van appeared.

26 *TT* E454/2 *The Moderate*, no. 2, 18–25 July 1648, report from Appleby 21 July.

27 See Chapter 6, n. 25.

28 Burnet, p. 356; Braye p. 168, gives the time at which the guards were pushed back towards the town as one o'clock. The date, sender, and recipient are not known.

29 *TT* E454/10 *A Bloody Fight in the North on Munday last, July 17 1648*, letter from Liverpool 21 July; *TT* E525/9 *Perfect Occurrences of Every Daies iournall in Parliament*, no. 82, 21–28 July 1648, letter from Bowes 19 July; *TT* E454/14 *A True Relation of the Fight between Maior Gen. Lambert and the Scots Army neer Appleby July 24 1648*, undated pamphlet, with ms 'July 27th' on title page.

30 Not the Henry Sheeres who was later Surveyor General of the Tangier mole.

31 Burnet, p. 356.

32 John F. Curwen, *The Later Records Relating to North Westmorland or the Barony of Appleby*, (Cumberland & Westmorland Antiquarian & Archaeological Society Record Series, vol. VIII), 1932. p. 159.

33 Rushworth, pp. 1200–1, 24 July 1648.

34 *TT* E525/9 *Perfect Occurrences of Every Daies iournall in Parliament*, no. 82, 21–28 July 1648, letter from Bowes 19 July; *TT* E525/10 *A Perfect Diurnall of some Passages in Parliament*, no. 261, 24–31 July 1648, letter from Bowes 19 July; *TT* E454/14 *A True Relation of the Fight between Maior Gen. Lambert and the Scots Army neer Appleby July 24 1648*, undated pamphlet, with ms 'July 27th' on title page, is the only one to say that the party was foot, the rest are silent on the point. Rushworth, pp. 1200–1, 24 July 1648 gives the rank as Capt, the rest, Col. or no rank.

35 Firth and Davies, pp. 258, 260, 262.

36 *TT* E454/19 *Packets of Letters*, no. 19, letter from Bowes 19 July 1648; *TT* E454/10 *A Bloody Fight in the North on Munday last, July 17 1648*, letter from Liverpool 21 July; *TT* E454/14 *A True Relation of the Fight between Maior Gen. Lambert and the Scots Army neer Appleby July 24 1648*, undated pamphlet with ms 'July 27th' on title page.

37 See Chapter 6, n. 28.

38 *TT* E454/10 *A Bloody Fight in the North on Munday last, July 17 1648*, letter from Liverpool 21 July, and *TT* E454/21 *A Message Sent From His Highness the Prince of Wales to the Maior of Yarmouth*, letter from Robert Green, Kendal 13 [*recte* 23rd see Chapter 6, n. 57] July 1648, both say sixty were discovered and all put to the sword; *TT* E454/3 *The Perfect Weekly Account*, no. 19, 19–29 July 1648, gives a hundred killed and taken in the barn.

39 *TT* E454/6 *The Kingdomes Weekly Intelligencer*, no. 269, 18–25 July 1648, report read on 24 July.

40 Burnet, p. 356; *Letter from Holland*.

41 E.g. *TT* E454/14 *A True Relation of the Fight between Maior Gen. Lambert and the Scots Army neer Appleby July 24 1648*, undated pamphlet, with ms 'July 27th' on title page. S. Birch, 'A true and perfect account of the receipts and disbursements of Captaine Samuel Birch . . .', *Portland Papers*, vol. III, pp. 173–86, mentions leaving at daybreak. A letter in Braye, p. 168, says 'that night towards morning, our men retreated'. *Ane Information* says that Lambert left about midnight 'towards Lancashire'.

42 Burnet, p. 356.

43 See Chapter 5, n. 39.

44 *Portland Papers*, vol. I, p. 488, Lambert to William Lenthall, Barnard Castle, 20 July 1648; Hesilrige, DG21/275/h, Lambert to Hesilrige, Barnard Castle 19 July 1648. *TT* E454/14 *A True Relation of the Fight between Maior Gen. Lambert and the Scots Army neer Appleby July 24 1648*, undated pamphlet, with ms 'July 27th' on title page.

45 Charles Carlton, *Going to the Wars: The Experience of the English Civil Wars 1638–1651*, London: Routledge, 1992, p. 325.

46 *TT* E454/14 *A True Relation of the Fight between Maior Gen. Lambert and the Scots Army neer Appleby July 24 1648*, undated pamphlet, with ms 'July 27th' on title page; Hesilrige, DG21/275/h, Lambert to Hesilrige, Barnard Castle 19 July 1648.

47 *Portland Papers*, vol. I, p. 488, Lambert to William Lenthall, Barnard Castle, 20 July 1648.

48 *TT* E454/14 *A True Relation of the Fight between Maior Gen. Lambert and the Scots Army neer Appleby July 24 1648*, undated pamphlet, with ms 'July 27th' on title page. The date in the title must be that of the letter, rather than the action.

49 Burnet, p. 356.

50 Curwen, pp. 52–5. Each arch had a span of 45 feet and a rise of 12 feet.

51 *FSPB, Field Service Pocket Book*, London: HMSO, 1914, p. 118, gives a figures of about 44 lb for a bridge of the dimensions of Appleby. This is based on the efficiency of gunpowder in 1914. In 1648, perhaps twice as much would be needed but this would depend on the quality of the ingredients, and the manufacturing standard and fineness of the particular batch of powder.

52 See Chapter 6, n. 50.

53 See Chapter 6, n. 48.

54 Aylmer, f. 147r, Hamilton to Langdale, Kirby [Thore] 19 July 1648.

55 *Ane Information.*

56 *TT* E456/5 *Another great and bloudy Fight in the North*, letter from Barnard Castle 27 July 1648.

57 *TT* E454/21 *A Message Sent From His Highness the Prince of Wales to the Maior of Yarmouth*, letter from Robert Green, Kendal 13 [*recte* 23rd] July 1648. The 1 in the date is indistinct, but is certainly not a straight line. It is in fact a very worn figure 2 – *vide* a small and badly printed 4 in the line below. The J of July is also worn. In any case a date of 13th cannot have been intended, as the reference to Wednesday and Thursday would then have been to 5 and 6 July, when Lambert was moving from Warwick Bridge to Penrith through Dalston and Sowerby, and not in contact with the enemy.

58 Wanklyn, 2006, p. 190 n. 2.

59 *TT* E454/16 *The Moderate Intelligencer*, no. 175, 20–27 July 1648, letter from Newcastle 21 July 1648.

60 Hill and Watkinson, pp. 59, 116.

61 E.g. Richard Holmes, *Preston 1648*, Market Drayton: Mercia, 1985, p. 16; Reid, p. 226; Woolrych, 1961, p. 164.

62 See Chapter 6, n. 57.

63 Rushworth, p. 1211, Monday July 30 [*sic, recte* 31] 1648.

64 *TT* E525/10 *A Perfect Diurnall of some Passages in Parliament*, no. 261, 24–31 July 1648, letter from Lambert to the Commons dated 25 July.

65 Braye, p. 168; *TT* E454/14 *A True Relation of the Fight between Maior Gen. Lambert and the Scots Army neer Appleby July 24 1648*, undated pamphlet, with ms 'July 27th' on title page.

66 *TT* E454/16 *The Moderate Intelligencer*, no. 175, 20–27 July 1648, letter from Newcastle 21 July 1648.

67 *CSPD 1648–1649*, p. 208, 21 July 1648.

68 D. W. King, 'The High Command of the New Model Army', *Journal of the Society for Army Historical Research*, vol. 56 (1978), p. 57.

69 See Chapter 3, n. 68.

70 *TT* E456/1 *Another Fight between the Two Armies of Scotch and English*, letter from Barnard Castle 25 July 1648.

71 *TT* E525/9 *Perfect Occurrences of Every Daies iournall in Parliament*, no. 82, 21–28 July 1648, report from Bowes 20 July.

72 Abbott, vol. 1, pp. 618–9, Cromwell to Lord Fairfax, 28 July 1648.

73 Rushworth, p. 1211, Monday July 30 [*sic, recte* 31] 1648; Whitelocke, p. 325, 31 August 1648; both refer to a letter from Lambert's quarters 28 July.

74 Whitelocke, p. 325, 31 August 1648, letter from Lambert, text and date not given.

75 *CSPD 1648–1649*, p. 69, 15 May 1648.

76 *CSPD 1648–1649*, p. 221, 28 July 1648; *Portland Papers*, vol. I, pp. 490–2, four letters about the loss of Scarborough; *CJ*, vol. 5, p. 673, 16 August 1648.

77 *TT* E454/21 *A Message Sent From His Highness the Prince of Wales to the Maior of Yarmouth*, letter from Robert Green, Kendal 13th [*recte* 23rd, see Chapter 6, n. 57] July 1648.

78 Turner, p. 59.

79 *TT* E456/1 *Another Fight between the Two Armies of Scotch and English*, letter from Barnard Castle 25 July 1648.

80 *TT* E522/10 *Perfect Occurrences of Every Daies iournall in Parliament*, no. 65, 24–31 March 1648, a List of the Field Officers and Captains.

Notes – Chapter 6: Appleby, Stainmore and Bowes

81 It is also possible that this was the Captain Robert Atkinson of Mallerstang, who was active there in June 1648 when Hesilrige asked Lambert to send him forty muskets and bandoliers (Hesilrige, DG21/275/d, Lambert to Hesilrige, Penrith 11 June 1648).

82 *TT* E457/28 *Packets of Letters*, no. 21, letter from Helmsley 4 August 1648; Rushworth, p. 1219, 7 August 1648, letter from Appleby 4 August giving 'Saturday last' as the date of surrender; Whitelocke, p. 326, 7 August 1648, says that both a Scot and an English solder were killed. Gardiner and others give 31 July for the surrender, but contemporary reports give Saturday 29th.

83 *TT* E457/33 *The Moderate Intelligencer*, no. 177, 3–10 August 1648, report from Newcastle 4 August.

84 *TT* E525/15 *Perfect Occurrences of Every Daies iournall in Parliament*, no. 84, 4–11 August 1648, report from Durham 3 August. See also Chapter 3, n. 43.

85 *TT* E456/5 *Another great and bloudy Fight in the North*, letter from Barnard Castle 27 July 1648.

86 Burnet, p. 356; Turner, p. 77.

Chapter 7: To Preston and Back

1 Rushworth, p. 1219, letter dated 4 August; *TT* E525/16 *A Perfect Diurnall of some Passages in Parliament*, no. 263, 7–14 August 1648, report from Newcastle 4 August.

2 Hesilrige, DG21/275/i, Lambert to Hesilrige, Richmond 3 August 1648. A contemporary note on the outside of the letter wrongly gives the date as Wednesday 3 July.

3 *TT* E525/15 *Perfect Occurrences of Every Daies iournall in Parliament*, no. 84, 4–11 August 1648, report from Richmond 3 August.

4 Rushworth, p. 1218, 7 August 1648, letter from York dated 4 August 1648; *TT* E457/21 *The Moderate*, no. 4, 1–8 August 1648, report of letters from York to the Commons 4 August; *TT* E457/24 *The Perfect Weekly Account*, no. 21, 2–9 August 1647 [*sic*], report of letters from York 4 August. Punctuation and orthography vary slightly in each report.

5 *TT* E525/15 *Perfect Occurrences of Every Daies iournall in Parliament*, no. 84, 4–11 August 1648.

6 Royle, p. 465.

7 H. C. B. Rogers, *Battles and Generals of the Civil Wars 1642–1651*, London: Seeley Service, 1968, p. 280.

8 *TT* E459/2 *Packets of Letters*, no. 22, letter from Helmsley Castle 10 August 1648.

9 National Library of Scotland, Add. Mss 35.5.11, ff. 28–9, letter from Thomas Margetts to William Clarke, York, 9 June 1648, printed in part in Firth, *The Clarke Papers*, vol. ii, p. 25.

10 *CSPD 1648–1649*, pp. 208, 227, 21 July and 1 August 1648.

11 Abbott, vol. 1, pp. 624–5; Rushworth, p. 1191, 15 July 1648, reports Cromwell as intending to march north 'on Friday last' [14th]; it was not until 18th that Derby House issued an order for him to march north with all the troops which could safely be spared (*CSPD 1648–1649*, p. 199). Rushworth, p. 1206, 28 July 1648, reports him as in Gloucester on 'Wednesday last', which must be 26th to allow for marching over 150 miles.

12 See Chapter 1, n. 59.

13 See Chapter 6, n. 14.

14 *TT* E457/24 *The Perfect Weekly Account*, no. 21, 2–9 August 1647 [*sic*], report of letters from Nottingham 7 August; *CSPD 1648–1649*, p. 230, 2 August 1648; Rushworth, p. 1227, 14 August 1648. A letter from Helmsley dated 4 August (*TT* E457/28 *Packets of Letters*, no. 21) falsely reported that Cromwell reached Doncaster on that date. The rebels were tried in London in April 1649 and Poyer was shot.

15 *TT* E459/4 *A Terrible and Bloudy Fight at Tinmouth Castle*, letter from Doncaster 11 August 1648; *TT* E459/19 *The Moderate Intelligencer*, no. 178, 10–17 August 1648, report from York 11 August.

16 Holmes, 1887, pp. 308, 320, Paulden's Account.

17 *TT* E459/2 *Packets of Letters*, no. 22, letter from Abersouth 11 August 1648. The original of the letter, written by Margetts to William Clarke, shows the place as Aberforth, i.e. Aberford (National Library of Scotland, Add. Mss 35.5.11, ff. 11–12.).

18 *TT* E460/12 *A Letter from the Earl of Norwich*, letter from York 14 August 1648. The text of the speech is not given.

19 Dawson, 1938, p. 79.

20 *TT* E462/17 *Mercurius Elencticus*, no. 41, 30 August–6 September 1648.

21 Wanklyn, 2006, p. 189, says that Cromwell did 'full justice to all the units under his command' but in fact he mentions every unit present, including the militia regiments, except Lambert's and Lilburne's. The nearest he comes to naming them is to describe them as 'the remaining horse' (Abbott, vol. 1, p. 635, Cromwell to the Speaker, 20 August). He does say in a letter to Derby House three days later that he had sent Lambert in pursuit of Hamilton and the cavalry (Abbott, vol. 1, pp. 641–2). Farr, pp. 119–20 comments on the positive relationship between Lambert and Lilburne.

22 Braye, p. 168, Thomas Margetts to John Browne Esq, Clerk of the Parliament, Brancepeth 14 September 1648.

23 See Chapter 7, n. 17.

24 There is probably an error in Birch's dates, as he says that on the 14th he went to Otley and thence to Skipton, a distance of thirty-one miles, a very long march for foot soldiers.

25 Abbott, vol. 1, p. 634, Cromwell to Speaker Lenthall, 20 August 1648.

26 *Letter from Holland* says the march took two days, but this is presumably from Brough not Kirkby Thore, as Hamilton is unlikely to have managed twenty miles a day over the hills.

27 Aylmer, f. 147r, Hamilton to Langdale, Hornby 12 August 1648, in which he announced his intention of marching on Monday [14th] towards Warrington; Turner, p. 62.

28 Ogilby, plate 38, shows this road as suitable for travel, and there is no reason to suspect that twenty-five years earlier it was not negotiable. The Lancashire reinforcements for Lambert had marched up through Kirkby Lonsdale, but they were then probably aiming for Appleby. It was only after diverting west to take Beetham House that they completed their journey on A6 and came up through Penrith.

29 See Chapter 7, n. 34.

30 Turner, p. 62.

31 Burnet, pp. 357–8; Firth, 1904, p. 309. On 1 July the Commons had asked the county to consider a commander and garrison for the castle.

32 Turner, pp. 62–3.

33 George Ormerod (ed.), 'An Impartiall Relation of the late Fight at Preston . . . by Sir Marmaduke Langdale', *Tracts Relating to Military Proceedings During the Great Civil War in Lancashire*, Chetham Society, vol. II (1844), p. 267.

34 Aylmer, f. 146v, Hamilton to Langdale, Kendal, 8 August 1648; f. 148r, Hamilton to Langdale, 7 August. The origin of the second letter is given as Hornby, but Hamilton was still in Kendal, so either place or date is in error.

35 Aylmer, f. 147v. The letter has no date or place of origin.

36 Currer was presumably of the family at Kildwick Hall, although his precise identification is uncertain. Mr Robin Greenwood, who has kindly shared his knowledge of the family and locality, suggests that Currer was not actually the governor of the castle but a local, somewhat lukewarm, supporter of Parliament.

37 Aylmer, f. 147v, Kendal 7 August; f. 147r, Hornby 12 August 1648.

38 Ormerod, p. 267.

39 See Chapter 7, n. 27.

40 William Beamont (ed.), *A Discourse of the Warr in Lancashire*, Manchester: Chetham Society, vol. LXII (1865), p. 65.

41 Burnet, p. 358.

42 Woolrych, 1961; Holmes, 1985; Bull and Seed. Wanklyn, 2006, Chapters 16–17, discusses the first day. All these sources are used to some extent for the following account, but Sanderson's diary and 'relation' of the battle (Hill and Watkinson, pp. 61–4, 119–21, 141–4) are used as the main source.

43 Following Holmes, 1985, p. 32; Bull and Seed, p. 64; Stephen Bull, *A General Plague of Madness: The Civil Wars in Lancashire 1640–1660*, Lancaster: Carnegie, 2009, p. 326. Hodgson, Sanderson, and Cromwell all say that the point was about a mile from Preston.

44 *TT* E460/35 *The Moderate Intelligencer*, no. 179, 17–24 August 1648, report from Warrington 20 August.

45 *CSPD 1649–1650, Calendar of State Papers, Domestic . . . 1649–1650,* ed by M. A. E. Green, London: HMSO, 1875, p. 358, 9 November 1649, when lead from Lancaster Castle was ordered to be sent to Preston to re-lead the chancel for the reason given.

46 On 7 August Derby House decided to write to the 'Deputy-Lieutenants and Committees of Cheshire, to raise what forces they can, to keep a good correspondence with those of Lancashire, and to assist them in keeping Warrington bridge, in regard of the Scots coming into that county,' but in their letter of the following day there was no mention of Warrington (*CSPD 1648–1649,* pp. 233, 237, 7 and 8 August 1648).

47 Abbott, vol. 1, pp. 641–2, Cromwell to Derby House, Wigan, 23 August 1648.

48 When Lambert marched from Berwick to Edinburgh late in September, he had with him his own, Cromwell's, Lilburne's and Twistleton's regiments, but this may have no relevance to the situation at Uttoxeter. *TT* E468/26 *A True Account of the great Expressions of Love from the Noblemen, Ministers & Commons of the Kingdom of Scotland,* letter from Carlisle 14 October 1648.

Chapter 8: To Scotland and Pontefract

1 Abbott, vol. 1, p. 640, Cromwell to the Committee at York, from Wigan, 23 August 1648. He could have written this, and the letter to Derby House (Chapter 7, n. 21), either in the evening on arrival, or in the morning before departure.

2 *TT* E462/11 *The Moderate,* no. 8, 29 August–5 September 1648, report from Knaresborough 2 September.

3 *TT* E462/18 *The Moderate Intelligencer,* no. 181, 31 August–7 September 1648, report from Skipton 28 August.

4 Fairfax, f. 98, letter from H. Cholmley to Col. Fairfax, Ferry bridge 1 September; *TT* E462/14 *Packets of Letters,* no. 25, letter from Helmsley 31 August.

5 *TT* E526/5 *Perfect Occurrences of Every Daie iournall in Parliament,* no. 89, 8–15 September 1648, report from Knaresborough 8 September.

6 *TT* E464/16 *A Remonstrance for Peace,* letter from Durham 14 September 1648.

7 Rushworth, p. 1261, 12 September 1648.

8 Hill and Watkinson, pp. 64, 121, where it was incorrectly assumed that Sanderson went first to Wroxeter. In fact, the place is Rocester in Staffordshire (SK 110393), only four miles north of Uttoxeter.

9 Fairfax, f. 92, letter from Lambert to Col. Fairfax, 4 September 1648.

10 *TT* E464/16 *A Remonstrance for Peace,* letter from Durham 14 September 1648; *TT* E463/8 *Packets of Letters,* no. 26, letter from York 9 September 1648; Rushworth, p. 1259, 11 September 1648.

11 Rushworth, pp. 1264–5, 18 September 1648, letter dated 14 September.

12 *TT* E526/5 *Perfect Occurrences of Every Daie iournall in Parliament,* no. 89, 8–15 September 1648, report from Knaresborough 8 September; Rushworth, p. 1250, 4 September.

13 Whitelocke, p. 336, 11 August 1648; *CSPD 1648–1649,* 24 August 1648; Rushworth, p. 1259, 11 September.

14 *CSPD 1648–1649,* pp. 264–6, 1 September 1648. They wrote in similar terms to both colonels and to Col. Bright by the same post.

15 Rushworth, p. 1339, 27 November 1648, letter dated 20 November; *TT* E473/1 *The Moderate,* no. 19, 14–21 November 1648, report from Pontefract 18 November.

16 See Chapter 8, n. 14.

17 *CSPD 1648–1649,* pp. 269, 274, 282, 4, 8 and 16 September 1648.

18 *TT* E462/18 *The Moderate Intelligencer,* no. 181, 31 August–7 September 1648, report from Newcastle 1 September; *TT* E463/2 *The Demands Of Lieutenant-Generall Crumwell,* letter from Newcastle 8 September 1648.

19 Hill and Watkinson, pp. 59, 109; *Portland Papers,* vol. I, p. 508, Statement by Major John Mayer, 28 January 1648[9], part of the examination of Captain Batten's record as governor.

20 State Papers Domestic, Supplementary, SP 46/95, March 1648[9].

21 *TT* E462/18 *The Moderate Intelligencer,* no. 181, 31 August–7 September 1648, report from Newcastle 1 September; *TT* E463/2 *The Demands Of Lieutenant-Generall Crumwell,* letter from Newcastle 8 September

1648; *TT* E462/11 *The Moderate*, no. 8, 29 August–5 September 1648, report from Knaresborough 2 September; *TT* E462/19 *Bloudy Nevves from the North*, letter from Helmsley 4 September 1648.

22 Le Fleming, pp. 19–20 (document 201–2), Orders issued by Sir Philip Musgrave, in the role of commander-in-chief, at Appleby.

23 *TT* E462/19 *Bloudy Nevves from the North*, letter from Helmsley 4 September 1648; Rushworth, p. 1250, 4 September 1648.

24 *TT* E462/18 *The Moderate Intelligencer*, no. 181, 31 August–7 September 1648, report from Newcastle 1 September, and report from Skipton 28 August; *TT* E462/19 *Bloudy Nevves from the North*, report from Helmsley 4 September 1648; *TT* E462/22 *The Resolution Of Major-Generall Munro*, letter from Richmond 4 September 1648; Rushworth, pp. 1250, 1253, 4 and 5 September, letter dated 1 September 1648.

25 *CSPD 1648–1649*, p. 112, 8 June 1648.

26 Rushworth, p. 1283, 2 October 1648; *CSPD 1648–1649*, pp. 287, 289, 20, 21, 22 September 1648.

27 Rushworth, pp. 1264–5, 18 September 1648, letter from Brandespeth [Brancepeth] 15 September 1648; Braye, pp. 168–9, letter from Margetts to Browne, Brancepeth, dated 14 September 1648; see *TT* E526/8 *A Perfect Diurnall of some Passages in Parliament*, no. 269, 18–25 September 1648 for a précis of the same letter; *CJ*, vol. 6, p. 32, 25 September 1648.

28 Rushworth, p. 1283, 2 October 1648.

29 Daniel Lysons and Samuel Lysons, *Magna Britannia, vol. 4 Cumberland*, London: T. Cadell & W. Davies, 1816, p. 41 and n. 4.

30 Rushworth, p. 1294, letters received in the House 16 October 1648; *TT* E468/7 *A Great Victory at Appleby*, letter from Appleby 11 October 1648.

31 *TT* E472/12 *A Message Sent to the King from both Houses of Parliament, On Wednesday 15 November 1648.*

32 *TT* E464/27 *Bloudy Newes from the North*, letter from R. Smith, Richmond 18 September 1648.

33 See previous note, and *TT* E463/14 *Victorious Nevves from the North*, letter from York 10 September 1648; Rushworth, p. 1277, 26 September 1648. Two reports of a letter from Brancepeth mention Tyldesley and Sir William Blackstone as being around Chillingham at this time (*TT* E526/7 *Perfect Occurrences of Every Daies iournall in Parliament*, no. 90, 15–22 September 1648, report from Brandspeth near Durham 15 September and *TT* E526/8 *A Perfect Diurnall of some Passages in Parliament*, no. 269, 18–25 September 1648). Among those who escaped was 'young Salkield' who may be the Captain Thomas Salkeld whose life Major Sanderson of Lilburne's had saved at Preston (Hill and Watkinson, p. 142).

34 See Hill and Watkinson, pp. 18–21 for a summary of the army careers of the several Sanderson brothers.

35 Rushworth, p. 1265, 18 September 1648, letter from York dated 15 September 1648; *CJ*, vol. 6, p. 32, 25 September 1648, letter from Cols. Lascelles and Bethell, 16 September, letter from Mr Robinson and Mr Anlaby, 16 September 1648; *TT* E526/7 *Perfect Occurrences of Every Daies iournall in Parliament*, no. 90, 15–22 September 1648.

36 Rushworth, p. 1259, 11 September, letter from York dated 9 September 1648; p. 1264, 14 September 1648, letter from Cromwell at Alnwick dated 14 September; *TT* E463/8 *Packets of Letters*, no. 26, letter from York 9 September 1648, says that Cromwell was at Durham on 7th and in Newcastle on 8th. Rushworth, p. 1260, 12 September 1648, says that Cromwell and his army were still about Durham on 8th, so a departure from there on 9th or 10th is to be preferred.

37 See Chapter 7, n. 25.

38 Abbott, vol. 1, p. 650 and n. 114.

39 Rushworth, p. 1260, 12 September 1648; *TT* E464/27 *Bloudy Newes from the North*, letter from R. Smith, Richmond 18 September 1648.

40 *TT* E463/2 *The Demands Of Lieutenant-Generall Crumwell*, letter from Newcastle 8 September 1648.

41 Rushworth, p. 1265, 18 September 1648, letter dated 15 September. A summary of this letter in Braye, pp. 168–9, shows that it was from Thomas Margetts to John Browne.

42 Rushworth, p. 1273, 25 September 1648, letter from Norham dated 20 September.

43 Abbott, vol. 1, p. 650, Cromwell to Sir William Armyn?, from Alnwick 14 September 1648.

44   Abbott, vol. 1, pp. 650–4, Cromwell to: the Governor of Berwick, 15 September; the Committee of Estates, 16 September; the Earl of Loudon, 18 September 1648. Abbott, vol. 1, p. 658, Cromwell to Derby House, 20 September.

45   Abbott, vol. 1, p. 659, Cromwell to the Committee of Estates, 21 September, and p. 656, Cromwell's Proclamation 20 September 1648; *TT* E465/39 *The Moderate Intelligencer*, no. 185, 28 September–5 October 1648, report from Mordington 27 September; *TT* E465/34 *Good News from Scotland*, letter from J. L. at Cromwell's quarters, Mordington near Berwick, 27 September 1648.

46   Rushworth, p. 1311, 30 October 1648, letters from York dated 22 October 1648.

47   Rushworth, p. 1306, 24 October 1648, letter from Newcastle dated 16 October 1648.

48   Margetts (Braye, p. 169, letter to John Browne, Belford 20 September 1648) says that it was Col. Bright and Major Strachan who were sent as commissioners to Argyll, but Major Strachan (or Straughan) was a messenger for the Scottish side (Abbott, vol. 1, p. 657, Cromwell to Derby House, from Norham 20 September 1648).

49   *TT* E466/7 *Letters from Lieutenant General Crumwels Quarters*. Lambert to Cromwell, Haggerston 16 September 1648; Abbott, vol. 1, p. 658, Cromwell to Derby House, 20 September; Rushworth, p. 1274, 25 September, letter from Cromwell's quarters at Norham dated 20 September (this letter also in *TT* E526/11 *A Perfect Diurnall of some Passages in Parliament*, no. 270, 25 September–2 October 1648); *TT* E465/34 *Good News from Scotland*, letter from J. L. at Cromwell's quarters, Mordington near Berwick, 27 September 1648.

50   Hill and Watkinson, pp. 118, 126, appendix 6.

51   *TT* E465/3 *The Kings Majesties Declaration for Peace* . . . *With a dangerous fight and the number of killed and wounded*, [printed] 28 September 1648.

52   Rushworth, p. 1284, 23 October 1648; Abbott, vol. 1, pp. 660–2, Cromwell to Speaker Lenthall from Berwick, 2 October; *TT* E465/39 *The Moderate Intelligencer*, no. 185, 28 September–5 October 1648, report from Mordington 27 September; Braye, pp. 171–2, Thomas Margetts to John Browne, Seaton, 3 October 1648.

53   Braye, pp. 171–2, Thomas Margetts to John Browne, 3 October 1648.

54   Braye, pp. 171–3, Thomas Margetts to John Browne, 3, 10 and 17 October 1648; Abbott, vol. 1, p. 669, Cromwell to Speaker Lenthall, 9 October 1648; Whitelocke, p. 345, 23 October 1648; Rushworth, p. 1305, 23 October 1648, letter from Lambert's quarters, Eaton [*sic, recte* Seton] 28 October 1648. There is a problem with the date of this letter, which cannot post-date the Rushworth entry. It is presumably a misprint for 18th.

55   Rushworth, p. 1313, 31 October 1648, letter from Edinburgh 24 October.

56   *TT* E468/26 *A True Account of The great Expressions of Love from the Noblemen Ministers & Commons of the Kingdom of Scotland*, letter from Carlisle 14 October 1648. Sanderson mentions only Lambert's and Lilburne's (Hill and Watkinson, p. 126).

57   *CJ*, vol. 6, p. 57, 20 October 1648.

58   Rushworth, p. 1310, 30 October 1648, letters from York 22 October 1648.

59   Abbott, vol. 1, p. 670.

60   Rushworth, p. 1317, 6 November 1648, letter to the Speaker from Barnard Castle 25 October.

61   Abbott, vol. 1, pp. 671–2, Cromwell to Speaker Lenthall, Boroughbridge, 28 October 1648; *TT* E469/19 *The Perfect Weekly Account*, 25 October–1 November 1648, letters read 31 October. Christopher Sanderson, 'Selections from the Diary of Christopher Sanderson of Barnard Castle', *Six North Country Diaries*, Surtees Society, vol. 118 (1910), p. 37, also refers to the visit to Barnard Castle and his move to Richmond.

62   *TT* E472/4 *The Moderate*, no. 18, 7–14 November 1648, report from Knottingley 10 November.

63   *TT* E472/11 *The Moderate Intelligencer*, no. 191, 9–16 November 1648, letter from Edinburgh 27 October; Rushworth, p. 1319, 6 October 1648, letter from Lambert's quarters dated 1 November (based on a letter in Braye, p. 173, from Margetts to John Brown, from Broxmouth 1 November).

64   Rushworth, p. 1325, 13 November 1648, letter dated 9 November from Lambert's quarters 'on his march back out of Scotland'; Hill and Watkinson, pp. 67, 128.

65   *TT* E473/1 *The Moderate*, no. 19, 14–21 November 1648, report from Pontefract 18 November. *TT*
     E472/4 *The Moderate*, no. 18, 7–14 November 1648, report from Knottingley 10 November, has the same
     information, but the date cannot be correct in view of the distances involved. The same letter said that three
     troops of Lambert's dragoons had reached Pontefract, although the only two such troops he had were still
     with him on 16th (see next note).
66   *TT* E473/1 *The Moderate*, no. 19, 14–21 November 1648, report from Newcastle 16 November.
67   Rushworth, p. 1339, 27 November 1648; *TT* E474/9 *Packets of Letters*, no. 37, letter from Doncaster
     25 November 1648. The letter in Rushworth begins: 'From the Leaguer before Pontefract by Letters this
     day November 20' but refers to Lambert arriving 'Monday last', that is, 13 November. But he did not leave
     Newcastle until the 17th, which means that this is a good example of editing of a letter to reflect the date
     of printing. It appears that Rushworth took his information from a printed version which has not been
     identified.

Chapter 9: The Siege of Pontefract

1   *TT* E448/16 *Packets of Letters*, no. 14, letter from Newcastle 15 June 1648.
2   Holmes, 1887, pp. 150, 321.
3   Rushworth, p. 1314, 31 October 1648, letter from York dated 28 October; Abbott, vol. 1, p. 683,
     Cromwell to Derby House, dated 15 November 1648 but *recte* 5th, see Chapter 9, n. 27.
4   Holmes, 1887, pp. 321–2, sees them as the same raid, but he has overlooked the widely differing dates.
5   *TT* E451/22 *A true and perfect Relation of a Great Victory obtained by the Parliaments Forces*.
6   *TT* E449/45 *The Kingdomes Weekly Intelligencer*, no. 266, 20–27 June 1648, report dated 26 June in which
     Tickhill 'if I am not mistaken is on the confines of *Derby-shire*'. It is actually well over twenty miles from
     Derbyshire as the crow flies.
7   E.g. Fairfax, f. 27, f. 31, f. 56, f. 57, f. 69, f. 103.
8   Fairfax, f. 27. In f. 82, Digby thanks Col. Fairfax for his civility in this matter.
9   Fairfax, f. 103, f. 104, f. 108, f. 109, f. 110, 20 and 30 September, 6 and 7 October. Morris, Fairfax, f. 109,
     said that he had paid dearly for a protection for his father. There are many more letters between the two in
     the same correspondence.
10   Rushworth, pp. 1294, 1314, 16 and 31 October 1648, letter from York dated 28 October.
11   Whitelocke, p. 344, 20 October 1648.
12   Rushworth, pp. 1300, 1305–6, 20 and 24 October 1648.
13   Fairfax, f. 106, General Fairfax to Col. Fairfax, 27 September 1648; F. W. Leyborne-Popham, *Report on
     the Manuscripts of F.W. Leyborne-Popham . . .*, Historical Manuscripts Commission [51st Report], London:
     HMSO, 1899, pp. 6–8, Rainsborough to General Fairfax, 15 October 1648.
14   Holmes, 1887, pp. 308–10.
15   *TT* E526/7 *Perfect Occurrences of Every Daies iournall in Parliament*, no. 90, 15–22 September 1648, letters from
     the north 18 September.
16   Fairfax, f. 105, letter from H. Chomley to C. Fairfax, 26 September 1648.
17   *TT* E469/4 *A Bloudy Fight at Pontefract Castle in York-shire on Sunday morning last*, letter from Pontefract Upper-
     town 20 October 1648.
18   Leyborne-Popham, pp. 6–8, Rainsborough to Lord Fairfax, Doncaster, 15 October 1648.
19   Rushworth, p. 1314, 31 October 1648, letter from York dated 28 October; Whitelocke, p. 346, 31 October
     1648.
20   *TT* E469/4 *A Bloudy Fight at Pontefract Castle in York-shire on Sunday morning last*, letter from Pontefract Upper-
     town 20 October 1648. It is not clear how long his regiment remained in Axholme.
21   There is still a Ferry Boat Lane on both sides of the river, just over half a mile west of the road bridge
     carrying the A6023. The first mention of the ferry other than by Paulden is in a dispute between William
     Savile and Sir William Reresby in 1694–1695. It ceased operating in 1964 just after the building of the
     bridge which now connects Mexborough to Old Denaby and Conisbrough. (Information on Mexborough
     kindly provided by J. R. Ashby, chair (2008–2011) of the Mexborough and District Heritage Society.)

22 Whitelocke, p. 346, 1 November 1648; Rushworth, p. 1315, 1 November 1648; Drake, pp. 98–9; Holmes, 1887 (both Letter and Account), pp. 151–2, 313–14.

23 Rushworth, p. 1319, 6 November 1648.

24 *CSPD 1648–1649*, p. 307, 17 October 1648; Rushworth, p. 1301, 23 October 1648; *CJ*, vol. 6, pp. 58, 61, 23 (Lancs) and 24 (Yorks) October 1648; *TT* E472/11 *The Moderate Intelligencer*, no. 191, 9–16 November 1648, report from Knottingley 11 November. See also Chapter 9, n. 81.

25 Abbott, vol. 1, p. 673, Cromwell to Col. Fairfax from Byron, 2 November at eight at night.

26 Abbott, vol. 1, p. 680, Cromwell to Col. Fairfax, from Knottingley, 6 November 1648.

27 Abbott, vol. 1, pp. 673–4, 683–4, Cromwell to Derby House, 15 November; *CSPD 1648–1649*, p. 321, 10 November 1648. Derby House sent the letter on the Commons, who on 15th referred it on to the Army Council. At this point the letter seems to have been copied with a date of 15 November, leading to a false belief that Cromwell wrote two letters. There is no record of two such letters being received at Derby House.

28 *CJ*, vol. 6, pp. 667, 681, 15 and 18 November 1648. Nottingham and Lincolnshire are a minimum of twenty miles away, and Sanderson's troop were sent ten miles towards Leeds to quarter.

29 *TT* E469/4 *A Bloudy Fight at Pontefract Castle in York-shire on Sunday morning last*, letter from Pontefract Upper-town 20 October 1648.

30 See Chapter 9, n. 18.

31 Fairfax, f. 121, York Committee to Col. Charles Fairfax, 3 November 1648.

32 *TT* E473/1 *The Moderate*, no. 19, 14–21 November 1648, report from Pontefract 18 November.

33 Rushworth, p. 1325, 13 November 1648, letter from near Pontefract dated 11 November.

34 *TT* E472/11 *The Moderate Intelligencer*, no. 191, 9–16 November 1648, report from Knottingly 11 November; *TT* E473/1 *The Moderate*, no. 19, 14–21 November 1648, report from Pontefract 18 November.

35 Abbott, vol. 1, pp. 681–2, Cromwell to Col. Fairfax from Knottingley 10 November 1648.

36 Rushworth, p. 1325, 13 November 1648, letter from near Pontefract dated 11 November; Holmes, 1887, p. 318, Paulden's Account; *TT* E472/4 *The Moderate*, no. 18, 7–14 November 1648, report from Knottingley 10 November; Baynes, Original Correspondence of Captain Adam Baynes, British Library Add. Mss. 21,417, f. 23, letter from John Baynes, Pontefract 30 December 1648; Rushworth, p. 1393, 16 January 1649.

37 *TT* E474/3 *The Moderate Intelligencer*, no. 193, 23–30 November 1648, letter from Pontefract 20 November; *TT* E474/9 *Packets of Letters*, no. 37, letter from Doncaster 25 November 1648.

38 Abbott, vol. 1, pp. 691–2, letter to Robert Jenner and John Ashe, 20 November, and p. 693, a *laisser passez* for Digby, 22 November 1648.

39 *CSPD 1648–1649*, p. 335, 28 November 1648.

40 *TT* E473/1 *The Moderate*, no. 19, 14–21 November 1648, report from Pontefract 18 November.

41 *TT* E474/3 *The Moderate Intelligencer*, no. 193, 23–30 November 1648, letter from Pontefract 20 November.

42 See Chapter 2, n. 34.

43 *CJ*, vol. 5, pp. 658, 673–4, 675; 2, 17, 19 August 1648.

44 *CJ*, vol. 5, pp. 415–6, 3 January 1647[8]; *CJ*, vol. 6, pp. 81, 88, 91, 20, 27 and 30 November 1648. Rushworth, p. 1331, 20 November 1648, gives the chief heads of the Remonstrance, which he had signed in his capacity as Secretary to the General Council of Officers.

45 Rushworth, pp. 1338, 1350, 27 November and 1 December 1648.

46 Rushworth, pp. 1340, 1351, 29 November and 4 December 1648; *CJ*, vol. 6, pp. 89, 91, 93, 27 and 29 November, 5 December 1648.

47 Rushworth, pp. 1356–7, 8 December 1648, T. Fairfax to the Lord Mayor, 8 December 1648.

48 *CJ*, vol. 6, pp. 95–6, 97, 13 and 14 December 1648; Rushworth, p. 1362, 13 and 14 December 1648.

49 *TT* E474/1 *The Perfect Weekly Account*, 22–29 November 1648, report of letter from headquarters 23 November.

50 *TT* E472/4 *The Moderate*, no. 18, 7–14 November 1648, report from Knottingley 10 November.

51 *TT* E474/3 *The Moderate Intelligencer*, no. 193, 23–30 November 1648, letter from Pontefract 20 November.

52 Firth, *The Clarke Papers*, vol. ii, pp. 62–3, Lord Fairfax to Cromwell, 28 November 1648.

53 See Hill and Watkinson, p. 152, for a discussion of rates of travel.

54 Abbott, vol. 1, p. 707, Cromwell to Lord Fairfax, dated by Abbot to ?29th, properly corrected by David Underdown, *Pride's Purge: Politics in the Puritan Revolution*, Oxford: Clarendon Press, 1971, p. 149 n. 17, to between 23 and 25 November 1648.

55 Hill and Watkinson, pp. 67–8, 131. From the handwriting it appears that Sanderson wrote up his diary on 1 December for that day and the previous two days, but there seems no reason to doubt that he was accurate about events occurring only two days earlier.

56 *TT* E475/26 *The Moderate Intelligencer*, no. 194, 30 November–7 December 1648. Cromwell had time before he left Knottingley on 29th to write an order concerning maintenance of the garrison of Wressell Castle before he left. The letter is incorrectly dated 23rd in *HMC Third Report*, p. 87 but the original (Alnwick Castle Archives, DNP Ms 16) has 'th' after the date and the final digit is certainly 9 rather than 3.

57 *TT* E474/3 *The Moderate Intelligencer*, no. 193, 23–30 November 1648, letter from Pontefract 20 November.

58 See Chapter 9, n. 54.

59 *TT* E476/8 *A Declaration of the Three Deputy-Governors of the Isle of Wight, with A Letter from the House of Commons to Col. Generall Lambert, Now Commander in Chief at the Leaguer before Pontefract* . . . The letter from the Commons is not dated, but the following item is dated 8 December, and the title page has ms date 12th December.

60 *TT* E476/4 *Mercurius Elencticus*, no. 55, 5–12 December 1648, report on 6 December.

61 See Chapter 9, n. 57.

62 *TT* E476/2 *Mercurius Pragmaticus*, no. 36.37 [*sic*], 5–12 December 1648, report on 6 December.

63 *TT* E474/9 *Packets of Letters*, no. 37, letter from Doncaster 25 November 1648; *TT* E474/3 *The Moderate Intelligencer*, no. 193, 23–30 November 1648, letter from Pontefract 20 November; *TT* E476/24 *The Moderate Intelligencer*, no. 195, 7–14 December 1648, report from Pontefract 5 December; Baynes, f. 23, letter from John Baynes to Adam Baynes, Pontefract 30 December 1648.

64 *TT* E475/8 *The Moderate*, no. 21, 28 November–5 December 1648, report from Pontefract 2 December; Rushworth, p. 1352, 4 December 1648, letter from Pontefract; *TT* E476/24 *The Moderate Intelligencer*, no. 195, 7–14 December 1648, report from Pontefract 5 December; *TT* E477/4 *The Moderate*, no. 23, 12–19 December 1648, letter from Pontefract 16 December; Rushworth, p. 1381, 1 January 1648[9], letter from Pontefract 30 December 1648; Baynes, f. 25, letter from John Baynes to Adam Baynes, 6 January 1648[9].

65 *TT* E475/8 *The Moderate*, no. 21, 28 November–5 December 1648, report from Pontefract 2 December, and see pp. 118–19 for earlier complaints.

66 Fairfax, f. 137, Morris to Col. Fairfax, 27 November 1648; f. 137, Col. Fairfax to Morris, 28 November; f. 139, Morris to Fairfax, 29 November 1648; f. 142, Morris to Fairfax, 27 December 1648.

67 *TT* E476/8 *A Declaration of the Three Deputy-Governors of the Isle of Wight* . . . *with A Letter from the House of Commons to Col. Generall Lambert, Now Commander in Chief at the Leaguer before Pontefract* . . . The letter from the Commons is not dated, but the following item is dated 8 December, and the title page is dated in ms 12th December.

68 *TT* E477/4 *The Moderate*, no. 23, 12–19 December 1648, letter from Pontefract 16 December.

69 Order Book, 'Council of the Northern Parliamentary Army, 1647–8. A book containing a modern [before *c*.1900] transcript of part of the order book of the Council, found in some old buildings by Mr W[illia]m Murgatroyd (Councils of War at Ripon, Knaresbro', York, etc.)'. York Minster Library, Hailstone Collection BB53, f. 30, f. 32. (The work is usually referred to as the Order Book, although it is in fact a record of meetings of the Council of War of the Northern Army, chiefly concerned with courts martial.) *TT* E476/24 *The Moderate Intelligencer*, no. 195, 7–14 December 1648, report from Pontefract 5 December; *TT* E477/10 *A Declaration of the Officers belonging to the Brigade of Col. Iohn Lambert*, letter from Pontefract signed by Margetts 12 December; *TT* E477/4 *The Moderate*, no. 23, 12–19 *December* 1648, letter from Pontefract 16 December; Rushworth, pp. 1365–7, 18 December 1648, letter from Lambert to the General and the General Council, dated 12 December 1648 from Pontefract, with a copy of their Remonstrance; Hill and Watkinson, p. 68, for discussion of Bradford's whereabouts.

70 See Chapter 9, n. 68.

71 *TT* E477/4 *The Moderate*, no. 23, 12–19 December 1648, letter from Scarborough 16 December; *TT* E477/13 *The Perfect Weekly Account*, 13–20 December 1648; Rushworth, p. 1352, 4 December 1648.

72 Rushworth, pp. 1370–1, 23 December 1648, letter from Bethell to General Fairfax, from Scarborough, dated 19 December 1648.

73 *TT* E536/34 *Heads of a Diarie Collected out of The Journalls of Both Houses of Parliament*, no. 5, 26 December–2 January 1648/9, letter from Lambert at Pontefract 23 December.

74 Hill and Watkinson, pp. 69, 133. Barnsdale was formerly a large area of forest centred on the village of Hampole, two miles south of Barnsdale Bar.

75 Rushworth, pp. 1365, 1371, 16 and 23 December 1648.

76 Rushworth, p. 1376, 27 December 1648.

77 *CJ*, vol. 6, pp. 107, 108, 109, 110–11, 113; 1, 2, 3, 4 and 8 January 1648[9].

78 Baynes, f. 23, f. 25, letters from John Baynes to Adam Baynes, 30 December 1648 and 6 January 1648[9].

79 Kitson and Clark, p. 193, recording payments made on 24 April 1649. Streeter is very likely to be the John Streeter sent to Ireland in 1650 as a fortifications engineer.

80 Fairfax, f. 149.

81 Baynes, f. 23, f. 24, letters from John Baynes to Adam Baynes, Pontefract 30 December 1648, and Margetts to Adam Baynes, 6 January 1649; Rushworth, p. 1386, 8 January 1648[9], letter from Pontefract 6 January. A report in *TT* E472/11 *The Moderate Intelligencer*, no. 191, 9–16 November 1648, from Knottingley 11 November, saying that Cholmley's horse had been discharged and their place taken by Harrison's probably referred to their removal from the besieging forces rather than to disbanding.

82 Rushworth, p. 1393, 16 January 1648[9], letter from Pontefract dated 13 January 1649 (and see fuller version in Fox, p. 133); Rushworth, pp. 1399–400, 22 January 1648[9]; *TT* E541/4 *The Moderate Intelligencer*, no. 202, 25 January–1 February 1649, report from Pontefract 27 January; Baynes, f. 36, letter from Margetts to Adam Baynes, 27 January 1649. The reference to disbanding Bethell's regiment conflicts with the letter to Col. Fairfax, previous note.

83 *CJ*, vol. 6, pp. 112–13, 120, 6 and 17 January 1648[9].

84 Baynes, f. 28, letter from Margetts to Adam Baynes, Pontefract 13 January 1649. Rushworth, p. 1386, 8 January 1648[9] has an extract from the letter.

85 Firth and Rait, vol. I, pp. 1253–5, the Act for the Trial and Judgment of Charles Stuart, listing all the commissioners. It is noteworthy that none of the commissioners was given their military rank, giving the outward appearance of a civilian trial.

86 See Chapter 9, n. 41.

87 *TT* E539/13 *The Moderate Intelligencer*, no. 201, 18–25 January 1649, report from Liverpool 19 January; *TT* E543/3 *The Moderate Intelligencer*, no. 204, 8–15 February 1649, report from Preston 9 February.

88 *TT* E546/18 *Mercurius Pragmaticus*, no. 45, 6–13 March 1648, report from Lancashire.

89 Fairfax, f. 171, Lambert to C. Fairfax from Knottingley 28 February [1649].

90 *TT* E548/19 *The Kingdomes Weekly Intelligencer*, no. 304, 20–27 March 1649.

91 *CSPD 1649–1650*, pp. 70, 98, 139, 163, 4 and 17 April, 14 and 29 May 1649; *TT* E551/12 *Mercurius Pragmaticus*, no. 1, 17–24 April 1649, report from Lancashire 20 April; *TT* E551/9 *A Modest Narrative of Intelligence*, no. 3, 14–21 April 1649, report of a letter from Lancaster 17 April; *TT* E552/21 *The Kingdomes Weekly Intelligencer*, no. 309, 24 April–1 May 1649, report on 25 April. Bamber had been troublesome from June 1648, when he had declared 'that he would sooner fight against his Excellencies Forces than against the Forces in Westmerland' (*TT* E447/4 *Packets of Letters*, no. 13, letter from Wigan 9 June 1648; Rushworth, p. 1148, 12 June 1648).

92 *TT* E539/13 *The Moderate Intelligencer*, no. 201, 18–25 January 1649, letter from Pontefract 20 January; Baynes, f. 36, letter from Margetts to Adam Baynes, 27 January 1649.

93 Baynes, f. 43, letter from Margetts to Adam Baynes, Pontefract 3 February 1649.

94 Baynes, f. 40, f. 43, letters from John Baynes to Adam Baynes, Pontefract 3 February 1649, and Margetts to Adam Baynes, Pontefract 3 February 1649; *TT* E541/17 *The Kingdomes Weekly Intelligencer*, no. 297,

30 January–6 February 1649, report from Pontefract 5 February; *TT* E541/27 *The Moderate Intelligencer*, no. 203, 1–8 February 1649, report from Pontefract 3 February; *TT* E542/11 *The Moderate*, no. 31, 6–13 *February* 1649, letter from Pontefract 10 February. At this time, most cannon fire was of inert shot, while mortars normally fired explosive shells but could project almost anything.

95 Rushworth, p. 1386, 8 January 1648[9]; Baynes, f. 24, letter from Margetts to Adam Baynes, Pontefract 6 January 1649.

96 Baynes, f. 36, letter from Margetts to Adam Baynes, 27 January 1649; *TT* E545/3 *The Armies Weekly Intelligencer*, no. 5, 15–22 February [1649], report from Pontefract; *TT* E541/4 *The Moderate Intelligencer*, no. 202, 25 January–1 February 1649, report from Pontefract 27 January; *TT* E545/2 *The Moderate Intelligencer*, no. 205, 15–22 February 1649, report from Pontefract 17 February; Whitelocke, p. 383, 19 February 1648. Fox, p. 139, says that Beaumont was chaplain to the garrison.

97 *TT* E545/3 *The Armies Weekly Intelligencer*, no. 5, 15–22 February [1649], report from Pontefract; *TT* E545/15 *Mercurius Pragmaticus*, no. 43 [sic], 20–27 February 1649, report on Pontefract.

98 *TT* E544/10 *The Moderate*, no. 32, 13–20 February 1649.

99 *TT* E541/27 *The Moderate Intelligencer*, no. 203, 1–8 February 1649, report from Pontefract 3 February; *TT* E542/2 *The Kingdomes Faithfull and impartiall Scout*, no. 2, 2–9 February 1648[9], report from Pontefract headed 5 February.

100 Holmes, 1887, p. 152.

101 Holmes, 1887, pp. 318–9.

102 Baynes, f. 40, letter from John Baynes to Adam Baynes, Pontefract 3 February 1649.

103 See Chapter 9, n. 105.

104 *TT* E542/2 *The Kingdomes Faithfull and impartiall Scout*, no. 2, 2–9 February 1648[9], report headed 2 February.

105 *TT* E542/11 *The Moderate*, no. 31, 6–13 February 1649, letter from Pontefract 10 February; *TT* E543/3 *The Moderate Intelligencer*, no. 204, 8–15 February 1649, report from Preston 10 February.

106 Fairfax, f. 150, Morris to Col. Fairfax 25 January 1648.

107 *TT* E544/9 *Mercurius Pragmaticus*, no. 45 [sic], 13–20 February 1649, report on Pontefract; *TT* E545/13 *The Kingdomes Weekly Intelligencer*, no. 300, 20–27 February 1649, letters reported from Pontefract 26 February

108 Fairfax, f. 181; Fox, p. 138.

109 Baynes, f. 53, letter from Margetts to Adam Baynes, 24 February 1648.

110 Baynes, f. 41, f. 61, letters from Robert Baynes to Adam Baynes, Pontefract 3 February and 9 March 1648[9].

111 *TT* E546/4 *Mercurius Pragmaticus*, no. 44, 27 February–5 March 1649, report from Pontefract.

112 Baynes, f. 59, letter from Margetts to Adam Baynes, 3 March 1649; *TT* E546/10 *The Perfect Weekly Account*, 28 February–7 March 1649, report from Pontefract 3 March.

113 Baynes, f. 62, f. 63, letters from John Baynes and Col. Bright to Adam Baynes, Pontefract 10 March 1649.

114 Baynes, f. 70, letter from John Baynes to Adam Baynes, Pontefract 17 March 1648[9]; Holmes, 1887, Paulden's Letter and Account, pp. 152–3, 322. Austwick's father was Mayor of Pontefract. Lilburne's regiment was represented in the signatures to the treaty by Major Smithson, as Colonel Lilburne had remained in London (Baynes, f. 59, letter from Margetts to Adam Baynes, 3 March 1649).

115 Fox, pp. 143–4.

116 *TT* E546/20 *The Moderate*, no. 35, 6–13 March 1649, letter from Pontefract 10 March; *TT* E546/22 *The Perfect Weekly Account*, 7–14 March 1649, report from Pontefract 3 March, letter from Pontefract 10 March; *TT* E546/24 *The Moderate Intelligencer*, no. 208, 8–15 March 1649, report from Pontefract 17 February; Fox, p. 144, Lambert to the Speaker, Knottingley, 22 March 1649.

117 *CJ*, vol. 6, p. 174, 27 March 1649.

118 Holmes, 1887, p. 330. This quantity of lead would cover around 40,000 square feet of roof, assuming a weight of 7 lb or 8 lb per square foot which was, and is, normal for the purpose. Some lead no doubt came from windows and water pipes, but the accounts in Holmes do not distinguish the source. The largest purchaser, a Mr Childe of Leeds, used £2 10s. 0d. worth of Parliamentary wood to smelt at least some of his

Notes – Chapter 9: The Siege of Pontefract

40 tons of lead, which may indicate that it came in part from windows and was melted down to separate it from broken glass and to make it more compact for transport.

119 See Chapter 9, n. 117.

Appendices

1 *ODNB, Oxford Dictionary of National Biography*, 60 vols, Oxford: Oxford University Press, 2004; Joad Raymond, *The Invention of the Newspaper: English Newsbooks 1641–1649*, Oxford: Oxford University Press, 1996, pp. 67–8.

2 See Chapter 7, n. 17.

3 David Scott, '"Particular businesses" in the Long Parliament: The Hull Letters 1644–1648', *Parliament, Politics and Elections 1604–1648*, edited by C. R. Kyle, Camden 5th series, vol. 17, (2001), pp. 334, 335, 341; Letter, no. 489, 25 April 1648; Letter, no. 492, 17 May 1648; Letter, no. 507, 25 August 1648.

4 See Chapter 6, n. 57.

5 *TT* E446/3, E447/4, E448/16, E449/40.

6 Quoted in Lois Spencer, 'The professional and literary connexions of George Thomason', *The Library*, 5th series, vol. XIII (1958), p. 114.

7 Michael Mendle, 'George Thomason's Intentions', in G. Mandelbrote and B. Taylor (eds), *Libraries within the Library: the Origins of the British Library's Printed Collections*, London: British Library, 2009, p. 180.

8 Jason Peacey, *Politicians and Pamphleteers: Propaganda During the English Civil Wars and Interregnum*, Aldershot: Ashgate, 2004, pp. 222–32.

9 Jurgen Diethe, '*The Moderate*: Politics and Allegiances of a Revolutionary Newspaper', *History of Political Thought*, vol. IV (1983), p. 277.

10 See Chapter 6, n. 1.

11 *CJ*, vol. 5, pp. 628, 635, 640, 646; 8, 14, 18 and 25 July 1648.

12 Howard J. Robinson, *The British Post Office: A History*, Princeton N.J.: Princeton University Press, 1948, p. 30 makes a similar point.

13 Syon mss Q.II.153, Alnwick Castle Archives, letters written by Robert Watson to Hugh Potteron 7 March and 20 December 1648.

14 *CSPD 1648–1649*, p. 210, 24 July 1648.

15 *TT* E451/7 *Packets of Letters*; *TT* E525/9 *Perfect Occurrences of Every Daies iournall in Parliament*, no. 82, 21–28 July 1648; *TT* E542/2 *The Kingdomes Faithfull and impartiall Scout*, no. 2, 2–9 February 1649.

16 *CSPD 1648–1649*, p. 177, 8 July 1648; *CJ*, vol. 5, pp. 628–9, 8 July 1648.

17 *TT* E451/41 *An Impartiall and true Relation of the Great Victory Obtained . . . by the Conjoyned Forces . . . Under the Command of Col. Edw. Rosseter.*

18 *TT* E460/24 *Lieut. General Cromwel's Letter To The Honorable William Lenthall . . . of the several great Victories obtained against the Scots.*

19 *TT* E460/28 *A Full Relation of The great Victory Obtained by the Parliament Forces . . .*

20 *TT* E460/16 *Lieutenant General Cromwell's Letter Concerning The Total Routing of the Scots Army . . .*; *TT* E460/17 *A Copy of Lieutenant General Crumwels Letter . . . Of a great and Bloody Fight neere Preston*; *ODNB*.

21 See appendix 1, n. 30.

22 *CSPD 1648–1649*, pp. 202–4, 20 July 1648.

23 *CSPD 1648–1649*, p. 211, 24 July 1648.

24 *CSPD 1648–1649*, pp. 158, 159, 4 July 1648.

25 Kitson and Clark, pp. 171, 178.

26 Syon Mss QII 153.

27 Baynes, f. 25, f. 40.

28 Royce Macgillivray, *Restoration Historians and the English Civil War*, International Archives of the History of Ideas, vol. 74, The Hague: Martinus Nijhoff, 1974, p. 108; Frances Henderson, '"Posterity to judge" – John Rushworth and his "Historical Collections"', *Bodleian Library Record*, vol. 15 (1996), p. 256.

29 *HMC Fourth Report of the Royal Commission on Historical Manuscripts*, London: HMSO, 1874, p. 100.

30 *CSPD 1648–1649*, pp. 91, 167, 212, 3 June, 6 and 25 July 1648; *TT* E448/7 *The Severall Fights neere Colchester in Essex*, letter signed J. R. 15 June 1648; Rushworth, pp. 1136, 1179, 1193, 2 June, 6 and 15 July 1648.

31 Wing S578A, printed in Hill and Watkinson, pp. 141–4; Sanderson's diary is transcribed in Hill and Watkinson; *CSPD 1648–1649*, p. 92, 3 June 1648.

32 *TT* E452/17 *Packets of Letters*, no. 17.

33 T. Carlyle, *Oliver Cromwell's Letters and Speeches:* with elucidations by Thomas Carlyle, 5 vols, London: Chapman & Hall, 1891, vol. ii, p. 15 n.1. He also (p. 15) describes Hodgson himself as 'an honest-hearted, pudding-headed Yorkshire Puritan'.

34 *Portland Papers*, vol. III, pp. 173–86. The original is in the British Library, Add. Mss. 70006 folios 148–65. In Hill and Watkinson, p. 9, the document was unwisely accepted as a diary by the authors.

35 Kitson and Clark, p. 195, show that on 3 July 1649 Capt Roger West received 'in parte of his arreares £200 0s. 0d'. This may be the same man, but there is no evidence either way.

36 *TT* E449/12 *The Perfect Weekly Account*, no. 14, 14–21 June 1647 [*sic*]. A Royalist report, *TT* E449/28 *Mercurius Psiticus*, no. 3, 21–26 June 1648, carries a similar story.

37 *TT* E456/5 *Another great and bloudy Fight in the North* . . . The title page is dated in ms July 31st.

38 *TT* E460/29 *Mercurius Melancholicus*, no. 53, *21–28 August 1648*.

39 *Portland Papers*, vol. III, pp. 173–86. The original is in the British Library, Add. MS. 70006 folios 148–65.

40 See Hill and Watkinson.

BIBLIOGRAPHY

Abbott, Wilbur Cortez, *The Writings and Speeches of Oliver Cromwell*, 4 vols, Cambridge, Mass.: Harvard University Press, 1937–1947

Ane Information of the Publicke Proceedings of the Kingdom of Scotland and Their Armies, Edinburgh?: Evan Tyler, 1648

Ashley, Maurice, *The English Civil War*, rev. edn, Gloucester: Alan Sutton, 1990

Ashton, Robert, *Counter-Revolution: The Second Civil War and Its Origins, 1646–8*, New Haven, Conn., and London: Yale University Press, 1994

Aveling, Hugh, 'The Catholic Recusancy of the Yorkshire Fairfaxes', pt 1 *Biographical Studies 1534–1829,* vol. 3, no. ii (1955), pp. 69–114; pt 2 *Recusant History*, vol. 4, no. ii (1957), pp. 61–101

Aylmer, G. E. (ed.), *Clarke Trials, Clarke Papers microfilm,* Reel 9 2/10 (LXX)

Barratt, J., 'The letters of the first baron Byron of Rochdale (1600–1652)', *Journal of the Society for Army Historical Research*, vol. 49 (1971), pp. 127–40

Bates, Cadwallader J., 'The Border Holds of Northumberland 1' *Archaeologia Aeliana*, 2nd series, vol. xiv (1891)

Baynes, Original Correspondence of Captain Adam Baynes, British Library Add. Mss. 21,417

Beamont, William (ed.), *A Discourse of the Warr in Lancashire*, Manchester: Chetham Society, vol. LXII (1865)

Beardsley, W. F., 'An Account of the Battle of Willoughby Field, in the County of Nottingham', *Leicester Archaeological and Historical Society*, vol. 10, pt 1–2 (1905–1906), pp. 79–88

Binns, J., 'Scarborough and the Civil Wars 1642–1651', *Northern History*, vol. xxii (1986), pp. 95–122

—— *Yorkshire in the Civil Wars: Origins, Impact and Outcome*, Pickering: Blackthorn Press, 2004

Birch, S., 'A true and perfect account of the receipts and disbursements of Captaine Samuel Birch . . .', *Portland Papers*, vol. III, 1894, pp. 173–86

Bowen, Emanuel, *Britannia Depicta or Ogilby Improved*, 1720, facsimile reprint Newcastle: Frank Graham, 1970

Braddick, Michael, *God's Fury, England's Fire: A New History of the English Civil Wars*, London: Allen Lane, 2008

Braye, *The manuscripts of . . . Lord Braye . . . &c*, Historical Manuscripts Commission 10th report, appendix, part VI, London: HMSO, 1887

Broxap, Ernest, *The Great Civil War in Lancashire*, 2nd edn, Manchester: Manchester University Press, 1973

Brunton, D. and Pennington, D. H., *Members of the Long Parliament*, London: Allen & Unwin, 1954

Bull, Stephen, *A General Plague of Madness: The Civil Wars in Lancashire 1640–1660*, Lancaster: Carnegie, 2009

——, and Seed, Mike, *Bloody Preston: The Battle of Preston, 1648*, Lancaster: Carnegie, 1998

Burnet, Gilbert, *The Memoires of the Lives and Actions of James and William Dukes of Hamilton and Castleherald . . .*, London: R. Royston, 1677

Capp, Bernard, *Cromwell's Navy: The Fleet and the English Revolution 1648–1660*, Oxford: Clarendon Press, 1989

——, 'Naval Operations', in Kenyon, J. and Ohlmeyer, Jane (eds), *The Civil Wars: A Military History of England, Scotland, and Ireland, 1638–1660*, Oxford: Oxford University Press, 1998, pp. 156–91

Carlton, Charles, *Going to the Wars: The Experience of the English Civil Wars 1638–1651*, London: Routledge, 1992

Carlyle, T., *Oliver Cromwell's Letters and Speeches:* with elucidations by Thomas Carlyle, 5 vols, London: Chapman & Hall, 1891

Bibliography

CJ, Journal of the House of Commons, vols 5–6, London: n.p., 1802

CSPD 1644–1645, Calendar of State Papers, Domestic . . . 1644–1645, ed. by W. D. Hamilton, London: HMSO, 1890

CSPD 1648–1649, Calendar of State Papers, Domestic . . . 1648–1649, ed. by W. D. Hamilton, London: HMSO, 1893

CSPD 1649–1650, Calendar of State Papers, Domestic . . . 1649–1650, ed. by M. A. E. Green, London: HMSO, 1875

Curwen, John F., *The Later Records Relating to North Westmorland or the Barony of Appleby* (Cumberland & Westmorland Antiquarian & Archaeological Society Record Series, vol. VIII), Kendal, 1932

Dawson, W. H., *History of Skipton,* London: Simpkin, Marshall, 1882

——, *Cromwell's Understudy: The Life and Times of General John Lambert and the Rise and Fall of the Protectorate*, London: Hodge, 1938

Defoe, Daniel, *A Tour Through the Whole Island of Great Britain Divided into Circuits or Journies*, edited by John Mcveagh, London: Pickering & Chatto, 2001

Diethe, Jurgen, '*The Moderate*: Politics and Allegiances of a Revolutionary Newspaper', *History of Political Thought*, vol. IV (1983), pp. 247–79

Donagan, Barbara, *War in England 1642–1649*, Oxford: Oxford University Press, 2008

Doubleday, H. A. and Page, W. (eds), *The Victoria County History of the County of Bedford*, 3 vols, London: Archibald Constable, 1904–1914

Drake, Nathan, 'A Journal of the First and Second Sieges of Pontefract Castle, 1644–1645, with an appendix of evidences relating to the Third Siege', edited by W. H. D. Longstaffe, *Miscellanea*, Surtees Society, vol. 37 (1860)

Dugdale, William, *The Visitation of the County of Yorke*, edited by R. Davies, Surtees Society, vol. 36 (1859)

Edwards, Peter, 'Logistics and supply', in Kenyon, J. and Ohlmeyer, Jane (eds), *The Civil Wars: A Military History of England, Scotland, and Ireland, 1638–1660*, Oxford: Oxford University Press, 1998, pp. 234–71

Fairfax, Transcripts of the Collection of Letters known as The Fairfax Correspondence 1645–1648, British Library, Add Mss 36,996 (late nineteenth/early twentieth century manuscript copy)

Farr, David, *John Lambert, Parliamentary Soldier and Cromwellian Major-General, 1619–1684*, Woodbridge: Boydell, 2003

Firth, C. H. (ed.), *The Clarke Papers*, vols i–ii, Camden Society new series, vols 49, 54 (1891–1894)

—— (ed.), 'Narratives illustrating the Duke of Hamilton's expedition to England in 1648 I: Mr Thomas Reade's Relation', *Miscellany of The Scottish History Society*, vol. 2 (1904), pp. 293–302

—— (ed.), 'Narratives illustrating the Duke of Hamilton's expedition to England in 1648 II: Sir Philip Musgrave's Relation', *Miscellany of The Scottish History Society,* vol. 2 (1904), pp. 302–11

——. and Davies, Godfrey, *The Regimental History of Cromwell's Army*, 2 vols, Oxford: Clarendon Press, 1940

——, and Rait, R. S. (eds), *Acts and Ordinances of the Interregnum 1642–1660*, 3 vols, London: HMSO, 1911

Fortescue, G. K. (ed.), *Catalogue of the Pamphlets, Books, Newspapers, and Manuscripts relating to the Civil War, the Commonwealth, and Restoration, collected by George Thomason, 1640–1661*, 2 vols, London: British Museum, 1908

Fotheringham, J. G. (ed.), *The Diplomatic Correspondence of Jean de Montereul and the brothers Bellievre . . .*, 2 vols, Scottish History Society, vols XXIX, XXX (1898–1899)

Fox, George, *The Three Sieges of Pontefract Castle*, Burton Salmon: Old Hall Press, 1987

Fraser, Antonia, *Cromwell: Our Chief of Men*, London: Weidenfeld & Nicolson, 1973

FSPB, Field Service Pocket Book, London: HMSO, 1914

Gardiner, S. R. (ed.), *The Hamilton Papers . . . relating to the years 1638–1650*, Camden Society, new series 27 (1880)

Gentles, Ian, *The New Model Army in England, Ireland, and Scotland, 1645–1653*, Oxford: Blackwell, 1992

——, 'The Civil Wars in England', in Kenyon, J. and Ohlmeyer, Jane (eds), *The Civil Wars: A Military History of England, Scotland, and Ireland, 1638–1660*, Oxford: Oxford University Press, 1998, pp. 103–55

——, *The English Revolution and the Wars in the Three Kingdoms 1638–1652*, Harlow: Longman, 2007

Godber, Joyce, *History of Bedfordshire 1066–1888*, Bedford: Bedfordshire County Council, 1969

Gooder, A. (ed.), *The Parliamentary Representation of the County of York 1258–1832*, vol. 2 (Yorkshire Archaeological Society Record Series, vol. XCVI), 1938

Gratton, J. M., *The Parliamentarian and Royalist War Effort in Lancashire 1642–1651*, Chetham Society, 3rd series, vol. XLVIII (2010)

Greaves, R. L. and Zaller, R., *Biographical Dictionary of British Radicals in the Seventeenth Century*, 3 vols, Brighton: Harvester Press, 1982

Green, M. A. E. (ed.), *Calendar of the Proceedings of the Committee for Compounding*, 5 vols., London: HMSO, 1889–1892

Greenberg, Stephen J., 'Dating Civil War pamphlets, 1641–1644', *Albion*, vol. 20 (1988), pp. 387–401

——, 'The Thomason Collection: Rebuttal to Michael Mendle', *Albion*, vol. 22 (1990), pp. 95–8

Greenwood, Robin, 'Kildwick 1485–1714 . . . with special reference to Kildwick in the 1642–49 Civil War' (unpublished monograph 2008)

Guthry, Henry, *The Memoirs of Henry Guthry . . . Containing an Impartial Relation of the Affairs of Scotland, Civil and Ecclesiastical, from the Year 1637, to the Death of King Charles I*, 2nd edn, Glasgow: A. Stalker, 1748

Haldane, A. R. B., *Three Centuries of Scottish Posts: An Historical Survey to 1836*, Edinburgh: Edinburgh University Press, 1971

Harrison, John, *The Battle of Willoughby Field*, Loughborough: Reprint Books, undated, c. 2008

Heath III, George D., 'Cromwell and Lambert 1653–57', in Roots, Ivan (ed.), *Cromwell: A Profile*, London: Macmillan, 1973, pp. 72–90

Henderson, Frances, '"Posterity to judge" – John Rushworth and his "Historical Collections"', *Bodleian Library Record*, vol. 15 (1996), pp. 247–59

—— (ed.), *Clarke Papers V: Further Selections from the Papers of William Clarke*, Camden Society 5th series, vol. 27 (2005)

Hesilrige, Arthur, Leicester Record Office, The Hazlerigg Collection, DG21/275 Letters to Sir Arthur Hesilrige, 2nd Bart c1648–1650 [Note: a typed transcript under DG21/276 is in inaccurate in places.]

Hill, P. R. and Watkinson, J. M., *Major Sanderson's War: The Diary of a Parliamentary Cavalry Officer in the English Civil War*, Stroud: Spellmount, 2008

HMC Third Report of the Royal Commission on Historical Manuscripts, London: HMSO, 1872

HMC Fourth Report of the Royal Commission on Historical Manuscripts, London: HMSO, 1874

HMC Various, Report on Manuscripts in Various Collections, vol. viii: The Manuscripts of the Hon. Frederick Lindley Wood; M.L. S. Clements Esq,; and S. Philip Unwin Esq., London: HMSO, 1913

Hodgson, *Original Memoirs, Written During the Great Civil War; Being the Life of Sir Henry Slingsby and Memoirs of Capt Hodgson etc.*, Edinburgh: Archibald Constable, 1806

Holmes, Clive, *Seventeenth-Century Lincolnshire (History of Lincolnshire, vol. vii)*, Lincoln: Society for Lincolnshire History & Archaeology, 1980

Holmes, Richard, *Preston 1648,* Market Drayton: Mercia, 1985

Holmes, Richard (ed.), *The Sieges of Pontefract Castle 1644–1648*, Pontefract: R. Holmes, 1887

Hoover, Charles, 'Cromwell's status and pay in 1646–47', *Historical Journal*, vol. 23 (1980), pp. 703–15

Hutchinson, Lucy, *Memoirs of the Life of Colonel Hutchinson*, ed. with introduction by J. Sutherland, Oxford: Oxford University Press, 1973

Jobey, George, 'A military redoubt on Burnswark Hill, Dumfriesshire', *Transactions of the Dumfriesshire and Galloway Natural History and Antiquarian Society* 3rd series, vol. i (1973), pp. 72–81

Kenyon, J. and Ohlmeyer, Jane (eds), *The Civil Wars: A Military History of England, Scotland, and Ireland, 1638–1660*, Oxford: Oxford University Press, 1998

King, D. W., 'The High Command of the New Model Army', *Journal of the Society for Army Historical Research*, vol. 56 (1978), p. 57

Kitson, Ethel, and Clark, E. K., 'Some Civil War Accounts 1647–1650', *Thoresby Society Publication XI: Miscellanea* (1904), pp. 137–235

Latham, Robert, and Matthews, William (eds), *The Diary of Samuel Pepys*, 11 vols, London: Bell, 1983

Le Fleming, *The Manuscripts of S .H. Le Fleming Esq. of Rydal Hall*, Historical Manuscripts Commission 12th report, appendix part VII, London: HMSO, 1890

Letter from Holland, Rotterdam, 23 September 1648, *TT* E467/21

Bibliography

Leyborne-Popham, F. W., *Report on the Manuscripts of F.W. Leyborne-Popham* . . ., Historical Manuscripts
Commission [51st Report], London: HMSO, 1899

LJ, Journal of the House of Lords, vols 9–10, London: n.p., 1802

Lyndon, B. P., 'The Parliament's Army in Essex, 1648', *Journal of the Society for Army Historical Research*, vol. 54
(1981), pp. 140–60

Lysons, Daniel, and Lysons, Samuel, *Magna Britannia, vol. 4 Cumberland*, London: T. Cadell & W. Davies, 1816

Macgillivray, Royce, *Restoration Historians and the English Civil War,* International Archives of the History of Ideas,
vol. 74, The Hague: Martinus Nijhoff, 1974

Mannix, William and Whellan, William, *History, Gazetteer and Directory of Cumberland*, Beverley: Johnson, 1847

Markham, Clements R., *A Life of the Great Lord Fairfax*, London: Macmillan, 1870

McElligott, Jason, *Royalism, Print and Censorship in Revolutionary England*, Studies in Early Modern Cultural,
Politcal and Social History, vol. 6, Woodbridge: Boydell, 2007

Mendle, Michael, 'The Thomason Collection: A Reply to Stephen J. Greenberg', *Albion*, vol. 22 (1990),
pp. 85–93

——, 'George Thomason's Intentions', in Mandelbrote, G. and Taylor, B. (eds), *Libraries within the Library: the
Origins of the British Library's Printed Collections*, London: British Library, 2009, pp. 171–86

Nelson, Carolyn, and Seccombe, Matthew, *British Newspapers and Periodicals, 1641–1700: A Short-Title Catalogue*,
New York: Modern Language Association of America, 1987

Nuttall, W. L. F., 'The Yorkshire Commissioners appointed for the trial of King Charles the First', *Yorkshire
Archaeological Journal*, vol. 43 (1972), pp. 147–57

ODNB, Oxford Dictionary of National Biography, 60 vols, Oxford: Oxford University Press, 2004

Ogilby, John, *Britannia, Volume the First, or an Illustration of the Kingdom of England and Dominion of Wales*, London:
printed by the author, 1675 (facsimile reprint, n. p., 1939)

Order Book, 'Council of the Northern Parliamentary Army, 1647–8. A book containing a modern [before
c.1900] transcript of part of the order book of the Council, found in some old buildings by Mr W[illia]m
Murgatroyd (Councils of War at Ripon, Knaresbro', York, etc.)'. York Minster Library, Hailstone Collection
BB53. (The work is usually referred to as the Order Book, although it is in fact a record of meetings of the
Council of War of the Northern Army, chiefly concerned with courts martial.)

Ormerod, George (ed.), 'An Impartiall Relation of the late Fight at Preston . . . by Sir Marmaduke Langdale',
Tracts Relating to Military Proceedings During the Great Civil War in Lancashire, Chetham Society, vol. II (1844),
pp. 267–70

Page, William (ed.), *The Victoria County History of York, North Riding*, 3 vols, London: Constable, 1914–1925

Paulden, Captain Thomas, undated account, in Holmes, Richard (ed.), *The Sieges of Pontefract Castle 1644–1648*,
Pontefract: R. Holmes, 1887, pp. 291–322

——, letter dated 31 March 1702, in Holmes, Richard (ed.), *The Sieges of Pontefract Castle 1644–1648*, Pontefract:
R. Holmes, 1887, pp. 149–54

*PCHE, The Parliamentary or Constitutional History of England; From the Earliest Times, to the Restoration of Charles II
. . . By Several Hands*, 2nd edn, 24 vols, London: J. Tonson, A. Millar & W. Sandby, 1761–1763

Peacey, Jason, *Politicians and Pamphleteers: Propaganda During the English Civil Wars and Interregnum*, Aldershot:
Ashgate, 2004

Phillips, John Roland, *Memoirs of the Civil War in Wales and the Marches 1642–1649*, 2 vols, London: Longman,
1874

Pococke, Richard, *Tours in Scotland 1747, 1750, 1760*, ed. by D. W. Kemp, Scottish History Society, vol. I (1887)

Portland Papers, The Manuscripts of His Grace the Duke of Portland preserved at Welbeck Abbey, 10 vols, Historical
Manuscripts Commission, London: HMSO, 1891–1931

Powell, J. R. and Timings, E. K. (eds), *Documents Relating to the Civil War 1642–1648*, Publications of the Navy
Records Society, vol. 105 (1963)

Raymond, Joad, *The Invention of the Newspaper: English Newsbooks 1641–1649*, Oxford: Oxford University Press,
2005

Reece, H. M., 'The Military Presence in England, 1649–1660': a thesis submitted for the degree of Doctor of

Philosophy at the University of Oxford, 1981 (unpublished)

Reid, Stuart, *All the King's Armies: A Military History of the English Civil War 1642–1651*, Stroud: Spellmount, 2007

Roberts, Sir Howard, and Godfrey, Walter H. (eds), *Survey of London*, vol. 23, London: London County Council, 1951

Roberts, Ian, *Pontefract Castle*, Wakefield: West Yorkshire Archaeology Service, 1990

——, *Pontefract Castle: Archaeological Excavations 1982–86*, Yorkshire Archaeology, vol. 8 (2002)

Robinson, Howard J., *The British Post Office: A History*, Princeton N.J.: Princeton University Press, 1948

Rogers, H. C. B., *Battles and Generals of the Civil Wars 1642–1651*, London: Seeley Service, 1968

Roots, Ivan (ed.), *Cromwell: A Profile*, London: Macmillan, 1973

Royle, Trevor, *Civil War: The Wars of the Three Kingdoms 1638–1660*, London: Abacus, 2005

Rushworth, John, *Historical Collections Fourth and Last Part.*, 2 vols, London: R. Chiswell & T. Cockerill, 1701

Sanderson, Christopher, 'Selections from the Diary of Christopher Sanderson of Barnard Castle', *Six North Country Diaries*, Surtees Society, vol. 118 (1910), pp. 35–42

Sanderson's Diary, in Hill, P. R. and Watkinson, J. M., *Major Sanderson's War: The Diary of a Parliamentary Cavalry Officer in the English Civil War*, Stroud: Spellmount, 2008, pp. 90–135

Scott, David, '"Particular businesses" in the Long Parliament: The Hull Letters 1644–1648', *Parliament, Politics and Elections 1604–1648*, edited by C. R. Kyle, Camden 5th series, vol. 17, (2001), pp. 273–341

——, *Politics and War in the Three Stuart Kingdoms, 1637–49*, Basingstoke: Houndsmills, 2004

Skirmish, A Skirmish in Northumberland. Being a Reprint of a Very Rare Tract in Quarto Entitled 'Packets of Letters . . . 1648' (Sunderland, 1842). Letter from Major Sanderson, printed in Sunderland, 1842, reprinted in Hill, P. R. and Watkinson, J. M., *Major Sanderson's War: The Diary of a Parliamentary Cavalry Officer in the English Civil War*, Stroud: Spellmount, 2008, pp. 139–41

Spencer, Lois, 'The professional and literary connexions of George Thomason', *The Library*, 5th series, vol. XIII (1958), pp. 102–18

Stevenson, David, *Revolution and Counter-Revolution in Scotland. 1644–1651*, rev. edn, Edinburgh: John Donald, 2003

Syon Q.II.153, Alnwick Castle Archives.

Temple, R. K. G., 'The Original Officer List of the New Model Army', *Bulletin of the Institute of Historical Research*, vol. LIX (1986), pp. 50–77

Turner, Sir James, *Memoirs of His Own Life and Times 1632–1670*, Edinburgh: Bannatyne Club, 1829

Underdown, David, *Pride's Purge: Politics in the Puritan Revolution*, Oxford: Clarendon Press, 1971

——, *Revel, Riot and Rebellion: Popular Politics and Culture in England 1603–1660*, Oxford: Oxford University Press, 1987

Vyner, Blaise, *Stainmore: The Archaeology of a North Pennine Pass*, Tees Archaeology Monograph, no. 1 (2002)

Wanklyn, Malcolm, *Decisive Battles of the English Civil War: Myth and Reality*, Barnsley: Pen & Sword, 2006

——, *The Warrior Generals: Winning the British Civil Wars 1642–1652*, New Haven, Conn., and London: Yale University Press, 2010

Welfare, Humphrey, 'Maiden Castle Fortlet', in Vyner, Blaise, *Stainmore: The Archaeology of a North Pennine Pass*, Tees Archaeology Monograph, no. 1 (2002), pp. 96–8

Whellan, William, *The History and Topography of the Counties of Cumberland and Westmorland*, Pontefract: Whellan, 1860

Whitelocke, Bulstrode, *Memorials of the English Affairs . . . From the Beginning of the Reign of Charles the First, to King Charles the Second His Happy Restoration . . .* new edn, London: J. Tonson, 1732

Woolrych, Austin, *Battles of the English Civil War*, London: Batsford, 1961

——, *Britain in Revolution 1625–1660*, Oxford: Oxford University Press, 2002

Young, Peter, and Holmes, Richard, *The English Civil War: A Military History of the Three Civil Wars 1642–1651*, Ware: Wordsworth, 2000

Yule, George, *The Independents in the English Civil War*, Cambridge: Cambridge University Press, 1958

INDEX

(Timeline and Appendix 4 Birch's 'Diary' are not indexed)

Index

214

Index